MERVYN ᴘ
TWO LIVES

Maeve Patricia Mary Theresa Gilmore was born in London in 1918. Her Irish father was a surgeon from Co. Down and her mother the daughter of the owner of the *Western Mail*. Maeve grew up in Chelsea and was sent as a boarder to the Convent of the Holy Child in Hastings. At seventeen she spent a year at a Swiss finishing school. When she returned to London she enrolled as a student at the Westminster School of Art, where on her first day she met Mervyn Peake. Despite disapproval from her father Maeve continued to meet with him and they married in December 1937. Maeve Gilmore died in August 1983 at the age of sixty-five, surviving her husband by fifteen years.

The eldest of Mervyn Peake and Maeve Gilmore's three children, Sebastian was brought up in London, Kent, Surrey and Sark and in his childhood attended nine different schools. A keen interest in languages took him to Europe where he lived in various countries for almost five years. On his return he worked in shops and breweries and set up his own transport, and painting and decorating companies before becoming involved in the wine trade. He now runs his own wine company. Sebastian Peake has a son and three daughters and lives in London.

MERVYN PEAKE: TWO LIVES

FOREWORD BY
Sebastian Peake

A WORLD AWAY
A Memoir of Mervyn Peake
By Maeve Gilmore

PREFACE BY
Michael Moorcock

A CHILD OF BLISS
Growing Up With Mervyn Peake
By Sebastian Peake

V

VINTAGE

Published by Vintage 1999

2 4 6 8 10 9 7 5 3 1

A World Away
Copyright © by Maeve Gilmore 1970
Preface copyright © Michael Moorcock 1970
First published in Great Britain in 1970 by
Victor Gollancz.
Mandarin edition 1992.

A Child of Bliss
Copyright © Sebastian Peake 1989
Foreword copyright © Sebastian Peake 1999
First published in Great Britain in 1989 by
Lennard Books Ltd

Vintage
Random House, 20 Vauxhall Bridge Road,
London SW1V 2SA

Random House Australia (Pty) Limited
20 Alfred Street, Milsons Point, Sydney
New South Wales 2061, Australia

Random House New Zealand Limited
18 Poland Road, Glenfield,
Auckland 10, New Zealand

Random House South Africa (Pty) Limited
Endulini, 5A Jubilee Road, Parktown 2193,
South Africa

The Random House Group Limited Reg. No. 954009
www.randomhouse.co.uk

A CIP catalogue record for this book
is available from the British Library

ISBN 0 09 928286 0

Papers used by Random House are natural, recyclable
products made from wood grown in sustainable forests.
The manufacturing processes conform to the environ-
mental regulations of the country of origin

Printed and bound in Great Britain by
Cox & Wyman Limited, Reading, Berkshire

CONTENTS

FOREWORD

Immediately after my father died in November 1968, my mother began writing her memoir *A World Away*, and within six months had completed what in reality became not only her *cri de coeur* at a cruel physical loss, but also an open-hearted statement and clear testament to her experience of life with Mervyn Peake. A celebration in words of 'a marriage made in heaven', as one of her sisters described Maeve and Mervyn's life together. A marriage which lasted thirty-one years, and can only be described as having been unique. Until at different stages in their own destinies incurable diseases brought them down, they lived the lives that many might envy, built as they were around the accumulated treasure troves of nuances and personal, but intimate, understandings that only those privy to them ever seemed to grasp. They worked together, loved together, and developed together, both as humans and artists, and even if, in my father's professional life, many of the commissions and projects, which they had often brought about together, were poorly paid, there was artistically always something about the work, which was unusual, and which set him apart. 'Peake never offers us less,' observed one commentator, 'than the full breadth of his idiosyncratic and singular visionary individualism. Many of the classics that he illustrated, now unbelievably half a century ago, retain the timelessness of his observation, and show us Long John Silver still as dangerous as ever, Alice just as intelligently fey, and the Ancient Mariner as hauntingly powerful, as any previous, or subsequently illustrated interpretation by the artists, of these seminal figures in literature.

On page one of *A World Away*, the Irish convent-reared girl of seventeen, describes meeting my father on the very first day of her course at the Westminster School of Art, and her nerves at being introduced to him as her tutor, having she writes, had enough trouble even entering the building. Dramatic enough surely, for a nature she herself describes as 'having a built-in shyness about it.' One can only speculate at what would have been her reaction to him, had she known then of the impact he was later to have on English writing, illustration, and poetry. The course at Westminster gave her latent artistic talent the discipline and structure it required, and in her early *faux-naif* oil paintings, the atmosphere of the idyllic early days of marriage at their homes in Sussex, Chelsea, and later Sark, she captures a mood of love and happiness. Always encouraged and supported by my father to experiment with any of her own ideas, her painting and writing developed and grew in originality, as she herself did, both as wife and mother. But it was in her role as supporter and ubiquitous presence, that my father was often able to bring to fruition the talents that lay in such abundance deep within his being.

To a great extent, the prodigious output in both words and drawings that he sustained throughout his career was due to my mother, and her consummate and all-pervading belief in him. Until he was so incapacitated that the pencil literally and metaphorically dropped from his grasp, my father continued until the very end of his life to practice the art of drawing. To 'make a drawing,' he wrote, 'was to record an idea, and to hold back from the brink of oblivion, that fleeting glimpse, that shape or structure suddenly perceived, imaginary or visual. Anything seen without prejudice, is enormous'. My life did not begin until I met Mervyn Peake, my mother would often say to friends and family alike, and in the months following his death when the totality of the loss sank in, and co-incidentally his name and financial fortunes were at their lowest ebb, she decided to offer his entire *oeuvre* for sale, in the hope of reviving an interest in his work, while at the same time paying off some of their bills. Humiliated, and heartbroken by the Tate Gallery's offer of £1500 for my father's whole artistic output, she walked home in tears along the Thames embankment to Kensington, carrying the large artists' portfolio, containing many of his masterpieces as samples, vowing never to compromise his dignity again. How overjoyed she would be, now that the BBC Television's adaptation of *Gormenghast* is in production as its Millennium Drama, that a Sadler's Wells opera of the same name opens in January 2000, that translations of his novel are now available in many languages, and other publications and ideas are in hand.

A *faux pas* by the ill-informed R. A. Butler, then Home Secretary, when presenting my father with the Fellow of the Society of Literature award in 1951 for his *Gormenghast* novels, describing him at the ceremony as 'the greatest living illustrator', was rectified a few minutes later by a prestigious and lucrative commission. On being presented to the Queen Mother, who was also attending, my father was asked to produce several drawings for her new grandson, Charles. The work was later delivered to Buckingham Palace and hung in the nursery of the young prince. It would have given my father great pleasure, I'm sure, to know that the letter I received from St. James' Palace recently, stating that 'The Prince of Wales would be delighted to accept the 1999 award as honorary member of the Mervyn Peake Society,' was not unconnected with the impression the drawings must have left on him as a young boy. The first part of this compendium, is both a homage to a husband and the man as artist, while the second refers to him as a father, who still, thirty years after his death, continues to influence me on a daily basis, whether in the way I choose to see life, or in the way I choose to live it.

★　　　★　　　★

In this introduction to the paperback edition of both *A World Away* and *A Child of Bliss,* in compendium form, I am not only paying my respects to a man who happened to be my father, but also to someone who still, over thirty years after his death, is generally considered to have been a genius. And despite the twenty years separating the writing of the two books, and the very different atmospheres in which they were both written, my mother reflects in her memoir, the same belief in him as multi-talented renaissance man, as I attempt to convey in mine, even if obviously our voices differ, in the way in which we remember him.

Inspired to write *A World Away* in the weeks following my father's death, my mother's memoir must have influenced me at least in post trauma timing, for I similarly began writing down my memories of life at home with my parents shortly after she herself died in August 1983. She completed her book in six months, a somewhat shorter time than I laboured over the writing of mine. To begin with, I jotted down in various notebooks ideas and events from childhood that had lodged themselves firmly in my mind, but these jottings were irregular and sporadic, sometimes with long intervals before either energy or desire to continue returned. Only after I had been at it for several years did I feel that I should collate the notes.

In the summer of 1988 I drove to Tangiers, where I rented a room in a hotel overlooking the wide bay, and spent three weeks putting the accumulated material into chronological order. Having done so, I began the process of writing the whole thing again, dividing the narrative into short chapters, each one of which, to my mind, constituted an important and salient block of memory. Instead of going down to the dining room for breakfast in the mornings, I arranged to have coffee and croissants brought to my room at 8am every day, after which, feeling ready for the day, I would begin work. Never stopping until 8pm, when I usually felt quite exhausted, I would leave the hotel to buy bread, cheese and red wine from a local shop, with which I would return and consume, while looking down on the bay below, through the open window of my room on the sixth floor. So bright were the stars at night that their reflection off the broad sweep of yellow sand, radiated a light so luminous it could have been day, and with the gently lapping waves on the shore below as background music, I would fall asleep. I kept up this strict routine every day until the three weeks were up, and then, feeling that my stay had produced something like the result I had hoped for, I left to drive across the Sahara to Senegal. But that is another story.

Most of us retain certain evocative memories from our earliest childhood, and however hazy they might become later in life, they can, if really willed back into consciousness, form powerful atmospheric links with our distant past. In my case the openly joyous sound of the common garden bird, which sang its little song to the world from a perch outside my bedroom, can, if I concentrate, still bring back the clearest and most vivid of echoes from those days. Even now its musical reveille is so sharply etched on my subconscious, that I can only think of it as primal sound. Today, whenever I hear a similar chant of *joie de vivre*, I zoom back down my tunnel of remembrances to my feathered friend, and the little thatched cottage beneath the Sussex Down. From about the age of three I would place my Dinky toys in a row on the windowsill at night, so that they would be the first things I noticed on waking in the morning. I loved them. When still very young I remember my father trying in vain to get me to say the word 'beauty', to which request I would always reply with my favourite word, 'car'. 'Beauty,' he would persevere; 'car,' I would counter. The first thing my father would do when arriving home on leave from the army, would be to place his regimental cap on my head, almost submerging it, and while running around the garden with me astride his shoulders, would whoop out loud, both at the pleasure of being home, and for the chance at last, to show my mother the work he had been doing, while stationed at some far flung provincial barracks. It was at this time, in the early 1940's, that he was sowing the seeds of his literary and artistic future, which now, over fifty years later, is resulting in a bumper harvest. Now, with a greater general acceptance by the thinking public of him as an influential English writer and illustrator, poet and painter, his eponymous novel, *Gormenghast*, is allied and almost synonymous with viewing life and its machination in an original way.

After returning to England from my Tangiers sojourn, I was given a recommendation to an established London publisher, who I am pleased to say accepted my manuscript. Writing, as I have discovered since, is a tough solitary business with no guarantee of success, so when this, my first book, came out in the autumn of the following year, I was delighted when the publisher informed me after six months that the hard cover edition had sold out. I dedicated the first edition to my parents, which I would like to repeat here, while hoping that, flaws and all, the current reader will enjoy this, my own *'recherche du temps perdu'*.

Sebastian Peake
London
December 1999

Maeve Gilmore

A WORLD AWAY
A Memoir of Mervyn Peake

WITH A PREFACE BY
Michael Moorcock

LIST OF ILLUSTRATIONS

ACKNOWLEDGEMENTS

I am extremely grateful to the following for allowing me to reproduce here letters which they wrote to Mervyn Peake: Sir John Clements, Mr Michael Codron, Mr Graham Greene, Mr Peter Hall, Sir Laurence Olivier, Mr Anthony Quayle and Mr Kenneth Tynan. The B.B.C. have kindly allowed me to reproduce letters written to my husband by Mr David Jones when he was in their employment.

I also gratefully acknowledge the original publishers of poems quoted in this book:

Messrs Bertram Rota for poems from *A Reverie of Bone* ('How foreign to the spirit's early beauty . . .'; 'We are the haunted people'; 'Be proud, slow trees'; 'They had no quiet and smoothed sheets of death . . .'; 'They spire terrific bodies into heaven . . .'; 'Heads float about me . . .'; and '. . . I ponder on sun–lit spires . . .').

Messrs Chatto and Windus for poems from *Shapes and Sounds* ('You walk unaware . . .'; 'The Rhondda Valley'; 'The Cocky Walkers'; 'Coloured Money'; and 'Rather than a little pain . . .').

Messrs Dent for four stanzas from *The Rhyme of the Flying Bomb* ('This isn't no place for the likes of you . . .').

Messrs Eyre and Spottiswoode for two stanzas from a poem in *The Glassblowers* ('With people, so with trees . . .').

'Out of the overlapping leaves . . .' has not previously been published.

PREFACE

My admiration for Mervyn Peake has been one of the few constants in my life. I find it hard to distance myself from the enthusiasm I feel for his work and the affection I felt for him and continue to feel for Maeve Gilmore. This memoir, which was published soon after Mervyn's death in 1968, is still the best and most accurate picture of a remarkable artistic genius and a loveable man whose decline into illness was profoundly terrifying and appallingly unjust. The simplicity and directness of Maeve Gilmore's account of her life with her husband and their children speaks of the rare honesty she and Mervyn shared and which her sons and daughter inherited. No amount of academic interpretation or romantic myth-making can diminish the book's truthfulness.

Since Mervyn's death his reputation and his audience have grown enormously. The public sometimes receives an image of him as a doomed, driven, Byronic artist (perhaps a more suitable personality for the author of the Titus Groan books) when in fact he was a talented, hard-working man of considerable charm and humour, an inspiring, tactful, sensitive teacher, a wonderful friend and parent. As an artist he was constantly developing his range and his techniques. One cannot fail to regret the great loss to the world of all he would have accomplished if he had continued to live in good health.

For the basic facts of Mervyn's life, the most accurate source is John Watney's biography (*Mervyn Peake*, 1976). I was a boy when I first met him in the 1950s, after I had written him an enthusiastic letter, and was invited to tea by Maeve. Their

house in Wallington, as Maeve says in this book, was rather
like Gormenghast in miniature and my main impression of the
interior was of books, pictures and seemingly hundreds of
stuffed birds perched on every available surface (Mervyn had
bought a job lot some time before). He was already ill and
easily tired, but at that time his illness had not been identified
as Parkinson's Disease and there was every hope that he would
get better. I remember writing, after that first meeting (when
I'm certain I outstayed my welcome), that I felt I had for the
first time been in the presence of an original genius. I was
surprised, too, by the lack of public success Mervyn had
received. I began trying to find publishers who would publish
or reprint his work. Later this passion was shared by Langdon
Jones, who painstakingly put *Titus Alone* back into its original
form (the first edition had been somewhat thoughtlessly
copy-edited). It was not until Penguin's decision to publish the
Titus books that Mervyn's work reached a wide audience. By
then Mervyn was too ill to appreciate his success. Since the
mid-60s virtually all his work has been republished and his
drawings and paintings now change hands for amounts
which, had he received a fraction of them at the time, might
have made a vast difference to his state of mind.

The person chiefly responsible for Mervyn's increasing
recognition is, of course, Maeve Gilmore herself. A gifted
painter in her own right she frequently set her own career aside
in order to ensure that Mervyn's work received its proper due.
As a result it could be argued she gave up the opportunity for
consolation as well as personal success, yet there is no hint of
self-sacrifice or misdirected piety in this memoir any more
than she displays in her own life. A person of enormous
courage and dignity, exhibiting the same sense of humour and
straightforwardness she reveals in this memoir; a person of
great substance, passion and sensibility with a loathing for
small-mindedness, meanness and cruelty which, try as she

might sometimes, she can never disguise, she has had more than her fair share of misfortune, yet her integrity and love of life has remained fundamentally undamaged. Although I'm sure she would be embarrassed to hear it, *A World Away* is a record of her own love and generosity of soul as much as it is a memoir of Mervyn.

Mervyn was fifty-seven when he died, though his illness made him look considerably older. The illness produced a gradual physical and mental decline and, as his condition worsened, the hope many of us fostered, contrary to the medical evidence, that he would by some miracle get well, began to fade. At the small establishment run by his wife's brother, James Gilmore, Mervyn developed a haemorrhage and died peacefully and, as far as one could tell, happily, for his last months were spent with people who loved and respected him.

I had visited him about a year before. As usual for me the visit had been pleasurable, for although he could remember very little and could rarely finish a sentence, his spirit and his sensibility (as well as his humour) remained. My love for him could not be diminished by the superficial characteristics of his illness. On one level he almost always seemed aware of what had happened to him and at times when strangers patronized him it was possible to see a distinct glint of irony in his eyes. When I heard that he had died, I was filled with rage and then with bitterness. The bitterness, impossible to express still, remains as strong after fifteen years. Mervyn was a man who enjoyed life and gave more to life than anyone I ever knew.

He was a man of great gifts. His vitality was expressed through thousands of drawings and poems and through four novels and two plays. His vision was personal, unselfconscious and to do not with abstractions but with people, of whom he was a wry and sympathetic observer. What gives his Titus books their power and quality is not so much their fantastic elements as their characters—the Earl and Countess of Groan, Flay and Swelter, Steerpike, Fuchsia Groan, Irma Prunesquallor and Doctor Prunesquallor, the mad twins Cora and Clarice, Barquentine and a hundred others—who have bizarre names, certainly, but are as alive and credible as Dickens's characters. Like Dickens, Peake had the gusto, the energy, the invention, the powers of observation, the language, the skill to direct his flood of original invention.

One of Peake's most remarkable qualities was his craftsmanship, his control over the creations of his unique imagination. This control was observable in everything he drew and wrote. He is generally considered the finest illustrator of his day, although the commissions he received were comparatively few—*The Rime of the Ancient Mariner, Treasure Island, Alice in Wonderland, Grimm's Household Tales, The Hunting of the Snark* and a handful of others—and not always as well-paid as they should have been. Dozens of drawings could be mentioned: his portraits of children, his drawings of Belsen inmates, his sketches of Sark, Spain and all the other places he lived in or visited. His talent was unmarred by any hint of the morbid neurosis frequently identified with artists of such intensity; he had no political axes to grind, no messianic notions, no manifestoes to justify or rationalize his particular view of the world. Such things amused him and were often his subject-matter (the emphasis in the Titus books, for instance, on ritual and the quest for power). He was concerned with the business of living, astonished by earnest discussions on the Nature of Art and Life, reduced to laughter by the antics of bureaucrats and politicians and, as his old friend the Rev. A. C. Bridge told those who attended, would have been acutely embarrassed by his own Memorial Service which was held at St James's Church, Piccadilly, on 6 December 1968.

Mervyn had a fine eye for irony. His work could often be

sardonic, but there was no malice in him; merely a considerable sympathy for the individual, particularly the underdog. His amusement at fixed ideologies was neither innocent nor naive, but it was frequently disbelieving. Perhaps it was his refusal to rationalize and explain his work that made it hard for critics to 'place' him and why his work made many, whose attitudes were conventionally moulded, uncomfortable or antagonistic, why, as a consequence, a large public took so long to 'find' him.

Mervyn would have been particularly amused to hear himself called a seminal figure, yet there is no doubt he influenced and continues to influence many new writers, especially in subject-matter and technique. He certainly had considerable influence on what I think is my own best work. His spirit lives on in those he has inspired, in his remarkable family (Maeve now has ten grandchildren) and, of course, in his own work, which so accurately reflects his attitude to the world:

> To live at all is miracle enough,
> The doom of nations is another thing.
> Here is my hammering blood-pulse is my proof.
>
> Let every painter paint and poet sing
> And all the sons of music ply their trade;
> Machines are weaker than a beetle's wing.
>
> Swung out of sunlight into cosmic shade,
> Come what come may the imagination's heart
> Is constellation high and can't be weighed.
>
> Nor greed nor fear can tear our faith apart
> When every heart-beat hammers out the proof
> That life itself is miracle enough.

(*The Glassblowers*, 1950)

In one of his rare published statements about work (*Drawings of Mervyn Peake*, 1949) he said: 'After all, there are no rules. With the wealth, skill, daring, vision of many centuries at one's back, yet one is ultimately quite alone. For it is one's ambition to create one's *own* world in a style germane to its substance, and to people it with its native forms and denizens that never were before, yet have their roots in one's experience. As the earth was thrown from the sun, so from the earth the artist must fling out into space, complete from pole to pole, his own world which, whatsoever form it takes, is the colour of the globe it flew from, as the world itself is coloured by the sun.'

Mervyn Peake succeeded splendidly in creating his own world—a richly populated world—and he left it for us to enjoy.

Since this memoir was first published Mervyn's work has appeared all over the world and film rights have been bought for *Gormenghast*. His main fiction has never been long out of print. Books which he illustrated have been republished because there is now a large audience for his drawings. He is 'collected' (copies of first editions, particularly of illustrated books, sometimes selling for more than the advance he originally received) and he is 'taught'. There is a Mervyn Peake Society, publishing a regular journal, and he is the subject of academic theses. His reputation and his audience is assured; he is recognized as one of the important figures in post-war English literature. I suppose it is unrealistic to wish that some of this recognition had come a little earlier (if only in the form of somewhat larger advances) and to continue to regret the fact that Mervyn never really understood what his work meant to the generations who followed him; he so thoroughly deserved the rewards of his own generosity.

A World Away is a unique book, capturing experience and intensity of feeling without a note of false sentiment or bathos.

Maeve Gilmore is no more capable of self-consciousness in her writing than was her husband. It is, as I've said, a book of remarkable truthfulness. It remains one of the most moving books I have ever read. It will endure, in its own right, for as long as the work of that great artist whose humanity it so effortlessly celebrates.

Michael Moorcock
Fulham Road
London
May 1983

Into the sculpture room he came, quick and sudden and dark, and when he left the room they said, 'That's Mervyn Peake; he's dying of consumption.' For me, at seventeen, someone dying of consumption (even though he was not) had a terrible romance about it.

He returned a few minutes later to the sculpture room, went to the tin trunk where the damp clay was kept, scooped out a handful of it, then went to work on it. In a very short space of time, a vigorous figure emerged from the hitherto shapeless clay; it had nothing to do with the prosaic pose of the model, or the even more prosaic efforts of the students. It had grown out of a native exuberance, and it was the first time I had seen such vitality manifest itself.

During the break, this volatile, dark man came over to where I stood, palpitating, in front of my own clay. He asked me to meet him that evening when the classes were over—perhaps to go to a park for a walk. Out of my appalling shyness I said that I never went for walks, and I didn't like parks. Perhaps such a bald answer should have ended everything before it began, but I did manage to ask, 'What do you paint?' and the answer, 'I'd paint a dust-bin if I thought it beautiful,' was by far the strangest thing I had ever heard, especially coming from the most romantic looking man I had ever seen, that I managed to accept an invitation to tea, which followed this startling dust-bin manifesto.

It had been my first day at an art school, September 1936. I was a convent-reared girl, with a built-in nervousness. It took me an half-hour to enter the school, the cloak-rooms, and eventually the class. It was an experience that I had never before encountered, and the inhibitions with which I had commenced adolescence were too intense to accept without questioning the world of easy banter, in which everyone seemed to know what they were doing and saying. Perhaps no one knew but when one is unsure everyone else seems to be perfectly at ease.

He left the sculpture room, leaving behind him the clay figure he had modelled. The rest of the day for me seemed as long as a climb up Everest.

It did end though, and I went down the stairs to the hall of the school, feeling now as though I was descending Everest, such trepidation and fright did I feel at entering an unknown world. The experience of climbing Everest had changed the world from which I had come. It could no longer be the same—would one's feet ever touch the ground again?

He was waiting in the hall, in the longest, shabbiest, darkest-grey mackintosh that I had ever seen. He looked like a young handsome gypsy, or a young tramp, slim and dark, with the deep-set eyes, and heavy eyelids that were so very striking, and the deep furrows down his cheeks—too deep for so young a man.

*   *   *

There were still trams at that time, and we went upstairs in one. Along Vauxhall Bridge Road it went, and rattled loud enough to make conversation very difficult, like talking or listening through chain mail. That was good for me, as all thoughts, or rather all intelligent thoughts, had completely vanished, and I could think of nothing to say of my own volition, and nothing to answer.

Eventually, we arrived at a Lyons Corner House, and went upstairs to a balcony where one could see the gypsy ladies' band downstairs. In memory they almost seem like carica-tures, but the music was being played with electrifying gusto. It was in this Corner House that for us both love began to the strains of 'The Desert song'. What a desert, what a song.

I was put back on a tram: it couldn't have been the end of an evening, only the beginning of living. I arrived home somehow, and to me the whole world was vibrating. I couldn't imagine a world without Peake—as I thought of him. It was some time before I could use his first name to myself or to anyone else. It was private, and it hurt.

At the time when I first saw Mervyn, and first met him, I had no previous knowledge of him, although he had had exhibitions in a Soho gallery with a group of painters who called themselves the 'Twenties Group', mainly his fellow students from the Royal Academy Schools; and all, as the name implies, in their twenties. Looking through old catalogues which have survived the years, the prices seem very modest, usually between five and fifteen guineas.

Peake was not a student in the sculpture room, but he was teaching—life-drawing. A different part of life. I longed to see him again. He phoned to ask me to go to see him in the place where he lived and worked, and painted. I was given directions. They seemed remote, but as directions always seemed remote to me I knew that I should have to have them transcribed by someone who read maps. A warehouse just over Battersea Bridge, and past a bus station depot. I had seen for years, across the river, a huge signpost which read 'Thousands of tons wasted daily'. I had seen it, and it had meant nothing—just one of those things, like disease, and old age, which we know about but have no inkling of, because it has not touched one personally. 'Thousands of tons wasted daily' was the slogan which pulled one into life.

My first visit was very circumspect. I gave the directions to Penfold, my mother's chauffeur—'Hester Road', just across Battersea Bridge, past the bus station.

Oh, how I love the memory of that place. The incongruousness of it, and my particular form of arrival never struck me as

strange. How could it? When one is in a trance, reality seems
the strange thing.

I knocked at a battered door, and I heard steps descending.
The door opened. Penfold stayed outside, and I never gave
another thought to him. He must have been in an alien world
himself more so even than me, but he waited patiently outside
for several hours, until I stepped down the stairs, another girl
in another clime, never to return to what I had thought I knew.

There was a flight of stairs leading directly from the
door—the steps were painted a crude chrome yellow, and the
top of the banisters vermilion. At the top of the stairs there was
a succession of rooms. I had never seen anything like them.
They were not furnished. They were simply alive. Paintings
and drawings everywhere. Dark patches on the walls, which I
presume must have been patches of damp, but faces and
landscapes had been woven into them, so that what should
have been detrimental was turned into a world of angels and
monsters.

A hissing of an ancient gasfire welcomed one, an old
chaise-longue in front of it; and in the corners of each of the
rooms, and not in corners, were collections of more empty
and half-empty milk bottles than I had ever seen. The most
beautiful and the most romantic place I had been to.

I can remember nothing of that first visit, except that I knew
that I must and would return there.

*　　　　*　　　　*

After this first visit, I was able to find my own way, down
Hester Road, past the bus-drivers and the conductors. I hated
going past them, because of the jokes and the whistles. But
once in those rooms, I entered a new world. Silent, except for
the intermittent, or perhaps regular, vulgar noises of the
ancient gasfire, which was also inefficient as a means of

Mervyn Peake, 1946

Mervyn Peake,
1935

The family,
Sark, 1949

heating. Such beautiful rooms, bare of comfort. Mervyn, as I was beginning to be able to call him, did drawings and paintings of me: a head turning; a body standing; a half head; an eye; a mouth; a hand; half-draped; half-nude; draped or nude; lying; sitting; asleep; awake; laughing; crying; singing; sulking; pencil; pen; oil; chalk; and over-all the nostalgic smell of turpentine.

And afterwards, toasted crumpets by the fire, and indifferent tea.

The stairway to the attic—the stairway to Fuchsia's attic in *Titus Groan*—was larger than life, though what could be larger than life as it was lived in those days?

Sitting by the fire, in this quiet enchanted world, there would sometimes and suddenly be the sound of thuds, and unexpected sound overhead. This island was after all an island surrounded by water, by the Thames. Warehouses on rivers are the refuges of large river rats. Large river rats can jump dexterously, and can pilfer ingeniously; paper and canvas could be quite a pleasant diet. Romance survived on the sound, and only once the sight of these huge and frightening river inhabitants disturbed us.

Once in the candlelight, in front of the black gas monster, the floorboards of the room seemed to move very gently, undulating with the lazy ease of a hammock. It wasn't the candlelight which was playing tricks, because there was also an accompaniment of sound, the sound of the trumpeting of an elephant. The sound and the movement seemed like a minor earth tremor. The sound of an elephant trumpeting was the sound of an elephant trumpeting, and the sight of the floorboards moving was the heaving of the elephant moving underneath. It was being housed for the night in the warehouse below on its way to dance and sing in a travelling circus.

*   *   *

These days were translucent—with light, if love is light, or light is love. They were days of love, but of discovery also. To see everything in a new way. Everything was new. Battersea Bridge, the Embankment, have never been more beautiful. Walking along by the river at dusk and going into 'The Blue Cockatoo', which has now disappeared, for some tea by candlelight. Talking of the future, of the present, of painting, of poetry, jokes. Watching, and being watched, for certainly then Mervyn was an unusual sight. His hair was long and very dark, and he wore bright red waistcoats, orange velvet ties, and occasionally odd socks: one red, one white, not to be looked at, but because he was even then absent-minded. He had a black cloak, with a red lining. People always seemed to stare, at what today would pass unnoticed. But apart from being looked at himself, Mervyn looked and taught me to look, to see people and incidents, objects, and to store up knowledge. People were the raw material for many of his illustrations. Sometimes he would stop a stranger in the street—it could be a tramp, it could be a girl, or a spiv—and ask him to pose, perhaps on the spot, a quick drawing (sometimes on the inside of a cigarette carton, if he had no sketch-book with him); and sometimes to go to his studio, when he would do drawings or paintings of him.

When I was still a somewhat young bride, the girls he stopped always seemed to have good 'bone structure', which eased the small green seed of jealousy, and later on 'bone structure' became one of those jokes enjoyed only between ourselves.

Apart from this, the drawings made of an old tramp asleep in Trafalgar Square were used for the Baker in *Hunting of the Snark*, which was one of the first books he illustrated. I remember seeing a man coming out of Hatchards in Piccadilly with a copy under his arm, and I walked up to him and said, 'My husband did those drawings.' I was frozen by a look. I had invaded a private universe, and I decided that it were better to remain silent, always.

*   *   *

For Mervyn, going down into the underground was not a straightforward, upright, and still journey down an escalator, but a sliding descent down the rail. I could never summon up courage to follow, so that sometimes he would reach the bottom, go up the other escalator, and pass me by once more at, it seemed, even greater speed, in time to take my hand as I staidly tripped off the bottom step.

We often went to Lyons for meals, and I suppose we were neither of us the most regular looking customers: Mervyn, I know, was unique, dark and majestic. How can I say what I was? I think: pale and blonde and a good foil for such a dark one. Mervyn sometimes ordered stewed camel. It probably wasn't very funny, and the waitresses obviously thought not. They raised their eyebrows, and tapped their pencil on their pad, until the conventions were observed, and they were back in the world of brunch or eggs and chips, which they understood.

In the first years we found Lyons shops a kind of home. Once we met James Stephens, the Irish poet, like a little leprechaun, curly haired and lively, witty and from a world of fairies, and we all went in to the Lyons in Leicester Square. This was just after we were married, and he wrote a little poem for me on a scrap of paper which I still have.

For all Young Brides
When a son you shall desire
Pray to water, and to fire.

But when you would have a daughter
Pray to fire and then to water.

Then he did a strange little drawing which he called 'Portrait of many Mervyn Peakes by his friend James Stephens. Given at this Court at Lyons Dive 1938'.

*   *   *

Before our love went too far, I was sent away. For some strange and now quite forgotten reason I wished to learn German. So I went to a castle (probably a minor one) on the Rhine. The father, killed in the First World War, and the mother, a Baronin, picking up bits of silver paper on the spike of her walking-stick for munitions for the next war. Oh, how stupid, how ignorant one was as a girl. The terrible demonstrations for Hitler that I saw, but didn't understand, thinking only of love. The Nazi salutes, which one unthinkingly returned, as though it were a charade. The joke which was beyond one. I saw Hitler once at a parade in Nuremberg, and I saw Hess, and my mind had only one thought. Love.

My first letter from Mervyn in Germany was a drawing, a group of girls all walking with their feet fixed on back to front; and the caption: 'Is this how they walk?' Where has the drawing gone? Lost, anyway.

But love was not lost. It survived a year, and we met again as though only a flutter of an eyelid had passed.

*   *   *

I went down to see Mervyn's parents in Wallington, Surrey. I felt frightened to meet them. I couldn't imagine him having parents. I couldn't imagine him coming from anywhere but from himself, and I didn't want to see him in any kind of environment but his own.

I was wrong. His father was kind and slow of speech, searching always for the apposite word, and always finding it, however long it took. His mother was small, dark, lively, and

Mervyn's dark looks were from Wales, his mother's native land.

His father was now a general practitioner, having returned from China. The change of environment must have been like the difference between space travel and under-sea diving.

The house was large, Victorian and Gothic, and much of its interior had reminders of the life which had been left behind: rice bowls and dragons, Chinese carpets, ornate brass ornaments. Later, as I learned to know them better, many of the horrifying experiences they had undergone during the Boxer Rising, and the violence they received as 'white devils', came to light, and I felt a pride in their achievements, which now have been erased in Communist China, but which must have taken them so very much courage and foresight.

Mervyn's father drew delicate little drawings, and his mother sang and played the piano, and from these must have sprung his own gifts. I think they themselves must have often wondered how such a gifted son had arrived through them. They were rather shocked by his first exhibition of line drawings, which had a sensuousness not to be expected from the son of a medical missionary.

I know that his father had seen very dreadful and appalling sights during the Rebellion, and his own work amongst people who were suspicious of the foreign devil was carried on under conditions which would appal and deter the surgeons of today. It was a long time before he was accepted in Tientsin, where he wished to build a hospital, and the occasion which made it possible is, or must be, medically bizarre. The local mandarin had a son who was blind, and he was brought to Dr Peake, after a great deal of courteous and non-committal exchange of pleasantries.

On examination, he was found to have cataract in both eyes. It must have been almost impossible to explain in the most difficult language of Mandarin China the effect that an operation on the eyes might have. Somehow there was a mutual understanding, and it was decided that an operation would be acceptable, but only if it were performed in public with the father and his entourage watching.

I do not know the details, as there is no one living who can substantiate them. All I know is that Mervyn's father was a man of courage. If he had failed, his life—or perhaps less so, his reputation—was at stake.

The operation was duly performed, and it had in some way been conveyed to the father that there would be no immediate result. It would take time before the bandages were removed from the eyes, and the result would be slow in manifesting itself.

After a length of time, perhaps two weeks, the bandages were removed for the first time, and an object held in front of the eyes. Before an audience of father and courtiers, there was a flicker of sight.

This happened over another period of time, and the young man saw. The foreign devil had expunged himself and the mandarin gave financial help to the building of a hospital.

A sad aftermath of this successful operation was the sight of a column of very poor blind Chinese, one behind the other, each holding the pigtail of the one in front, making their way to the surgery and falling down on their knees, praying for sight, to the man they could neither see nor understand. Impossible to explain in a distant language that theirs was blindness, and congenital. How could they understand? They left the way they had arrived, with their only security the pigtail of their blind friend or enemy in front of them, and only thinking that they were sinful and unworthy of the miracle that had been worked on the mandarin's son.

*　　　*　　　*

The digression to Mervyn's parents is not a digression. His

childhood was unusual, and I can see in his work so much that sprang from the surroundings that enveloped him, although to everyone in this particular world, which retained so much a flavour of England, but surrounded by China, it must have seemed quite mundane.

A strange childhood. Such a mixture of English noncon- formity, and almost bourgeois convention. Congregational hymns, tea-parties, a straight-laced upbringing, and outside surrounded by dragons and carvings of ancient imagination and disastrous beauty.

He rode on a mule to Tientsin Grammar School, where he received the most English of educations. His most vivid recollection seems to be of the raw red elbows of the spinster teacher who ran the school, although for some reason his parents lived in the Russian compound. So many things which are called 'Gothic' in his *Titus Groan* trilogy must spring from the fantasies which presented themselves to him, years later, from his childhood in China.

One day, on his mule, he stretched out his hand to stroke a camel. They are vicious creatures and not used to love. He could hear for ever after the livid meeting of the camel's jaws, as they opened and closed on what should have been his hand. A coolie, in a quick gesture, had pulled Mervyn's hand away, and he was left trembling, silent, and tearful, but with a right hand intact.

That camel made an appearance, perhaps thirty-five years later, in *Titus Alone*. It was a vile camel.

On his way to school he passed the tragic huts outside the compound, where the poorest lived, and the stray dogs, scrawny with hunger, sniffed and dug and scratched for what little sustenance they could find.

Mervyn was perhaps seven years old. Did he understand? And where did he store these sights, this knowledge, for the compound to make its way into *Titus Groan*, thirty years later, as the habitation of the mud-dwellers, who carved for their love, and their life, and the dreadful lean dogs, stalking their way through the dwellings?

He returned to England at the age of eleven with his parents and his brother. They came via the Trans-Siberian Railway. A few adolescent memories recurred to him. His brother, getting off the train, whilst it was being refuelled, in mid-Siberia, and the slow advance of the train in this desolate grey ice-pack. As it mounted speed, the small speck of humanity being left behind for the wolves. The mother, calling and calling for her child, who ran, faster than was thought possible, and being pulled by his father as though his arms would be torn to shreds, on to the high steps of the train—and the small younger brother, agog with excitement and trepidation. In his excitement, throwing out shoes, socks, gloves, but in such a situation, who cares what is expended! The small or larger boy was saved from the wolves, and life lay ahead, unexpected and unforearmed.

The carvings were everywhere, buildings were not functional but full of fantasy. How could it not have influenced a mind which from somewhere had a vision that finally betrayed it by its richness?

*   *   *

The visit to Wallington in Surrey, to meet Mervyn's parents, seemed to bring closer an event which now had an inevitability about it. Neither of us could imagine a life ahead which was not shared with the other.

Formalities seemed necessary, although we would both have liked to marry in some remote, isolated church, close to the sea, or dark and candlelit. But what one wants is not necessarily what is decided upon.

My parents met Mervyn. He had many things which were

not in his favour. Certainly, no one in the family had seen anyone quite like him before—with his dark, long hair, his deep-sunken eyes, shielded by black eyelashes, his red waistcoats, his purple socks, his orange velvet tie, all this and his lack of money. Perhaps most of all, the creed in which he had spent his childhood. Nonconformity. But religious nonconformity. His own life was nonconformist in ideas, his ideas were nonconformist in his life.

Somehow the divergencies had to be met. Divergencies are always met by the charitable. The practising Christians with their creeds, with their small partitions and lack of charity are the ones who win outwardly.

How foreign to the spirit's early beauty
And to the amoral integrity of the mind
And to all those whose reserve of living is lovely
Are the tired Creeds that can be so unkind.

There is brotherhood among the kindly,
Closer and defter and more integral
Than any brotherhood of aisle or coven
For love rang out before the chapel bell.

There is no intolerance and no bitterness
As between sects where the full-hearted are
And to pray for the non-natural and to have pity
On those of alien faith whose eyes are clear

Is to be insolent, is to be ignorant,
Is to deny the god-head—is to withhold
The focal Christ of love; is to renounce
The only selfless language in the world.

Jesus—where are you?
That is me speaking, after Mervyn. It seems it is not

possible to live by love alone. Dogma—laws of the church, laws of man—are essential to respectability.

I loved my mother very much. Mervyn loved me, and I loved Mervyn. No one wants to hurt anyone they love. I would have lived with Mervyn without any of the formalities, although I was devout to a degree of intensity.

I still don't want to hurt—but why is it that they hurt me? because my creed has changed; and I hurt them. Mervyn can no longer be hurt or hurt, although he was the gentlest man alive—a gentleness that came from his father who, having seen the cruelties of human beings, had retained an innocence that was touching and impossible to understand.

*　　　*　　　*

We were married very conventionally in St James's, Spanish Place. All the concessions came from the other side. From people who had spent their lives with a creed that had little to do with popery, who did not understand the dogma and the ritual but who were willing to concede on behalf of a son who loved a being so different as to be almost from another planet.

Theirs was the generous spirit.

*　　　*　　　*

So life began.

Could one possibly know what life was? How could one know what love was, before living it? How could one know what life was before loving it?

We lived in a flat overlooking Battersea Park, from December 1937. It didn't matter to me where we lived, and such mundane things as eating or meeting people or earning a living seemed utterly extraneous, vulgar and not germane to us. The gentle veil of love surrounded us—oh, why do we wake?

About this time, there was a great deal of abuse against a piece of sculpture by Jacob Epstein, called Adam. Strange that people no longer become incensed by painting or sculpture in the way that they used to. Mervyn wrote a poem, called 'Epstein's Adam', and sent it to *Picture Post*, where it was given quite a bit of space. It was written as a protest at protest. A few days later Epstein wrote to ask Mervyn to come to see him. We both went to tea in a mansion of a house in Hyde Park Gardens. There was sculpture everywhere. It was a moving manifestation of a man obsessed. We had tea at a huge table presided over by his first wife, an over-life-size woman, with deep red hair. I always think of her as Gertrude in *Titus Groan*—whether she was some kind of inspiration for her (although that sounds an archaic word) I have no idea.

Apart from the abundance of work everywhere, the only thing I remember is a detailed and absorbing description by his son, a small intelligent boy, of the refuelling of aeroplanes in the air, a subject about which neither Mervyn nor I was knowledgeable.

I knew nothing of cooking, nothing of cleaning; it seems on looking back that I simply knew nothing of anything. I had very little conversation; I had hardly heard of ideas as ideas. I can think of no one more boring. When we went out to meet people, if I was addressed personally, I simply went red, stuttered, and burst into tears. One of the first occasions this happened was when we went into a group of what I presume were intellectuals, and I was asked point-blank what I thought of the new Peter Jones building. Quite honestly, I had never thought it was a subject to be thought about. In the deathly silence which awaited my answer, and the white blankness which enveloped me, there was nothing to say, except; 'I think . . . it's negative', and then a burst of tears, and the embarrassment which followed such anti-social behaviour took us off home before our time.

The main source of income then was still the teaching—life-drawing twice a week at the Westminster School of Art where we had met, and commissions by the now defunct *London Mercury* (which was published monthly, and brought a small addition to our budget) to do drawings of already famous authors, artists, actors and actresses.

There was never any organized time for working—how could there be? An idea for a poem would grow as suddenly as the flight of a meteor. It might be jotted down quickly on the inside of a cigarette carton, to be worked on later. In the middle of the night words were eased into birth, to grow into a poem, the next day and following days or weeks, difficult as life itself.

Twice a week teaching, and the remaining five days filled with creative activity so rich and varied that one wonders how one man could survive such an onslaught on his eyes, ears, and brain.

*　　　*　　　*

It was in 1938 that the first exhibition of drawings of Mervyn's had been arranged. An exhibition of line drawings at a gallery called The Calmann Gallery just off St James's. It seemed to presage hope.

Hitler marched into, oh God, was it Czechoslovakia? or was it Vienna? on the day of the private view. So much does history impinge on our individual lives. A desperate air. As desperate as today. I remember standing on the balcony overlooking Battersea Park the night before the exhibition opened, and the dreadful feeling of foreboding. Not because for the first time in his life Mervyn was putting himself in view of a public who might be antagonistic or receptive, but because of a malaise—a political tremor which shook everyone; for even then it was hard to remain aloof, although the world has shrunk further since those days.

The first taste of a personal success, even a minor one, was damaged by outside events, which were the beginning of total world damage.

The sale of the first drawing was to me like selling my body. It was a drawing of me, which seemed to be intimate, and entirely belonging to us, as was the love we generated. Private and alone. It seemed inconceivable that a drawing, made alone and imperatively, should go into a house of strangers, hang on their walls, and be looked at, liked or disliked, spoken of by people we didn't know or care about. I wept once more at this concession to the philistine world. Gradually one's tears dry, and the cliché that time heals begins to rear its practical head.

Eddie Marsh, who collected pictures like butterflies, bought a drawing, and later a very large oil painting. He asked us both to come to see him, in one of the Inns of Court. Even though my house has an infinity of pictures, I have never seen anything quite like his! Pictures three or four deep wherever one looked. I think he was the first example of a really erudite man that I had ever met. Mervyn remained solely himself in whatever company he kept, whilst I was intimidated and frightened by such a superior brain.

★   ★   ★

The exhibition was financially a moderate success. There had been reviews. The first taste. Now I can read, on Mervyn's behalf, the good, the bad, the indifferent with a cauterized mind and still survive the day.

★   ★   ★

Just before we were married, Mervyn took me down to see Walter de la Mare in Buckinghamshire. Our meeting came about through a poem which Mervyn had written to me, and which Walter de la Mare wished to include in an anthology called *Love* which he was editing.

How can I say that the poem was not one which brought pride and love to me?

> You walk unaware
> Of the slender gazelle
> That moves as you move
> And is one with the limbs
> That you have.
>
> You live unaware
> Of the faint, the unearthly
> Echo of hooves
> That throughout your white streams
> Of clear clay that I love
>
> Are in flight as you turn
> As you stand, as you move,
> As you sleep, for the slender
> Gazelle never rests
> In your ivory groove.

He had been almost a myth for so long, since my school days and the learning of 'The Traveller', that I couldn't believe he existed, and he was the first famous person that I ever met.

We went by train to Penn, then walked to his house from the station. I was sick from apprehension on the walk to his house, but little I knew how unnecessary that was, for the man was gentle and fanciful, able to make the most diffident of guests at home in his house. He was small, and bright eyed. His wife also had the gift of putting at ease anyone who seemed uneasy.

We had tea at a candlelit table, and the talk ranged from

subject to subject—ghosts, love, fancy, stories—and as de la Mare wrote a little later in a letter which seems apposite:

One sips at a subject, and then passes on to flower No. 2, and so forth, does show up the peculiar evanescence of one's thoughts and fancies. These can be so infernally rapid; and yet I'm rather inclined to think that mine are like one of those charming little toys of my childhood when you peeped at a succession of the same figure in different attitudes etc.—whirled him round and he became alive. In quite other words, don't you think one finds oneself dishing out the same little obsessions over and over again. I simply cannot resist anything in the nature of apparitional.

That is almost how the conversation went. After tea, we went into the drawing-room, where de la Mare showed us his collection of miniature books. Beautifully made and perfect. It was some years later that I read a book of his, *Memoirs of a Midget*, and recollected this unusual and strangely personal set of tiny books.

There was a dream-like quality over the whole of that first meeting, and all the subsequent times. There was nothing to be frightened of in such a dulcet man.

★   ★   ★

The first commission for an illustrated book of Nursery Rhymes came at about this time. It was called *Ride a Cock-Horse* and had fourteen illustrations. It was quite easily the most beautifully produced of the books that Mervyn illustrated. The war had started, but the paper shortage and the many restrictions connected with publishing hadn't yet begun to make their indelible and ugly mark on wartime books.

Walter de la Mare wrote to say:

I have been engrossed in Nursery Rhyme pictures again and
again. Fantasy and the grotesque, indeed; a rare layer of the
imagination, and a touch now and then, and more than a
touch of the genuinely sinister. But, as I think, not a trace of
the morbid—that very convenient word. How many
nurseries you may have appalled is another matter. How
many scandalized parents may have written to you,
possibly enclosing doctor's and neurologist's bills, you will
probably not disclose. Anyhow, most other illustrated
books for children look just silly by comparison.

*   *   *

In 1938 we moved from Battersea to two floors of a house in
Portsdown Road in Maida Vale. A very short walk to the
canal, and a district which seemed rather dingy. The rooms we
had were the precursors of the succession of houses and flats in
which we lived afterwards. They were nearly always large,
very high-ceilinged, and usually in need of decoration, except
that books and pictures in profusion were always our major
decorative effort. Often murals on the walls, and doors
decorated like rococo cathedrals.

In a flat downstairs to which we were invited the owners
had a passion for red. Both had dyed red hair, but on being
shown into their rooms we were smothered and felt
claustrophobic with vermilion—walls, carpets, ceiling,
chairs, sofas, all in more tones and shades of red than could be
imagined. We wondered what their politics were! But I don't
think fanatical manifestoes made their way out of all this
decorative fantasia. They just loved red.

In our own home we had a tortoise who appropriated the
fire with our two cats: a black one called Chakka, the Black
Napoleon, and a white one called Moby Dick. The tortoise
roamed round the room gently and quietly, poking its little

Mervyn Peake in Soho whilst on leave, 1944

The author, 1937

raddled head out of its shell with the serenity of a cave-bound hermit, and eating up what greens there were. I found it strange that one could even grow to have a little affection for such an unknown quantity which housed itself in a shell.

Early in 1939 Mervyn had his second exhibition of paintings and drawings, at the Leicester Galleries; and I had my first exhibition at the Wertheim Galleries. There was a radio programme called 'In Town To-night', and we were asked to be on it, on the strength of our having concurrent exhibitions.

Quite naturally, we were in the usual state of inadequate finances, and we were told that we would each receive £3, which seemed a fortune in minuscule. We had one rehearsal, and on the evening went up to Broadcasting House, as two of the interesting people 'In Town To-night'! One of the others was Lilli Palmer, and her sister, and we all sat outside the studio, feeling vastly uninteresting.

It was far less arduous than we imagined, and we left the studio £6 the richer, and made our way straight to the Café Royal. Instead of the usual coffee, sitting on red plush seats at marble tables, we went beyond the barrier to the tables laid for eating. The £6 receded, as the meal proceeded, and there was very little left of the riches received that evening.

Sometimes we had a group of people in to do drawings from a model, and then we would have coffee and talk, or dance after drawing. It seems like a pre-historic way of spending an evening now, but then there was the dreadful malaise of an imminent war that diversions, of work or play, could not eliminate.

We had passed 'Peace in our Time', in which people believed because they so wished for it—although how could we have believed it, with so much menace, so much flavour of despair or inevitability surrounding us all?

Nevertheless, individuals still made their plans, had their hopes and aspirations.

My mother lent us a car to go to Stratford-on-Avon for a few days, in the beginning of September 1939. England looked invitingly beautiful—we were afraid for its vulnerability, aware of how easily the beauty could be damaged. We went to see *As You Like It* at the Stratford Memorial Theatre, and I remember an old man sitting in front of us, who so entered into the excitement of the fight between the wrestlers on stage that he stood up and encouraged his chosen one in a hoarse and excitable voice, flinging his arms around menacingly at the opponent, and shouting belligerently as though he were truly in a wrestling ring.

Such anti-social behaviour could not be allowed to last long, and he was asked by the manager to remove himself. We thought it was a marvellous tribute to the actors that he had so entered into the spirit of the play.

It was a time when one could be lost for a short while in dreams, but there was always the awakening to reality, knowing that life as we were living it then could not, would not, ever be the same again. Outside events would engulf everyone.

We were in Chipping Campden. The Cotswolds hurt us by their opulence; and Mervyn wrote this poem:

> We are the haunted people.
> We, who guess blindly at the seed
> That flowers
> Into the crimson caption,
> Hazarding
> The birth of that inflamed
> Portentous placard that will lose its flavour
> Within the hour,
> The while the dark deeds move that gave the words
> A bastard birth
> And hour by hour

Bursts a new gentian flower
Of bitter savour
We have no power . . . no power . . .
We are the haunted people,
We . . .
The last loose tassellated fringe that flies
Into the cold of aeons from a dark
Dynastic gown.

*　　　*　　　*

We were staying in a hotel in the square, and on the morning of 3 September 1939, we heard the bell of a town-crier ringing with an urgency that could only presage one thing. The tricorne hat and the long cape-coat, the bell, and the parchment had something about them of permanence, and the announcement of war seemed less dreadful, couched in the archaic language and setting of what seemed to be an England of ancient custom.

Just as the town-crier finished calling out the news which everyone was hearing in so many different ways and environments all over England, an almost apocalyptical figure, a man, appeared from one side of the square on a white horse and rode to the other side, disappearing as suddenly as he came, so that one hardly knew if it were a vision or not. He remained as a symbol always, through the war years to come.

What did one feel at that time? A dreadful fear of the unknown. But even in the time of such overwhelming fear, our own personal lives cannot but have importance to us, and hearing the announcement of war with the knowledge that we were expecting our first child could only cast gloom on an event which in itself is so mysterious.

We left Gloucestershire and returned to London. To the flat in Maida Vale. Everything had a strangeness: the atmosphere was uncertain, yet people still laughed and quarrelled, made love, were apprehensive, knew nothing, wished to do something positive, loved England, and more and more floundered in a negative abyss. Mervyn volunteered to fit gas masks, and was accepted; for the world, or England at war, was still uncertain, and until he was called up this seemed the only occupation for which he was suited.

These months from September onwards had an unreality about them that is like the unreality one feels before an operation—or before the birth of a child—the ominousness that precedes a violent change, so that one is never the same again.

The first Christmas of the war came, and the expected violence was non-existent, at least as we had visualized it over England, in England. We were still in Maida Vale. Our red friends downstairs blacked out, our friends upstairs with a fencing studio were gone; and we were left with our huge windows, criss-crossed with tape, hung with black draperies.

We wished to make Christmas memorable in a way to do with peace, as though life was as it had always been. Our finances were not outstandingly affluent—in fact, were as they had always been, a little strained—but we decided to buy as many packets of cigarettes as could stand the strain, and then for Mervyn to go with them to the Arches, and give a packet, to whomsoever he saw, as a minute gesture of Christmas. The Arches were beneath Waterloo Bridge where the derelict and the homeless congregated, the sordid and the lonely.

About midnight on Christmas morning he returned, empty of cigarettes, but with a young Welsh coal-miner whom he had found in the Arches. He had the gallantry of the Welsh, and then: .

> I heard them sing,
> And loose the Celtic bird that has no wing,

No body, eye, nor feather,
Only song,
That indestructible, that golden thing.

His voice rang out, as praise, or as a heathen offering. He shared our home for some days. It could not have been simply on account of:

The little flower
That lights the palm into a nightmare land,
A bloody basin of the sterile moon,
That lights the face that sprouts the cigarette
Into a sudden passion of fierce colour.

There was no difference between us. Mervyn gave him a suit, and he went off one morning for a job, and never returned. He had said that if he didn't return he would end his life.

It is easy to be cynical.

   ★   ★   ★

Because of the fear of air-raids we gave up the flat in Maida Vale, and went to a cottage in Sussex in an ominously named hamlet called Warningcamp. The ancient Britons fearing a Roman invasion.

Our child was due within a few months. Mervyn received his call-up papers, and for us the war had really begun.

He had applied some time before for a job as a war artist, and had a testimonial from Augustus John, which he sent with his application to (could it be?) the War Office.

Dec. 28. 1939.

To whom it may concern.
 I wish to recommend Mr. Mervyn Peake as a draughts-

man of great distinction, who might be most suitably employed in war records.

AUGUSTUS JOHN.

Needless to say this made no impression on anyone at all, and he was sent to Dartford as a prospective gunner, non-commissioned.

*   *   *

The day that he left couldn't be imagined. We had never been parted, except for a few hours at a time, and during the time of the advent of our son, Sebastian. He was two weeks old when Mervyn had to leave.

Although it was winter, it was moderately mild. The hollowness that we felt at this first parting lingers still. It seemed impossible that strangers could so cruelly separate one. Until the last moment we would not believe it.

But the time for the train departure from Arundel came, and leaving Sebastian asleep in the cottage we walked together along the towpath, by the side of the river Arun, unbelieving, almost as though we had both been and were under sentence of death.

Be proud, slow trees. Be glad you stones and birds,
And you brown Arun river and all things
That grow in silence through the hours of maytime—
Be glad you are not fashioned in God's image.

Impossible to say goodbye, to contemplate a life apart. Mervyn made his way to an unknown world, and I, more luckily, back to the warmth of home.

When I returned to the cottage, under a tree in the front garden was a bicycle, with a note pinned to its handlebars.

A present which seemed the most extravagant I could ever receive. It had been put there whilst I was out by a neighbour, but was from Mervyn.

It was to be my only means of transport from the village to Arundel, with one and then two babies, for shopping. But I never thought of it as a bicycle. How could I have done so? I loved it, and for fifteen years at least in wartime and out it took me, my children, and my cat, with no effort along country lanes in England, and later in Sark.

To be separated after never having been separated is like losing a limb. The acute sense of loss. How can one know until one is deprived of what one has always taken for granted?

The dream had given way to reality. It was a soldier's world, no longer a world of words and paint. Words and paint were an interlude, and the excitement of our first child, first words, first steps, first tooth, could only be shared through the post.

> There is no other link—only the sliding
> Second we share: this desperate edge of now.

★   ★   ★

Mervyn wrote to say that I could come to see him in Dartford. I made arrangements to leave the baby, and arrived in Dartford at the arranged time. How strange that the compartment in which I had been sitting stopped exactly where a soldier was standing. A soldier who looked familiar, but unfamiliar. Deep-sunken eyes, a lean face, but where was the long black hair? It was explained to me: the sergeant-major had said, 'Get your 'air cut—you look like a bloody poet.' It would have had to happen whatever the sergeant-major had said. You have to do what you are told.

★   ★   ★

There was leave due, and we moved to another cottage in Warningcamp, where maybe the warning was a little less imperative. Not so close to the river, nearer a mysterious wood, with rides that no one used any longer, it always reminded us of Kipling's poem, 'A way through the woods', and in the autumn an abundance of blackberries for jam and bottling and picnics.

It was during this leave that *Titus Groan* gestated. Mervyn began to write it in publishers' dummy books. At this time it had not been conceived as a whole, it was a book that grew under duress. Mervyn had many of these beautiful publishers' dummies, which came to him mainly from Chatto and Windus, and Eyre and Spottiswoode. The very sight of them seemed to tender, generate and promulgate ideas as generously as a Roman Catholic in the face of a family planning clinic. After the leave, he took what he could in his kitbag, and left at home the first small book. Strange, how something as familiar to me now, familiar as one's first child, was not familiar, was something to be known, or learned, and part of one's life.

He was sent to the Isle of Sheppey to a gun-site. Gunner Peake 5917577. I feel sick when I think of the waste, but he was always without pride, without resentment. I think of the drawings he could have made, and the futile waste of talent, but perhaps he made more use of everything he saw and lived with than he would have done in any official capacity. How he survived the world of army discipline is incomprehensible. I think the answer is that he didn't survive it. Physically perhaps, but not mentally.

Letters of love arrived. The imminence of everything perhaps accentuated our love:

My Maeve, my artist-girl—companion of the years, the first of many a fire—my little honey-haired, golden-eyed sweetheart from whom I receive so much of my strength and all my love, take care of your sweet feminine self until I come back. I love you so much more than ever before. It is as though there were something richer and fuller in it, and something hotter so that when we quarrel, which all full blooded people do, it seems worse than ever, and when we love one another, it is more wonderful than ever.

After being on the bomb site on the Isle of Sheppey for some months, the Commanding Officer asked if any of the squad could drive. Mervyn happened to be the only man who could do so.

He was transferred not many days later to Blackpool. He was met at the station, almost as foreign royalty is greeted at Victoria Station, with red carpet and full panoply. He learned that he was to be the new driving instructor in a regiment of Sappers. Sapper Peake 5917577, driving instructor for heavy army vehicles.

His knowledge of an engine was rudimentary. He could make a car go, but more often than not it would stop without any instructions from him. It just stopped because it wanted to.

It seems that the Army is no more noted for its common sense than any other branch of human nature, but that is assuming the Army is human.

It must have been, for it took one hour precisely to judge that Sapper Peake had no intimate knowledge of the temperamental workings of heavy army lorries. He was demoted. His major task thereafter in Blackpool was to print elaborately beautiful cards which said 'Only officers may use this lavatory'.

I had a wire from him to say that he would be in Blackpool for some time, and that I could join him there when all the various practical dispositions of cottage and furnishings (such as they were) could be made.

A friend came with me to London with the baby, nappies and all the trappings of an unknown future home. I was put on a train for Blackpool, a compartment crammed with soldiers, and wives, or women, and sat in a corner with, even at the beginning of the journey, a very vociferous male child. I can remember the dress I was wearing. Bright red jersey, buttoned all down the front to make feeding easier, and I was sick with excitement.

It took fourteen hours to reach Blackpool. The train was blacked out and stopped over and over again, with no seeming reason, except once when the train was a target for a lone German raider. It stopped still with the dread that a gentle antelope might feel when mesmerized by a boa constrictor. In the ominous darkness, my son's screams seemed to beckon to that alien pilot, heard but unseen. It was almost impossible to believe that he could not be heard in all that quiet.

In the over-crowded compartment the soldiers were infinitely kind and took the wailing baby on their knees, sang to him in Cockney, or dialect: kind and witty and gentle.

The train at last arrived in Blackpool. It was *heaven*. Mervyn had waited hours. We went to his billet in Coronation Drive. It was a bleak arrival, around four in the morning, and it was not until the next day, after exhausted sleep, that I saw my future companions and the landladies of the billet.

We had a tiny room, and Mervyn spent most of his time pouring 'Nurse Harvey's Mixture' down our son's throat to silence what seemed to be a permanent siren-sound of screams.

We had meals ending with high tea about 5.30 in a dingy room that, on recollection, could almost have won a prize for being the drabbest one could conceive.

We spoke to a young R.A.F. man who was billeted there with his wife and child. He told us that he wrote poetry, and over the next four weeks we spent in Coronation Drive we talked of everything that to him was a new world. Jack was his name, and after we left he sent us the poems that he wrote. It would be so easy, or it would have been so easy, to laugh at them but I have them still. They fill me with a terrible sadness, because he had the soul of a poet, without the knowledge. In one letter he says:

> Please convey my deepest regards to Mervyn. I have much indeed to thank him for. Each day in its circle has spasm of reflection in my mind, that can always be kept apart from the commonplace happenings. This practice was first initiated by Mervyn, and I can interpret the ugly and the weirdest thoughts, making them adopt a deeper meaning than that which is seen only by the naked eye.

Jack was killed a year later over Germany.

*   *   *

Because of the very cramped quarters in Coronation Drive, we applied for another billet. We were sent to one run by two spinsters, and we had a bedroom and sitting-room, which seemed almost immoral at that time.

Each morning I sat up in bed, polishing with Brasso the regimental buttons, and Mervyn polished his boots until they shone unnaturally. I wonder what his duties were during the day? There could not have been all that number of officers who were allowed to use those lavatories. There must surely be a saturation point!

There must have been a war on somewhere, but it was early days and it didn't seem to have found its feet.

In the evenings Mervyn wrote *Titus Groan*, and downstairs one of the R.A.F. men played Glenn Miller. 'In the Mood', 'Moonlight Serenade', 'Pennsylvania 65,000'. It's a strange association, but I still cannot read passages of his book without its awakening in me the sweet nostalgia of evenings which belonged to a nether world of waiting, a world that we all knew would end, and a world which hung suspended.

One day his Commanding Officer came to tea with us. He was not a Commanding Officer, but a man. Venerable in our company, unsure. He brought some of his poems and paintings, and he spoke of the loneliness and the deception of everything that he had felt was permanent, of how on his first leave he had returned to familiar places, familiar faces. After so short a time is one erased. People had forgotten his name and life had gone on. He simply felt alienated, and was glad to be back with his regiment. For a short space of time, for tea with us (and our 'little blossom', as the two spinster ladies in a thick Blackpudlian accent called our son) he was a human being with aspirations far removed from military splendour.

★　　　★　　　★

Although the war had not reached Blackpool, it seemed that a sapper who was no longer any use as a driving instructor to the Army was also no longer any use as a sign-writer for officers' lavatories.

The command came. Some remote authority thought it advisable that Sapper Peake should be transferred to the Lake District, where there were no facilities for wives.

Goodbye to Blackpool.

Near Warningcamp was a village on the Downs called Burpham, about three miles from Arundel. We found a thatched cottage at three shillings a week. No water inside, but a tap outside the back door. What a minute inconvenience!

I went to 94, Wepham, with Sebastian, and an imminent second arrival. Mervyn went to the Lake District. He was living in tents with a Negro regiment, and when he was free

from discipline he walked and savoured the mystery of the
district. It was, strangely enough, at this time that he was
asked by Batsford to illustrate a book called *Witchcraft in
England*. They sent reference books to him at the camp, and he
illustrated the book, in the very vicinity where witchcraft still
seemed to be particularly alive.

My sweetest, my most dear darling Maeve,

    To-day you will be going into the Nursing Home. I have
had no definite news whether I can come or not, but I will
do my utmost. How wonderful it was to be able to talk to
you last night, dear Maeve. As I told you I was talking from
that family I told you about. They gave me high tea when I
dropped in about 6 p.m., and I told them about you . . .

    Maevie, I am in love. Deeply, un-endingly. For ever and
ever.

Your Mervyn.

I cannot think how he found the materials with which to
work, but he did, and produced a most marvellously vigorous
set of drawings. The book was published within a year.

*   *   *

Apart from whatever he was doing on behalf of the war
effort, illustrating *Witchcraft in England*, and writing poems,
some of which were published in the *London Mercury*, the
Listener, the *New English Weekly*, and the *Spectator*, his book
was progressing as fast as a hunted stag. As each dummy book
was completed he sent it back to me, and I kept all his
manuscripts by my bed, together with a bagful of nappies in
case of a sudden air-raid. Baby, books, nappies: the three most
important things in life.

*   *   *

Where was the war? The countryside in Sussex was heavily beautiful. The downs, with their Piero della Francesca clumps of thorn bushes, were out of bounds. There was target practice, and fear of invasion made them especially venerable.

My second son, Fabian, was born in 1942 in 'The Peter Pan Nursing Home', and—is it possible?—a young nurse called Wendy looked after us.

Mervyn went to his sergeant and asked for compassionate leave, on the grounds of his wife having produced a baby, to be answered with 'What's so new about that?'

He forged a pass and came down for a brief visit.

It seemed when I returned to the cottage with Fabian, and Mervyn came home on leave, that there was a tenseness and a sense of withdrawal, that was shared and only partly shared. Perhaps the first time in our lives that we were not one. Was it the alien world that deprived one? It was certainly no loss of love. It grew and grew, but the world had intervened. A feeling of something amiss. To save the pain, he did not speak, but used the words that poetry alone can convey.

> O, this estrangement forms a distance vaster
> Than great seas and great lands
> Could lay between us, though in my hands
> Yours lie, that are less your hands than the plaster
> Casts of your hands. Your face, made in your likeness
> Floats like a ghost through its own clay from me,
> Even from you—O it has left us, we
> Are parted by a tract of thorn and water
> The bitter
> Knowledge of failure damns us where we stand
> Withdrawn, lonely, powerless, and
> Hand in hand.

★　　　★　　　★

Just after he returned to the Lake District, I had an official letter from the War Office saying that he had been sent to Southport with a nervous breakdown. It was six months before I saw him again, although we had desoltory phone calls and he wrote many letters, with drawings. One of the funniest was of him with his fellow sick-men queuing up for their meals, in long nightshirts, huge army boots, and cropped hair. They would then traipse back to their beds, remove the lumbering boots and sit up with their trays to eat—I wonder what?

His next-door neighbour in bed was a man who was also suffering from a breakdown. Being a spiritualist, he had been in the habit of receiving a visit from his mother (who had passed over) every evening at a certain time. On account of the Army time-table, she had never been able to find him, but in hospital they had been able to re-establish their old routine, and she came to see her son every evening at six o'clock promptly.

Because I know that Mervyn was unable to use his gifts as a war artist at this time I am flippant, and seek in the uselessness of Army life a joke. The only way to remain sane. Out of his breakdown he learned to make a bamboo recorder, and to play it. Unmilitary music, music like 'Plaisir d'amour', 'Jesu, joy of man's desiring', 'Parlez-moi d'amour'. A strange mixture of the serene and the sentimental. When he eventually came home on leave, his recorder was an essential part of him. I accompanied him on the piano, and once more nostalgia breaks through on hearing any of those songs.

*   *   *

After leave, following the breakdown and recuperation, his orders were to proceed to Salisbury Plain, for a course in 'theodolites'. I wonder whose strange twisted mind could think up so incongruous an idea. Certainly, although we had both heard of, and been to, Salisbury Plain neither of us knew the meaning of theodolite, and although Mervyn went to Salisbury on the course he never came any nearer to knowing.

At the end of the first lecture he asked to speak to the Commanding Officer.

He was allowed to speak, and explained that he felt he was out of his depth; that when, for instance, he saw a 6 or a 9, or an 0, he always thought of them as female shapes, a 7 or a 1 as masculine, and he then asked permission to continue writing his book at the back of the room. He spoke a little of *Titus Groan*, and the Commanding Officer, who had been puffing at a pipe, removed it, cleaned out the bowl carefully with a pipe-cleaner, and then tapped it gently on his right hand. There was a positive sound of wood hitting wood. It *was* a sound of wood hitting wood, for his right hand was a wooden hand. He told Mervyn that until he could be transferred to another unit, more within his own world of thought, he might continue to write his book.

He *must* have been an enlightened man.

*   *   *

It was whilst on weekend leave from the theodolite nightmare that we decided to spend it in London. Mervyn had been lent a room in Frith Street. We found a kind friend to look after Sebastian in the country, and because I was feeding Fabian at the time we took him with us. His bed was like a beautifully made nest in the largest drawer of a chest of drawers, and we never even shut it by mistake.

We went on the first night in London to the Café Royal, where we knew an infinite number of people. It is a nostalgic memory, and even then we were always told by older people that it was not as it had been. Red plush couches and marble

The author, 1940

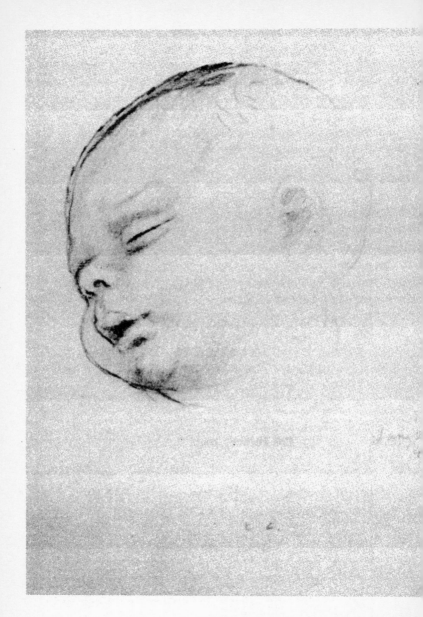

Sebastian, 1940

tables, and an evening spent if need be with just one cup of coffee. The elixir came from the lively minds of so many people now dead—John Davenport, Dylan Thomas, Roy Campbell. And on that particular night, Graham Greene. He asked Mervyn what he was doing, apart from being such a notable part of the war effort. Mervyn described, but not at length, the book he was writing, as yet untitled but possibly to be called *Titus Groan*.

We never thought again of that random conversation until a year or two later when Mervyn received a telegram from Graham Greene, asking him to submit the manuscript to Eyre and Spottiswoode of which he was then a director. It was finished and typed with great difficulty, as the writing became more obscure to read as the story proceeded.

Nevertheless, it was sent in typescript, and after some space of time was accepted in 1945. This is all rather after the time that I'm writing about, but it followed from our conversation with Graham Greene.

It was, or seemed, a miracle that a book written on compulsion, with no idea of publication, written as only, I think, true things are written, because it *had* to be, with no sense of future, past or present, that the message of interest came as a shock. A shock of complete amazement, that perhaps it would reach out, speak to people, make them laugh or cry, and in some cases hate, what had been written with an ebullience, a joy that the world of war in which we were living was trying hard to destroy.

The galley proofs which arrived were practically rewritten—ideas grew upon ideas on seeing in print what had been written in long-hand on those publishers' virgin dummy books. There was a tremendous sense of excitement, an almost impossible sense. We shared it. Those words, those characters written and brought alone to life, were to enter a world they knew not of, were frightened of, had no knowledge of. Like entering a party where one knew no one, and felt all around an animosity. Alien people, until you find that everyone else is frightened, then a sudden smile or joke invites you into their world.

*   *   *

Then the Army decided that Sapper Peake 5917577 was really no asset to them, and as he was on the edge of another breakdown he was invalided out, and sent home. He came back to Sussex, and after a week or so of rest he began his illustrations to *The Ancient Mariner*. Apart from making drawings of the children and myself everywhere, anywhere, writing poems, and doing illustrations for a magazine called *Lilliput*, we lived for a short space of time the life which had been interrupted in 1939.

Mervyn still had his room in Frith Street, and that is where the unique photographer, Bill Brandt, went to take some photos of him. It was a moderately sordid room in a moderately sordid house, and on the first photo the entire lights of the house fused. After a number of vicissitudes they were repaired, and one of the photographs appeared later in *Lilliput*.

Mervyn went to work at the Ministry of Information, and took a room in Store Street, close by. I've never been strong on facts or on dates, but I think it was through Graham Greene that he found himself in the Civil Service.

He had been commissioned to do two large paintings about this time. One was called 'The Glassblowers', which was shown at the National Gallery during the war. He went to Birmingham to do more drawings in the factory—the glassblowing was something to do with radar, and he made innumerable drawings. It was a theme full of fantasy and poetry, and the jacket of his book of poems called *The Glassblowers* was a reproduction of the final painting.

Another commission was done at an R.A.F. Bomber Station in Sussex. The scope for his imagination seemed less intense and he made a picture of The Squadron, small in a large space, which is now the Imperial War Museum. I think it interesting because it seems very untypical of him or his work.

He did drawings for propaganda leaflets, and was for the first time used in a small way as he should have been. I went to London from time to time with both the boys, although the air-raids were still a hazard. I have almost forgotten the fear in which one went to bed during those nights, and the wailing witchiness of sirens. How can one forget?

*   *   *

I remember standing in the garden in Sussex with both my sons, watching armadas of planes appearing from behind the Downs, disappearing towards the sea. A plethora of planes. Avenging angels. It was D-Day, only we didn't know it.

*   *   *

Past the rural flint wall of the cottage, with sunflowers straining over the flints, went columns of American soldiers, as curious as we were. Homesick men, who spoke and joked, and whistled at the two small boys astride the wall, playing with toy tanks. One soldier broke the line, and asked if he could visit me one evening. He came laden with chocolate and cigarettes, and spoke of home—the loneliness and fear of war, and nothing more. The *savour* of home.

*   *   *

This is not a chronicle of the war. It is trying to remember a lifetime ago. I am wishing to confine and savour a personal time amidst a public upheaval.

It was about now that the air-raids on London were

diminishing, and as our cottage, at 3s. a week, rates and all, was required by the Norfolk Estate, we decided to take a risk and return to London.

Mervyn had found a studio in Glebe Place, Chelsea, at a rent which seemed possible, for all the uncertainties of living, and we went to live there. A marvellous, spacious studio, with a few rooms as well for sleeping and living and cooking in.

We both painted. We had friends to coffee. It was cold, and one Christmas we were given a sack of coal. The ceiling was so high, and the studio was so large that there were always difficulties in keeping warm.

This was the time of the V.2s. Air-raids, as had been understood before, had changed their tune. Sitting huddled over the small fire with friends, talking of painting, listening to music, laughing or fooling, there would suddenly be a giant jerk, a reverberation, a jolt through coffee cups, then silence. Somewhere that crafty craft had landed, and ended someone else's laughter and tears.

The flying-bomb was also a part of our lives for a time—the sudden sickening stoppage of the engine, then the waiting for its arbitrary target. It wasn't bravery that kept one going, but the senseless faith that human nature has in human nature.

Mervyn wrote a long ballad called *The Rhyme of the Flying Bomb* a year or two later when everything could be seen a little more in perspective. It is very moving. A sailor in London during one of the flying-bomb attacks finds a baby, new-born but abandoned, and the ballad is his conversation and the baby's in the jagged burning city.

Just four verses out of a hundred or so:

> This isn't no place for the likes of you
> Nor it is for the likes of me
> We'd be better asleep in a hammock, we would
> On the wet of the mine-filled sea.

We'd be far better off where the soldiers are
Than naked in London town
Where a house can rock like a rocking-horse
And the bright bricks tumble down

All bare and cold in that gutter of gold
You had no cause to be,
No more than it's right for the likes of you
To be born in this century

But the sky is bright though its late at night
And the colours are gay as gay
And the glass that is lodged in my hip bone now
Is jabbing from far away.

★   ★   ★

It did end. It was coming to an end. Everything, everywhere had that ominous feeling which portends something beyond our control. The fear which we had had for years before the war had begun gave way, to an elation damaged by the violence and the bestiality of which we had read but scarcely believed possible.

The war in Europe was over. It was possible to go to bed at nights without fear. There were still relatives and friends abroad, who might still come to harm, but selfishly one could not but feel a lightening of living.

On V.E. night some friends of ours, who had a young baby, said that they would bring him round in a pram, and stay with our sons, so that we could go up to the celebrations in the West End.

A bonfire had already been lit in Glebe Place before we left to meet some friends to go 'to town'.

I don't suppose one will ever feel again the madness of that night, even though we knew there was still a war in the East, and despite the knowledge that the end of a war is not really the end of war. It was not the time for introspection. Can I really believe that we danced the entire way up Piccadilly, linked with soldiers, sailors, airmen, tarts and the whole world? Singing 'Knees-up Mother Brown', laughing, crying, being kissed, kissing, until our voices were hoarse, our eyes closed with sleep and weeping, our feet swollen with dancing on the hard roads. Everybody loved everyone.

*   *   *

Such an occasion could inevitably only lead to an anti-climax. It came quicker for some than for others, but we were lucky in many ways.

Mervyn's brother, who had been a prisoner-of-war in Changi Gaol, Singapore, was alive and safe.

One day as I was bringing my sons back from a nursery school a taxi drew up outside our studio. A man got out of it with a kitbag. He seemed familiar, and he looked rather like Mervyn. It was his brother. I rushed up to him, and we wept. The taxi-driver would take no fare. Mervyn's brother met his nephews for the first time, and we went into the studio.

I had made some cakes for tea, and within a second they had all disappeared. He told us later that whilst in the prisoner-of-war camp he had dreamed not of esoteric meals but of bread and butter—always bread and butter—and these cakes were for the moment the nearest he could get to that. Because of his having been a prisoner we were supplied with extra rations for him, and in a modest way we were able to indulge him in all that he had missed over the last year.

It must have been traumatic to be carried from the harshness of Changi to the freedom of a studio in Chelsea. He stayed with us for several months whilst awaiting transport to

America, where his wife and family had been living during the whole time of his imprisonment.

*   *   *

The proofs of *Titus Groan* had been corrected, the book jacket had been designed, the blurb written, and we awaited the day of publication.

The very first review we saw was by a man called Edward Shanks. I don't remember for which paper he wrote, but it was a cold douche. Mervyn wanted to send a telegram 'Shanks a million', but we felt we had our pride. I can hear the people who level 'facetious' at his writing repeating it tenfold at this proposal. It *was* facetious, but also sad that the first review should have been starkly superior. He didn't send the telegram, and the majority of the reviews which followed were unexpectedly and fully in his favour. Since those days it has been called the literary sensation of 1945, but we still went on living, loving, working, fighting, in extreme ignorance of this fact. It certainly made very little practical difference to us. It was as difficult to pay the phone bill on being a literary sensation as before those august days.

Mervyn seemed able to swallow whole the good and the bad reviews. It's only now that I wonder if he really could, for it was cruel reviews many years later of a play in which he had placed too much hope that unhinged him in mind and spirit.

*   *   *

The war *was* over, but who could really pretend to themselves that life was or could ever again be the same? It is strange that Mervyn had to wait until it was all over to do the work which he had wished to do during it. He was sent with Tom Pocock, the journalist, to Germany to cover in drawings what Tom would cover in words. The nether land of horror.

Today we have been to the trial of Peter Bach. It was held in
a private house—a big one and about eight American
Colonels were the jury. I think it was carried out very fairly,
but the sentence was not read out. I made a lot of drawings
of the German witnesses as they came in and were
cross-questioned and of the German lawyer who defended
BACK—it is BACK not Bach as I originally thought. He (the
lawyer) was a huge, massive and portly man, and was I
think extremely good. Everything had to be translated into
English and German all the time, which made it very long.
He could not justify Back's action which he deplored, but he
tried to show the background which Back had had—how he
had been warped, and how being so self-conscious of his
being a cripple he had striven to excel himself as a party
man. None of this excuses him, but the lawyer quoted the
French phrase 'To know all is to forgive all'. Oh Maeve—it
was very tragic—its sadness is more upon me now than at
the time because the whole thing was informal in that big
room.

Tomorrow we go to Belsen.

He didn't write to me of Belsen, but I have seen drawings
and read poems.

They had no quiet and smoothed sheets of death to fold
    them, and no pillows whiter than the wings of Child-
    hood's angels
There was no hush of love. No silence flowered about them,
    and no bland, enormous petals opened with stillness.
    Where was lavender or gentle light? Where were the
    coverlets of quiet? Or white hands to hold their bleeding
    claws that grabbed horribly for child or lover?
In twisting flames their twisting bodies blackened,
For History, that witless chronicler
Continued writing his long manuscript.

In *Titus Alone*, the tragic woman 'Black Rose' who has suffered so much, and died as her head touched a white pillow, after so many years, must surely be one of the lonely and forsaken ones whom he drew and wrote of from Belsen.

*   *   *

There were many letters at this time, full of a mixture of love, homesickness, hatred for the violence and havoc of war, and a yearning to be able to write and paint unaffected by outside events.

The river bank was alive with Castles—I've never seen so many—some of them perched precariously on precipitous crags or half hidden among the forests that topped the rocks. It was Grimm's Fairy Tales—a legendary thing. But in the river were tiers of boats and barges and steamers of all kinds and nearly all of them half or wholly under water, and along the road were all types of Germans pushing hand-carts or riding ox-drawn carts or pushing prams, each with the remains of their furniture. It seems to me that they are absolutely hostile.

A young heavily built German we passed gave us a look of the intensest malice, and clapped his hand to his hip as though to draw a symbolic revolver. The children put out their tongues to jeer and whistle. It is a new thing for me to see hatred so manifest. I also saw a boy whose face looked about sixteen, but whose hair was grey, who was hobbling down the steps of a town-hall with a crutch and only one leg.

> War Correspondent,
> C/o P.R.D.
> Shaef

Most dearly beloved—oh my darling girl—
What a terrific lot has happened since I wrote to you from

Paris—yet I was in Paris this morning. I am now on the river near Wiesbaden, and tomorrow we are jeeping to Bonn.

After the impression I have received here of the way the Germans feel towards the Americans, and presumably towards the English too (we're in an American Zone at the moment) I don't feel too keen on introducing myself to one.

It is true that today a few peasants waved from the fields, and one or two oldish people bowed good morning and a few girls smiled hopefully, but in the main there is an intense feeling of hatred. Eyes are averted—or the stare is insolent. They are now doing what the Dutch, French and other subjugated races did when the Germans were in control. I have done today a drawing of a young Nazi—or Hitler Youth, wearing those strange short shorts—half way up the thighs and the sort of porter's cap they wear. It was the complete bully—rather impregnated with the spirit of Nazidom. The small children are openly cheeky or else when very young, cadging for rides on jeeps etc. Walking out this evening in this German town (Tom taking his revolver!!) was one of the strangest experiences I have ever had. Nearly every window had a head which stared at the opposite wall of the street as one came abreast. Sometimes looking quickly one would see a face staring at one from between the blinds, which would immediately shift its gaze on its being met. We are right on the river which is very wide but not particularly attractive near here. One or two people canoeing and a lot of boats and fishing nets on the shore. Also a line of our invasion barges which were used for crossing the Rhine. But the main part of the town—a very big town—is like Mannheim (to which we flew this morning). Sights which it would be impossible to believe were one not to see them. They are no more. They are relics. Terrible as the bombing of London was, it is absolutely nothing—nothing compared with this unutterable desolation. Imagine Chelsea in fragments with not one single house with any more than a few weird shaped walls where it once stood, and you will get an idea in miniature of what Mannheim and Wiesbaden are like—yet these are the only two that we have seen, save for the broken streets of every small town we passed through on our jeep ride here today. The Ruhr to which we are going tomorrow is reputed to be the worst—but how could it be worse than what I've seen today.

There were many letters, but the main content was always the tragedy of the human condition—'I must never let anything get cold'.

You know I will do all that is in me to do what was in our minds when we decided, through your insight, that it was for me to make records of what humanity suffered through war. I will not forget the reasons which prompted me to try and go to where people suffer. I will miss you desperately, but I will be proud to do something which we both believe in. . . .

During this time, apart from the horrors that he was seeing, and the nightmare, there was another side to life. In Hamburg he met the Old Vic Company who were touring and playing to the troops. Laurence Olivier was playing Richard III, and Mervyn did several drawings of him as the hunchback king, of Sybil Thorndike, and of a host of other actors and actresses lending truth to 'All the world's a stage'.

In Paris, where he went with Tom Pocock after Germany, they went to night clubs where people were emerging from the chrysalis of war. Negro drummers, angels and gargoyles. Part of a Paris known before, but changed as everything had. As he had. A shadow, a man with a shadow.

*   *   *

He was away a month, and during that month the sights and sounds of Germany must have damaged him more than he ever said, except in his poems and his writing in *Titus Alone* many years later, and his drawings. Perhaps there was the seed of all this in his work—he had 'grotesque' used about most aspects of it from the time he started—but there is also tenderness and humour, which the myriads of drawings of children express, and the lyrical poems contain.

*   *   *

It was around this time that Mervyn met John Brophy. He came to the studio, and overwhelmed us by buying one very large oil, and several drawings, and leaving a cheque that seemed over-life-size. He was a most genial man, always kind and with humour. He became a very good friend, and remained so until he died.

There was a shelf out of reach in our studio where coins were thrown, of any denomination, at the end of the day. It needed a great deal of athletic prowess to recover them at the end of the month, but each time it was like opening our Christmas stockings. We didn't know what we would find, but it is surprising how quickly pennies and half pennies, and their more wealthy relatives, sixpences and shillings, even florins and half-crowns, become a small fortune when left on the shelf. Covered in dust they become a revelation.

The Peter Jones of 'negative' repute decided to become patron of the arts. They opened a gallery, through the dress materials and the haberdashery departments. We were both asked to exhibit self-portraits. This was one of the first exhibitions to be held there, and a strange happening arose out of Mervyn's self-portrait.

The exhibition was at a time of year when it was excruciatingly cold, both inside and without, and there were

layers of multi-coloured snow outside the studio. The front
door was directly on to the road.

It might be apposite to describe the painting. Mervyn had a
face that belonged to another age. Cadaverous, romantic
(women thought it beautiful), haggard and wild. He had
painted himself with a paint-brush through his teeth, as a
pirate might hold a cutlass, or a gypsy dancer a rose. It was a
painting of bravura.

★   ★   ★

The exhibition opened, and a few people went to look at the
pictures, but in the main the public were people matching
cotton to the materials they had chosen, and marching
intrepidly towards the large window to see if they had
correctly chosen their pinks, or yellows, or greens. A slight
glance to left and right gave on to a world that had no meaning
to them, and they walked with upright steps back to the
security of the world they knew.

But somewhere amongst the people who saw this painting
was someone to whom it was an insult against aesthetics and
beauty.

The evening of the private view (it was not private, but
perhaps a view) was icy cold, but we went to bed around
midnight, warming each other as well as possible. Presumably
we went to sleep, but around 2 a.m. we both awoke with a
sharp instinct of fear. Our bed was on the same level as the
front door—it was not a bedroom but an alcove. There was a
sound, a rattle at the letter-box, and muffled steps running, in
the snow. They could only have been muffled because of the
silence of snow. At the moment that the letter-box rattled
there was a piercing scream from a room at the diametric end
of the studio, where Sebastian was sleeping. Who was to do
what? I ran to my son, and Mervyn to the front door.

I found a small boy, frozen with terror, pointing to a window where the curtains were pulled tightly across, so that there was no possibility of seeing out of them, or into them, screaming of an old woman who had been peering through the glass. There was nothing, and no possibility of anything. I tried to calm the little creature, but waited with trepidation to hear what Mervyn had found at the door. To begin with, a wire had been stretched across the door, which would have cut a thoughtless throat, but he had withdrawn in time, and on the doorstep was a loaf of bread made into a face—currants (predictably) for eyes, and through where should have been the mouth a paint-brush.

I was trembling—the whole thing seemed unclean and devious. We called the police, and in our large, cold studio explained to them the sinister sound of padded footsteps, the wire, dirty collars full of congealed bacon-rind pushed through the letter-box, our son's insistence on an old woman. In cold blood the most strange details take on a prosaic quality, and after the policemen left it seemed quite obvious that nothing out of the normal had happened at all.

It was cold though, and before we could return to bed we had to calm down the boy who had seen the old woman through heavy curtains.

*   *   *

It was a few days later that the police again came to see us. The widow of an R.A. who had seen Mervyn's self-portrait, had hated it so vitriolically that she could only think of doing harm to someone who, in her eyes, had desecrated *art* and her husband. The strangest thing in the story was that our son had described this old woman at the back of the house through drawn curtains when she was busily thrusting bacon-rind through the letter-box at the front.

*   *   *

People of all kinds came in and went out of our lives at this time. One weekend, whilst I was away, Dylan Thomas arrived at the studio, far from well. Mervyn put him to bed, the same bed that had witnessed the old woman's fury from the inside-out. The doctor came, and administered whatever there was to be administered—it almost seems like the blind leading the blind, but whatever remedies were suggested must have had some effect, for he recovered and left. Mervyn had done some drawings of him in bed, two of which were reproduced in *Encounter*. They were never returned to us, as they had been lost in the office, although, according to a letter from Stephen Spender, Mervyn hadn't asked for them back until a year or two after their publication. They did make an *ex gratia* payment of £25 for the drawings.

Not long after the blind leading the blind, a note was pushed through the door.

Mervyn, dear Maeve,

Will you please lend me coat and trousers for a day. Any coat and trousers so long as they aren't my own. I am supposed to speak on a public platform tomorrow, Sunday, just after lunch. May I call early morning—
Love, Dylan

On the other side, with a scribbled drawing:

I must, unfortunately, call for coat and trousers—doesn't matter that M is taller than D before 11. Say 10.30.

M was quite a bit taller than D, and a fair bit slimmer, and D had the look of a tortoise coming out of its shell in M's coat and trousers. Where the public platform was and what he spoke about are both conjectural.

★　　　★　　　★

It was still impossible to believe that the days and the nights were silent from bombs. It is hardly credible that for six years going to bed was a query whether we would be there to get up. And because of the easing of life, life itself became more wondrous.

'To live at all, is miracle enough.'

It seemed so, that each day was a leprechaun—humorous and fanciful, adventurous and mystical.

It was a time for us, if only we had known it, when the world was bubbling. It was a time when Mervyn, particularly, met new and not new people. Important people! Our world was our cocoon, but I had no wish to meet anyone—turpentine and canvas, words and a pencil, paper and paint—my love.

Around this time I had an exhibition at the Redfern Gallery. Looking back, I wonder how I dared exhibit any of the pictures. It wasn't arrogance or confidence, but a kind of blindness.

Mervyn too had an exhibition at a gallery called the Adams Gallery, but he had a habit of painting over his canvases so that any which were not sold were completely metamorphosized, and the shapes beneath became the shapes to dominate the new painting. Strange, that above all things that he did he wished to be a painter, and I think it was perhaps the medium in which he was least sure.

We came to know Maurice Collis then, and he remained to me over the long years of Mervyn's illness someone to whom I could turn, and whose humour and wit sustained darkness and despair. But the days when we first knew him were happier and we met with him a new world of people. A little later Mervyn illustrated his book called *Quest for Sita*, which was a beautifully produced edition on hand-made paper. Rare for those days when wartime economy was still extant.

Fabian, our son, was known by a little girl at the nursery

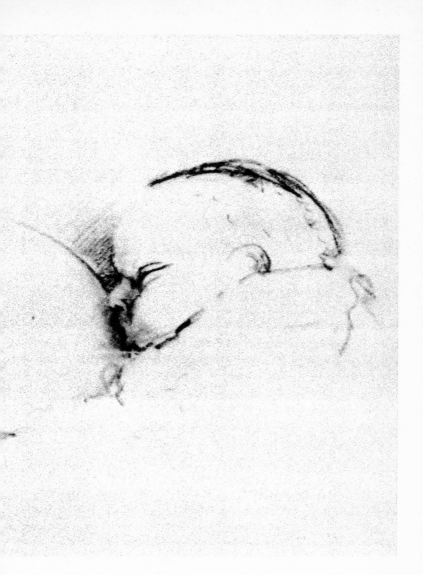

Clare, 1949

Blue-eyed thugs, 1943

school as the 'pinky-orange boy'; he had an angelic face which belied great mischievousness. One day when I was fetching him from school I watched him putting his arms gently round the little girl whose mother was standing close to me, and we were both sentimentally touched by such sibling sweetness, until a moment later it was shattered by a shrill scream. A large slice of tender cheek had been bitten into by the pinky-orange boy. Relations were never the same again.

Our two sons, who were later described by Louis MacNeice as 'blue-eyed thugs', lived wild lives with us in our studio. Mervyn would draw them at any moment, playing and fighting. We took them to the zoo, to tea-parties, where Fabian would lie anti-socially in the corner and speak to no one. They met Prince Lowenstein, son-in-law of Victor Gollancz, in Kings Road, and have never got over the shock of his head that sported no crown. Mervyn took them for walks along the river, and at low tide they took off their shoes and socks and paddled in the muddy slime, to return home smelling of all the unmentionable things that a river exudes.

*   *   *

Titus seemed to be selling; and one day Matthew Smith came to our studio to look at paintings. He was, in my memory, a very gentle man, and it seemed difficult to equate his personality with the rich and powerful pictures that he made. Mervyn gave him a copy of *Titus Groan*, and later on received a letter from him.

Dear Mervyn Peake,
    I felt it indeed a privilege to have a copy of your book. I am deep in it and entranced. I consider it a masterpiece. It must live.
    That wonderful foot that you manage to keep on the

ground! Thank you for a Gargantuan Feast and at the same
time an escape. So bless you and thank you.

> Yours,
> Matthew Smith.

Not to have illustrated it is alone a stroke of genius!

⌐

★   ★   ★

Although we had this big studio, a place for working in, we
longed to go away.

Mervyn had been given a retainer by Eyre and Spottiswoode to illustrate a certain number of books a year, and he
had many other ideas swimming and floating in his
ever-active, lively brain.

He went over to Sark to look for a house for us. He had
always felt a great love for this small island, since 1933, when
he had spent one or two years there, as a very young man, after
finishing at the Academy Schools, and where he had exhibited
in a most unlikely gallery.

★   ★   ★

Eric Drake had taught Mervyn English at Eltham College,
in Kent, and I think was a very positive influence in his life as
an artist, poet, and novelist; he decided to build a gallery in
Sark, and to start a colony of artists. It was a revolutionary
idea, for such a small island, 3½ miles by 1½ miles. The gallery
itself was something unforeseen in so remote a place. 'The
Directors do not subscribe to any set theory or school of
thought . . . they are looking for work that has a constructive
and integrating significance in modern life.'

Reviews galore appeared in the Channel Islands papers, and
one perhaps foreshadowed the future in the *Guernsey Press*.
'An outstanding exhibitor is Mervyn Peake who won the

Hacker Porticut Prize at the Royal Academy Schools in 1931, and has exhibited at the Royal Academy, the Redfern Gallery, and the London Group. His chalk and charcoal studies of venerable Sarkese are masterly. . . .'

'The standard throughout was on a particularly high level, and in some cases the work was stamped with something approaching genius. This was particularly so in the case of Mervyn Peake, a young man still on the sunny side of twenty-two whose versatility and imagination place him in a class of his own. . . . Mr Drake is very proud of the fact that it was whilst teaching this boy literature that he discovered his ability to draw, and encouraged him.'

Mervyn spent a few years in Sark in a small tin shack with a pet cormorant, painting, writing and living, and taking midnight swims in the beautiful lonely bays, and was then offered a job teaching at the Westminster School of Art by the principal of the school, on the strength of his drawings. He decided to take it, and to leave the island, despite all that he loved—and but for that we would never have met.

*   *   *

Sark, after the turmoil of the war, seemed to be a sanctuary, although it had itself been occupied by the Germans, and many people had been deported. Towards the end of the war there was a great deal of hunger among Germans and Sarkese alike.

He came back, full of houses that he had seen, one in particular, too large, comparatively ugly, but with immense space—a daffodil field, a bamboo hedge, pampas grass, no light, no electricity, no water, except by pumping, but alive, alive, with rooms for possibilities, and a whole island to explore.

We went together, after arranging for the boys to be looked

after, to see Le Châlet. It seemed a most inappropriate name. A large ungainly house, not endemic to the island, built by an elderly widow from England, used to better days and a staff of servants.

We saw it as an ugly house, prepared for anything, prepared above all to be lived in and worked in, loved and hated. Houses, like people, have their own peculiarities, and we both loved the peculiarities of this one. I've always thought of it as a spinster house, ready and willing to be invaded.

Mr Hirzel Baker from Guernsey was the landlord. The terms were £80 per annum for a ninety-nine-year lease. I think we were all completely unbusiness-like. We were getting what at the time was a white elephant, and he was getting rid of it. I don't *think* there was anything so ungentlemanly as a lease, only I can't remember. It was mutually agreed that at a certain date we would take possession of this ageing spinster, then after a few days staying and talking, walking, swimming, dreaming in Sark, we returned to London to dispose of our commitments, and to start thinking of living in an island where life was lived at a tempo unmolested by cleverness.

A small diversion: whilst Mervyn was away in Sark for the first time, someone living nearby tried to convert me to Christian Science.

During this short period when I was alone I happened, over a very trivial matter of opening a glass jar of boot polish, to get the glass into my thumb, and a jagged, bloody mess of skin hung suspended from my thumb. I had my small sons with me, terrified at the horrible sight, so I hurried round to our Christian Scientist friend, and asked him to look after them whilst I went to the doctor. His reply was, 'If that has happened, you must be guilty of a great sin. I'm sorry, I cannot help you.'

I rushed round to the doctor with my hand aloft, bleeding decoratively down my arm, like a Tachist painting, and on the way, met a white—I don't mean non-colonial, but colour-less—friend who seemed not to notice the gall, and would have kept me in conversation for many minutes, if my *sang-(chaud? froid!)* had not forsaken me. I rushed posthaste to the doctor's and had six stitches put in the thumb, with two poor little white-faced boys even more pallid. It was at this moment that I decided not to embrace Christian Science.

* * *

We were about to move into a house with at least twelve rooms from a studio that was comparatively under-nourished. What should or could we do? Nothing, just decide to go.

Our belongings were put into a pantechnicon. A railway van that would go oversea to Guernsey. Our cat, an essential, was to come with us.

* * *

I don't forget. I never will. All that was beyond what we were doing. A man with a family who is also a man with enormous creative impetus, works in a different way from a bank-clerk, a financial tycoon, or a film-star. Maybe he doesn't, but Mervyn did.

It's a beautiful sight, arriving in the early morning, by ship, at Guernsey. The islands are mysterious, slowly coming to life—seal-like shapes, in a mist, and the fog-horns and sea-gulls add to the hallucinatory aura. It's a pity to land so prosaically, and to make one's way up the 'Pollet' for breakfast before taking the boat over to Sark. One should always be defended against reality.

* * *

Our cat had survived the journey with the first of her nine lives. We took a small boat with an outboard motor to Sark. I can always remember the excitement of trailing hands in the water, it was a calm day, and the shape of Sark slowly materializing, magically, no reality anywhere. Beautiful silence, except for the engine, the lapping of the sea against the boat, and the intermittent excited cries of children enjoying something quite new. They had seen a school of porpoises, gracefully submerging and reappearing, they had seen cormorants and puffins, and they saw looming ahead of them a shape that was to become for ever a part of their lives.

We landed, and were greeted by many of the Sarkese, who had known Mervyn for years, since his days as a painter, exhibiting pictures, unworried by family ties.

There were no cars, only horse-drawn carriages for everything. We were drawn up to our house by Charlie Penée, who later drew Princess Elizabeth up the steep harbour hill, and had a royal coat of arms painted on his carriage. I don't think such an honour ensued from us!

*   *   *

Our furniture was to arrive the next day, so we arrived at a house devoid of everything except space.

There was no light, no beds, no food.

We were given candles, and bread and butter. We slept on the floor.

It was a strange first night. Although it was a young house, it had an old feeling. As darkness fell and the wind rose, in the flickering candlelight the ghost of Mrs Judkins (who had built it) did not walk, but whispered as we all slept on the floor of a big bedroom from which the coast of France could be seen. Her whispers subsided as the dawn rose, and we were all only too happy to arise from the hard floor.

Our furniture, pathetically minuscule as it was, should begin to arrive around eight in the morning. It all came, by horse-drawn carriage up the harbour hill and into our drive, a beautiful sweep of bamboo, and up to the front door. Paintings, paintings, paintings. Singly they arrived in Victorian carriages. A little later, we heard that there had been a large-scale exhibition of them on the quay in St Peter Port, Guernsey, before they were put into the motor-boats for Sark. Oh, how I wish we could live those days again.

At the end of the day we could hardly say our house was furnished. We had one couch, two beds, a few chairs, books and books, two large easels and a host of drawings and paintings and work-to-be.

The excitement of two small boys let loose on an island with no cars was limpidly pure. To run wildly and exhaustingly nowhere in particular.

A strange, sharp little woman came to see us, and to say that she would do housework for us, as she had for Mrs Judkins. 'Gracie' from Derby (she pronounced it Durby), with a wit, humour, and maliciousness all her own. It was she who told us of all the sales in the island, after the occupation. We bought a kitchen table, with which I could never part, for ten shillings, beds for £1, carpets for I can't remember how much, and suddenly our house was furnished. Beautiful oil-lamps and heaters and a bookcase with supports made from tea chests. It was a home, and work could begin again.

*   *   *

Sebastian was old enough to go to the school in Sark, just next to the prison, which features in a book called *Mr Pye* which Mervyn wrote after we left the island. Both the children made friends with the Sarkese boys, and I can think of no more exciting childhood than that which they had. We had a donkey, called Judy, aged thirty, and it was Gracie who told us of a little carriage to be auctioned, with bridles and accoutrements, that we bought for a pound or two, and to which Judy was harnessed with no great willingness on her part. She knew how to open the kitchen window, and nuzzle the lid off the bread-bin, which stood on the sill, and go off with whatever bread she could find. A few years later our sons used to harness her, and take visitors to the island on journeys round it for a few shillings a time.

* * *

People used to say, 'What can you do all day? *what* do you do? what *can* you do? there's nothing to do.'

There was a world to do.

* * *

Mervyn woke, and either went downstairs if it wasn't too cold, or to his room to write. *Gormenghast* was progressing. Books were being illustrated. We were both painting. Or if it was cold, he wrote in bed until about twelve noon. We all had breakfast in bed together, then Sebastian would run down the hill to school and Fabian would sit and draw for hours.

Mervyn never sat alone in a study to write or draw. He hated to be cut off from the life going on in the house, and in his manuscripts of *Titus Groan* there are drawings of the children or of myself caught suddenly in an act of living. He often sat in an armchair with a drawing board across its arms, and no more props than those which came from his superabundant imagination. Some days he wrote more easily than others, but as the story unfolded he read it to me.

It is very strange that although to many people he is mostly known as a draughtsman and illustrator, I cannot now read his poems or his books without their evoking in me a more

intense sadness than his drawings. I hear him in every line and
every thought, in every humorous and extravagant fancy. The
tenderness that was germane to him and the quality of
clowning.

★   ★   ★

Every day was new. From our bedroom, on mornings
when there was no sea mist, we looked out on to the coast of
France. The trees, apart from those in the Dixcart Valley, a
sheltered valley in the centre of the island, were warped by the
wind into strange, grotesque and sometimes ghostly shapes. I
loved to paint them, against the sea, and their loneliness.
Mervyn wrote a poem because of them:

> With people, so with trees: when there are groups
> Of either, men or trees, some will remain
> Aloof while others cluster where one stoops
> To breathe some dusky secret. Some complain
>
> And some gesticulate and some are blind;
> Some toss their heads above green towns; some freeze
> For lack of love in copses of mankind;
> Some laugh; some mourn; with people, so with trees.

★   ★   ★

At times the gales surrounding the island became so
insistent that one longed for silence, the uncanny silence which
sea-mist carries, but the eerie sound of fog-horns was a poor
substitute for it.

There were moments when I particularly felt an intense
claustrophobia, knowing that in whichever direction one
went there was the sea, and one was trapped.

These feelings did not last very long, although there were

times when no boats could come from Guernsey with provisions or mail for a week or two at a time.

The days, weeks and years we spent in Sark were perhaps the most memorable of our life together. Our sons had their friends who were born and bred on the island. Our garden was large and wild, with a field of daffodils in the spring that could have inspired Wordsworth, and the freedom from fear of car accidents allowed the children to run like leverets where they wished.

Apart from a few months in the winter we used to go for picnics down to one of the many bays—with lonely stretches of beach, mysterious caves, rocks to climb, in some of the bays amethyst and topaz to be searched for, but never found.

We walked everywhere, although I still had my bicycle and used it quite often for all the paraphernalia of picnics. Our cat, called Chloe, often walked with us to the top of the bays, and would wait for our return.

Once a week there was a film in the hall. Very old films, George Formby, Will Hay, and once, Deanna Durbin with whom Sebastian fell in love.

The cheapest seats in the front row were benches, backless and hard, but the group of small boys in the front row were agog with excitement, and practically always asleep by the end of the film. They had to make their way home across a cemetery, not really knowing a great deal of what they had seen in the film, but thrilled to be out so late; and frightened by the grave-stones they ran as fast as their tiredness could carry them.

*   *   *

Judy, the donkey, often made her way into our sitting-room, and would stand for hours in front of the bookcase. A most intellectual donkey, who spoke little, and never disgraced herself. Sometimes, visitors who had come over from one of the other islands for the day, would drop in to see us, and found her a somewhat unusual hostess, one who contributed by her presence alone to the niceties of hospitality.

This was a time of great creative energy and inspiration in living. *Gormenghast* was growing and each day I longed to know how the people in it were progressing, sadly, tragically, humorously, over-life-size friends.

Although the book was the major concern to be finished, apart from a fairly modest advance, which must surely have been spent before being received, money had to be found to enable us to stay in Sark. Mervyn went over to London from time to time to keep in touch with the fount of finance.

He did a series of advertisements for the Brewers Society, which must have helped financially, but it didn't last long, as so many things extraneous to the drawings were always queried. I remember one drawing of a young couple sitting outside a country pub which was returned as unsuitable. The tree under which they were sitting with their tankards was apparently too close to the inn, and would thus have undermined the foundations. The tree must be placed further away. The uprooting of the tree was, perhaps, easier in a drawing than in nature, but it decided Mervyn to uproot himself from the Brewers Society and to look elsewhere for means of support.

He was illustrating *Treasure Island* for Eyre and Spottis-woode, and some of the caves in Sark were inspiration for Jim Hawkins on his lone adventure. Sebastian or Fabian would be asked in the middle of some wild game of Indians with their friends to pose in a tree as Jim, or with me as Blind Pew, covered in an ancient coat and transformed into the sinister man of Stevenson's book. They posed moderately willingly so long as their game was not interrupted too cruelly and they could return to the wonders of the Sioux before the tribe had been completely wiped out.

On one of his visits to London, Mervyn had become fascinated by toxophily, and he returned with very beautiful equipment for us all, bought from Lillywhites. It was a new word for me, and unpronounceable for the boys, but getting to know more about it added yet another dimension to a life already over-flowing.

Bows and arrows, a target, quivers, shields for the fingers, it was a magical idea. We set the target up in the garden, at the bottom of the daffodil field, and it was certainly more through luck than skill that the arrows didn't fly over the hedge and into an innocent horse or man or woman or child. I had very little talent for toxophily, although it is such a graceful achievement if done well. Our Red Indians were infinitely more adaptable, it being a major part of their lives, and Mervyn had the surety of eye that his draughtsmanship had instilled in him to hit the bull's-eye.

*   *   *

Grimm's Fairy Tales, also for Eyre and Spottiswoode, was being illustrated, and once again we were all called in to pose—Rumplestiltskin, a witch, a sprite, a queen, a princess, in a rage, laughing, holding a scythe, whatever was necessary to transform and fuse imagination and reality.

Whilst Mervyn did his illustrations, in the evenings, after the boys were in bed, and he sat ensconced behind his drawing board, trapped by it and the fine mapping pens and Indian ink which he used, I read to him: *Bleak House*, several other Dickens', *Candide*, *The Loved One*, a catholic selection.

The days were too short for all that we wanted to do. The two boys both went to school, and returned for lunch. Every lunchtime Mervyn did a drawing for each of them in a special book. Pirates or cars, boats or tigers, in coloured inks or water colour or pencil or pen, and off they would rush back to school with the intensity of excitement that only children feel. Even then, they both had to have extra lessons in mathematics—a subject which always eluded them, as it always had their parents. A complete blank, that world of numbers. Eight is a woman. Seven is a man.

*   *   *

In front of the house there was quite a wide gravel drive, and in front of that a lawn which called for decoration. Horticulture seemed to have got into our blood. One day Mervyn phoned a nursery in Guernsey and asked them to send a palm tree over to us in Sark. They were not surprised by such an order, but needed specifications. What kind of palm tree? A momentary hesitation, then a silence, then, we would ring back. We rushed to the *Encyclopaedia Britannica*, and searched for palm trees. I no longer have an encyclopaedia, so I cannot remember what exotic species it belonged to. It was shipped over from Guernsey, and arrived, a huge spiky, furry trunk, with all its hands folded over each other inside thick sacking. A deep hole had to be dug in which to house it. It spent its first night on the lawn, and was the next day heaved into its new home, where it seemed to sway unsteadily, as land-sick as a tree can be, until it finds its roots.

It was a sanctuary during the years we spent in Sark for our cat and our sons who climbed it as easily as monkeys, to survey the land and sea-scapes surrounding us. After we left the island, and the house was sold, it was one of the first things to be removed. Poor palm tree.

The other grandiose scheme we had for garden improvements was to make a pergola, but no ordinary pergola. Telegraph poles were being lopped down in the island, and Mervyn thought that they would make a pergola of wondrous proportions. We bought twelve poles. It took about six men to struggle with them into our garden, and to drop them like giant matchsticks at the side of a hedge, where they lay discarded and uncared for, with no more thought of being a pergola than a pergola has of being a telegraph pole. They stayed silently there until we left a few years later.

*   *   *

Louis MacNeice, whom Mervyn knew in London, asked if he and his wife and children could come over to stay with us, and they all came with their Italian maid one stormy day. He only stayed about three days, as he had a telegram from the B.B.C., recalling him for a programme that he was working on.

*   *   *

These were little asides of life. Not highly successful, but enough to know that gardening was not our *métier*. The over-life-size pergola, burgeoning with honeysuckle, climbing roses and wistaria never materialized.

We went to dances at the hall, which were primitive and generous. We left Gracie from Durby to sit in, and she smoked non-stop. She herself did the can-can whenever she felt like it, with enormous Northern vitality, high-kicking, red bloomers ahoy, and she cleaned our house with the rapidity of a lynx, and the cleanliness of a cat, garrulous and comical.

She went to all the sales, of which there were many in the island at this time. She bought a small carriage with its accoutrements for our use with the donkey, a beautiful Victorian case for drawings, which she gave to Mervyn, oil-lamps of ornate design, and a life-size lay-figure which, apart from being a period-piece, has served as a surrealistic prop in the home, a silent figure reading the paper, with gloves on its hands and a mute personality of its own.

Just now, during 1949, our third child was on the way, and when Gracie was told she left—she couldn't bear babies. We asked our sons to guess what surprise there was for them. One guess was a pig, one a bicycle, another a parrot or a monkey, all of which we would like to have had, or a dog. It never entered their minds that such a thing as a baby could possibly be of interest to them, and the reception of the news was greeted with very little enthusiasm.

Materializing almost from the sea-mist came Armand, who had heard we wanted someone to help us in the house. His real name was Ahmed Ben Ali, a Moroccan who had come to Sark to work on the building of a new harbour, and he wanted to stay in the island. He was a kind and infinitely gentle man, and we decided mutually that we all liked each other, so he would come to do garden and housework for us.

*   *   *

The months went by. *Gormenghast* progressed. I painted every afternoon, mostly the wild trees and boys surrounding us.

We exchanged a drawing of Mervyn's for six Khaki Campbells. The vicar wanted the drawing very much, and suggested a system of barter for it. We had never had ducks before, and had felt no blank space in our lives because of the absence of them. I imagined this particular species in kilts, and waking up in the morning to the sound of bagpipes, but they proved to be khaki-coloured ducks with very little talent for anything except laying eggs in out-of-the-way places. None of us really liked duck-eggs, even when we could find them. By elimination, we gradually found the things for which we were not suited, and keeping ducks was another. Nevertheless, we had no inferiority complex on this account.

Sometimes Mervyn, the children and I all played follow-my-leader round an intricate box hedge in the front of the house on an array of bicycles and tricycles, trying not to fall as we rounded the corners.

It was not far from *Titus*, this world where the mist hid one from another, and the wind howled as violently as the scarecrow dogs in the outer dwellings of Gormenghast, and the fog-horns wailed as one could imagine 'The Thing' in her melancholy. It grew, and progressed as much a part of each day as eating, sleeping, and making love. The children, and the advent of our third child, were interwoven in everything which Mervyn did. His manuscripts are filled with drawings of us all, in the moments when words ceased to flow and the pen or pencil took over, a child with a bow and arrow, screaming, laughing, or myself sleeping. Illustrating, writing, walking, climbing up trees and down to remote bays, watching schools of dolphins, hearing the screech of sea-gulls, puffin landing, all of this world entered everything upon which Mervyn embarked, and my own painting could not but be touched by the wildness, the beauty which surrounded us.

*   *   *

There was no hospital on Sark. A good doctor, but no midwife. I wanted to stay at home to have the baby, so we arranged for a nurse to come from England. She arrived, and must have been horrified at the absence of amenities. Most of her clients had been titled ladies, and indeed her only subject of conversation was the royal family, about which we had only rudimentary knowledge.

Mervyn had to go down first during her stay every morning to inspect the sitting-room. Quite often there were the desiccated remains of a rabbit or a bird or a rat brought in by our cat during the night, and left as a matter of pride in the middle of the floor, but when you have been used to stately

Boy on a donkey, 1948

Sketch for the Glassblowers, 1944
Sketch in Yugoslavia, 1953

homes you must protest at this anti-social lack of behaviour.

On account of some miscalculation, the baby arrived two and a half weeks late, so that we began to grow quite acquainted with the ramifications of the royal family.

During the days of waiting, in order to try to hasten the advent, I went for long walks with the nurse, and because she happened to have rather larger proportions than even I had, I pulled her over stiles and hedges, and we went for drives in one of the Victorian carriages over the uneven roads, with Fabian sitting up in front by the driver. Often he would turn round, particularly after a very bumpy patch, and ask if the baby had come yet.

It almost seemed as though everything was a mistake, and there was no baby due, but one night there were the unmistakable signs. Mervyn woke the nurse, and was told to put a blanket to warm on the Aga cooker, and heat some water. I thought of all the Western films in which these mysterious preparations were made. Soon there was a gentle smell of scorching, and the blanket carried until its end a circular patch imprinted on it by the hot-plate.

Mervyn took his book and a pen, and went to another room where he said he would write. I went to my painting room, and started painting a still-life, which under the circumstances doesn't seem quite appropriate. I walked round the house from room to room, hardly believing that within a few hours there would be a new life in it. All the platitudes one knows crowded through one's mind, of birth and living and death.

The nurse kept asking if I was having a good pain, and as time progressed the answer was more often in the affirmative. I dropped in to see Mervyn more than once, and found him in a deep sleep, pencil in his hand, his manuscript dropped on the floor.

At eight in the morning, a girl arrived and Mervyn was awakened to be told that he had a daughter. I can still hear

Armand shouting to the vicar's wife, whose house was at the end of our garden, '*C'est une fille. C'est une fille.*'

*   *   *

Things were pseudo-hygienic. Face-masks were an essential. I saw Mervyn soon after the birth when he came to see his daughter. He said that she looked like Winston Churchill, which nearly reduced the nurse to apoplexy.

In the afternoon, the door was pushed open and he came in, maskless, with a painting, still wet, that he had done to celebrate the birth. I hardly caught sight of it before he was pushed out of the room in a most irate fashion and told not to return without a face-mask, and certainly not with such a germ-laden anachronism as a huge canvas of three kindly monsters sitting at a table. In the eyes of the nurse there seemed to be little relation between the baby and the picture.

At nights, my cat used to creep stealthily into the room and sleep on the bed, until early morning when Mervyn removed her.

*   *   *

I had written to the parish priest in Guernsey a month or two before the time due, to say that I would like my child to be baptized at home, as it would be difficult to go to St Peter-Port with a new-born baby. There was some delay in receiving a reply, and when it came it was to say that a special dispensation had been granted, as normally it is only royalty who are baptized in their own homes.

A day was arranged for a priest to come, and Mervyn went down to the harbour to meet him. It was a day of gales, and perhaps that priest is nearer heaven for having wrenched one unbaptized child from limbo, at the cost of his own nausea and sea-sickness, than he might have been at the more normal baptismal font. He was ushered into our living-room, where the donkey awaited him. He seemed to have very little taste for whatever was offered in the way of nourishment. The main object was to make a Christian of the small pagan upstairs as quickly as possible. The ceremony was held in the bedroom, and Fabian, who had seen his sister Clare for the first time, was transfixed by the unreality of the object. He could only find it in him to laugh, and to compare it with the Khaki Campbell ducklings, which he infinitely preferred.

*　　　*　　　*

Unless one has a positive means of income, it is difficult to live on an island, away from the people who can make it possible for an artist to survive.

Dawning gradually was the knowledge that the life we were leading would have to change. There was not enough money coming in, and yet looking back we lived with no extravagance. The extravagance was the life we were living.

*　　　*　　　*

We made up our minds that we would have to leave, but before doing so we went over to stay in a farmhouse in Guernsey, where Sebastian was now at school. We wanted to show him his sister also. His reaction was slightly different from his brother's. Apart from the daily routine of lessons, he and his friends spent all their free time exploring the dug-outs left by the German occupation, finding bayonets, helmets, German hieroglyphics, and then, as is the way of boys, fighting pitched battles with their dangerous trophies.

How can a new baby compete with such wonders?

*　　　*　　　*

In the autumn of 1949 it was time to go. Our wild garden with the bamboo hedge, the scene of so much living, our house, with so very few conveniences, but full of work and loving. We left it, our lease unexpired, returned to the landlord for the next ninety-five years.

We had to go back to London, where there was work to be found, for painters and a writer. We found a flat on the Embankment overlooking the river, and began to try not to miss the expanse of freedom that we had known on Sark. There was water, and there were trees, and nearby the Royal Hospital Gardens in which to stretch one's limbs.

Our sons were still at school in Guernsey, so that we had just the baby and the cat.

Mervyn began teaching life-drawing at the Central School of Art in Holborn, which gave us some basic money, and then he began to work on many other ideas. A collected book of poems was due to be published, called *The Glassblowers*. It covered many of the poems during the war, and afterwards. As mentioned earlier, the long poem from which the book took its title was written during and after the visit to Birmingham to the glassblowing factory, which seemed to have given him great inspiration. He described the glassblowers themselves as having the skill and self-discipline of ballet-dancers, and yet at the same time because of the distortions that their faces were subject to they had the dedicated look of trombonists or trumpet players. Mervyn seemed to see many things in terms of ballet—one of the least likely perhaps was cricket. Before taking me to the Oval once to see a Gentlemen *v*. Players match, he described to me the ritual of the game, the archaic terminology, the movements of a dance, a poetic and incomprehensible language to a novice. It seemed to me that nothing happened all afternoon, except a repetitive act of throwing a ball, and someone at the other end managing to hit it or miss it, and at intervals an interchanging of men in white to other places on a green field.

Rugby, too, he saw as a ballet of violence. Perhaps ballet is really only a game of cricket, with different skills.

★   ★   ★

At this time we met many actors—Esmond Knight, who had been partially blinded in the war, and his wife Nora Swinburne, Cyril Cusack, with his Irish wit, and Anthony Quayle. A liveliness descended.

By 1950 Mervyn had begun to think in terms of a play. His over-abundant mind was excited by the idea of the theatre and the vivacity of the actors whom we met stimulated his ideas. All the same, it was not until a year later that he began to write a play, which had a desperate bearing on our lives.

It was as though the years in Sark were needed for refuelling, and now once again we were in a hectic world, meeting people, and being able to know of the latest films, books, paintings, plays. An island is full of natural violence, which does not prepare one for the violence of people.

★   ★   ★

We happened to be living above the flat of a middle-aged couple with a girl around the age of our second son. The mother took some violent dislike to me, and would wait at her open door until I came down, then slam the door shut with the dreadful omnipotence of the righteous as I passed her. That is the kind of thing which can turn one into some kind of neurotic, but we simply decided to move. Later, the poor daughter was murdered, and the murderer, a middle-aged man, was tried and found guilty.

Glancing through the *Sunday Times*, we saw advertised a house with studio in Kent, and we decided to look at it. I had been left some money by my mother, and it seemed that life in a flat in London with three children was not an ideal existence for them.

We went to see 'The Grange' in Smarden, Kent. It was a Queen Anne house with an orchard and a cottage where studios could be made, with long hot-houses and vegetable patches. It was not an artist's house. It was a house for a gentleman with visible means of support. Why did we take it, I wonder? Looking back, it is impossible to know, except that the slamming doors had begun to make too great an impact on our lives.

*   *   *

Neither of us had the slightest idea of leases, of the vicissitudes of borrowing money. We were warned against it, but we did it, and an incongruous cavalcade of paintings and people, children and cats, arrived to take up residence in this very beautiful house.

Mrs Bull, a lady who had worked for us in Chelsea, came with us, to help us settle in. She developed a boil, and Mervyn a carbuncle. It took a little time to attend to each, but somehow furniture is moved, paintings and books take their righteous places, and one becomes a member, even for a short time, of a community to which one does not belong. The boys went to the village school and learned a great deal about birds' eggs, although their mathematics still gave cause for great alarm.

We had far too much property. An orchard that would only disintegrate unless properly attended to. We let it, and sheep and pigs grazed in it, but we had the freedom of it, and at the right time of year were able to pluck for our modest demands plums, or apples or pears or mushrooms, if one was able to distinguish them from toadstools. None of us died.

We had picnics in the orchard, and were awakened by green-woodpeckers outside our bedroom window. *Gormenghast* was published, and on 4 April 1951 a letter came, which was perhaps the most beautiful that could arrive.

I remember standing in the hall, whilst Mervyn read it to me, as I wept. Why do tears always spring up so readily? It was from the Royal Society of Literature.

I have the honour to inform you that my Council wish to award you a prize in respect of your novel 'Gormenghast' and your book of poems 'The Glassblowers'.

£100 was to be ours, free of income tax; his wonderful world had been entered into, and lo and behold I still weep. We were both as thrilled as one was at school on receiving an award for good behaviour or French.

*   *   *

A friend of ours, an artist, whom we had not seen for several years, had discovered our address, and arrived one day with an English wife married in Italy. The last time we had seen him he was desperate at Churchill's parliamentary defeat after the war. He was now a communist, and also, after the year of being in Italy, had no home and no work, only a burning desire to paint. We suggested that they should come to stay in the cottage, where I had a big painting room, but it was self-contained, and could house a man and woman and several score of paintings. We stayed a year in our completely anachronistic house, and they stayed a year in the cottage.

It was they who suggested they would look after our children, whilst we went to Paris on the proceeds of the £100 award.

We went, and stayed in a hotel in Montparnasse where it

was said that Oscar Wilde died. It had no particular significance, as it had been recommended to us by someone who had never heard of Oscar Wilde, but who knew that it was moderate in price.

How sad life is. I was bitten by fleas on our first night, and awoke looking like a balloon. Mervyn went out to get some dark glasses, but even they couldn't hide the unsightliness, and such is the vanity that besets one that I wouldn't leave the room until the ointments had done their work, and I had attained a certain resemblance to *moi-même*. After this it seemed that we should flee (?!) from Paris. Small childish humour has always appealed.

We went to a place called Montigny-sur-Loing which was, as its chief claim to fame, the habitat of a film-star called Michele Morgan. Staying in a modest pension, we walked and slept and drank red wine, enough to enable us to join Alcoholics Anonymous. The only memorable thing at Montigny was a walk at midnight along the deserted lanes of the village, *alongside* and, thank God, *inside* a wire fence, accompanied by the insatiable panting of alsatians who longed to break loose from the fencing, but man had been too cunning and they were confined, only able to violate us at second-fence.

On our way home we stayed again in Paris, and saw a few of the things which had been our purpose in the first place: Le Jeu des Paumes, and the Louvre.

*   *   *

We returned home. I, personally, am not one to be transplanted too often—Mervyn less so—but the banners and flags, the laughter and tears, of our welcome was enough to eschew any further absence.

Because the train journeys were infrequent to London, and

it was essential for Mervyn to get there in time to teach, we
decided to buy a car. It was a momentous decision. Mervyn
had a licence to drive, and I had just enough money to buy
something on four wheels. Even in 1951 it was difficult, and
we had to know someone who knew someone. We eventually
found someone who knew someone, and a car was to arrive, at
a certain time on a certain date. Our sons had been told. To
them, the mystery of the advent of a car was a hundredfold
more thrilling than the advent of a prospective brother or
sister. I think we all expected a winged chariot, a miracle, a
humming-bird, but what we actually saw was a black beetle, a
thing of shreds and patches, a Wolseley, down at heel, and
having lived its life to the full. It was tired, worn out as an old
nag. It had little left to give, and to the two with dreams of
speed it could offer nothing but crutches. We never ended a
journey we had begun in it.

★   ★   ★

Such is the life of a man alive with an intensity of living. A
year before, a book called *The Drawings of Mervyn Peake* had
been published, to which he wrote a Foreword that included
the following:

This is the problem of the artist—to discover his language.
It is a lifelong search, for when the idiom is found it has then
to be developed and sharpened. But worse than no style is a
mannerism—a formula for producing effects, the first of
suicide.

   If I am asked whether all this is not just a little
'intense'—in other words, if it is suggested that it doesn't
really matter, I say that it matters fundamentally. For one
may as well be asked, Does life matter?—Does man matter?
If man matters, then the highest flights of his mind and his

imagination matter. His vision matters, his sense of wonder, his vitality matters. It gives the lie to the nihilists and those who cry 'woe' in the streets. For art is the voice of man, naked, militant, and unashamed.

*   *   *

I was painting a great deal, during the afternoon mainly, when Clare was asleep, tethered in the orchard to a sheep, and before the return from school of the blue-eyed thugs. It was just now that Mervyn began to write his play, as yet untitled. He became obsessed with the theatre. Esmond Knight came to stay with us, and it was read to him as it progressed. Being an actor of long standing, *and* a friend of long standing, he gave his opinions with forthrightness and courage.

The playwright who wrote *Strange Orchestra* and *The Old Ladies*, Rodney Ackland, also came for a weekend, but his first night was marred by the presence of a bat in his bedroom.

The drama society of Smarden put on a one-act play of Mervyn's, and it was then the nearest we had come to hearing words made in silence publicly pronounced. Of all mediums it seems to be the nearest to a public examination of conscience.

Being a parochial affair, there was no fear of being hurt. It was elucidating, thrilling, and the sight of the two boys sitting in front, yet again on hard benches, swelling with pride at their father's prowess, was almost more rewarding than the play itself.

*   *   *

There were oast-houses attached to the farms surrounding us, in which cider was made. A cider to knock one out. We had an American acquaintance who wanted to come to see us for the day. Mervyn met her at the station in our miracle car.

With old-world courtesy he saw her into her seat, and as he shut the door all the windows slid softly open. A three-mile journey was ahead, and unless one had foreknowledge one would expect to make it without 'let or hindrance'. A gentle wind stirred, enough to lift the sunshine roof and see it float unhindered over the fields and faraway. Perhaps our transatlantic friend should have been ready for anything, but on being offered a glass of cider, and yet another, she tossed it down uncaringly, with the indifference of one used to pink gins and martinis, and before long she was safely tucked up in bed where she stayed a day or two, the purpose of her visit never really materializing. A book to be illustrated, we believed.

★   ★   ★

Flippancy is the only weapon I have against tragedy. It couldn't be foreseen, but it was on its way. Tiny manifestations, not yet identifiable, but there was still time for joy.

Mr Pye, a story based on Sark, was begun now. It was written truly, but also in the hope that it might make some much needed money. How could we know that it would be remaindered? The hope and the enthusiasm were there, the pleasure and the difficulties of its growing, like children, the impossibilities of seeing which way it would go. Seeing ahead wouldn't have mattered in any case. The important thing was to make something, and to hope.

From Smarden, on 4 April 1951, we went up to the Royal Society of Literature for Mervyn to receive his award. Although I have already written of the fruits of this, I have not mentioned the ceremony. There was a lecture, and a speech by R. A. Butler about the book, and afterwards we were introduced to him, and Mervyn was made a Fellow of the Society.

To have public confirmation of something which one already knows is perhaps vain, but none the less a happy experience.

*　　*　　*

Everything seemed to be a mixture of so many things. Trying to make enough money to live on, but at the same time painting pictures which might never sell, writing poems for which, even if accepted, the remuneration would not be over £2, and the book, *Mr Pye*, progressing. Mowing the lawns that surrounded the house which we should not really be living in, too big and too expensive it was. Going to watch 'The Golden Arrow' flashing by at a certain time each day was a major event. Talking about painting to the artist who was living in our cottage, drinking cider in neighbouring farms, seeing the hops flower, the miracle of the orchards, a variety of birds to watch, and hear the woodpecker like an alarm clock outside our bedroom window punctually every morning tapping away at the bark, bats and a white owl flying at night, with all the mystery that whiteness endows on the earth, on beasts, on all that it inhabits.

One night Mervyn stayed up late, and around three in the morning he woke me to say that he had started the play which had been in his mind for some time. He had the title for it, *The Wit to Woo*, and had written for about four hours. He was tremendously excited, and read to me what he had written, and also outlined the theme and the story. There *was* a certain amount at this time to keep one's mind active.

*　　*　　*

There was a general election, also, to make life less exciting. It happened that the artist's wife (in the cottage) was pregnant and imminently so, on the day of the election. In the early hours of the morning after polling day, we were awakened by the gentle sound of small stones hitting our window, and a voice calling out what seemed to be 'Labour's in—Labour's in'. As none of us was heavily interested in the result, it seemed a little unnecessary to wake us up in the middle of the night to give this information. From a drugged sleep Mervyn managed to get to the window, and to open it in a kind of trance. The solitary figure was standing on the lawn, in the moonlight. The election, it slowly dawned on us, was not his major concern, but his wife who was *in* labour, and he had come to ask if he could borrow our car to drive to London, to the hospital where all arrangements had been made. The necessary keys were found, and thrown out or handed over, and a little later in a mist of sleep we heard the uncertain sound of our car, idiosyncratic and unreliable, on the road, puffing past our house.

The next morning, the woman who came to do our cleaning arrived, with red eyes, which became redder and more swollen as the results of the election became manifest. The midnight prognostication had not been correct. In fact, nothing of that evening had been correct. The car returned, with no baby. Everything had been a false alarm.

*　　　*　　　*

A man we knew was organizing an exhibition of children's book illustrations for spastic children, and Mervyn was asked to contribute. He sent several drawings, amongst them one for *The Hunting of the Snark*. The exhibition was to be opened by the Queen, and she was also asked if she would accept one of Mervyn's drawings.

The place where the exhibition was held was unbelievably incongruous, in the basement of Gorringes in Buckingham

Palace Road, through the garden furniture department and the hardware. Not having seen or been close to any member of the royal family before, it was a matter of curiosity. The main thing I remember was the officiousness and bumbledom of the tail-coated members of the staff and entourage, herding the viewers into sheep pens, probably from the gardening department. Mervyn was given a little more respect as he was to be presented to the Queen, but his attire was perhaps not in the highest echelon of sartorial excellence, and therefore the respect was perhaps a shade less obsequious than to those of more perfect appearance.

It may be that I was prejudiced, but it seemed to me that in this dour world of handshaking and petty exchanges, as the Queen went down the line of bowing and handshaking, her eyes lit slightly as they came upon Mervyn. I know mine would have, but then I wasn't the Queen.

*   *   *

It slowly dawned that buying a house which one couldn't afford was not the way to make money. Apart from the fact that the bank had begun to query everything to do with us, we knew that once more it was time to go. Money is something we simply did not understand.

The house was put up for sale. Anyway, it hadn't belonged to us. It had been there for years before we went there, and it will be there for years to come, so little impact does one make on the history of a house.

In the meantime we continued to do all the things that we were doing anyway. Mervyn was finishing *Mr Pye*, and writing his play, at full speed ahead, painting, mowing lawns, teaching. (Oh Jesus, take me away.)

We went to Ashford, the nearest market town, to shop, and pulling up near a bus stop we saw a policeman watching us. I think to say with the eyes of a hawk would be a compliment to the policeman but, watching us sharply, and the moment that we had come to a stop, parked the car, and gone to wherever we wanted to go, up he came to Mervyn, shoulder tapping, and asking to see his insurance, and his this and his that. We had nothing. We thought you bought a car, and that was that. I know better now. Beautiful insurance, it was.

The policeman had never heard of people who had never heard of insurance, and road tax and licences. We were told to go to the nearest police-station, and our story was so ludicrous that we were let off whatever it was that we should have been guilty of, on condition that we armed ourselves with all civilized impedimenta such as little round discs on the front of the car to prove that we were worthy, and bits of paper for insurance to prove that we were even worthier.

We used to drive to the woods in Smarden, where there lived a tramp entirely dressed in newspaper. The woods were his home. In them he lived, slept, ate, and did everything else that is necessary for a human being to do. The smell from his black cauldron was delectable. We never spoke to him. His privacy had something sacrosanct in it. To have invaded it would have been crude to a degree. He had a natural courtesy, and dignity, and said good-evening with all the gentleness that one thinks nuns should be gifted with.

*　　　*　　　*

It was a beautiful part of the world in which to live, but too beautiful when our foolishness became manifest. All the wise people had been right. Not only could we not begin to pay anyone back for the house, we couldn't even pay the interest, which was something only just beginning to be understood by me. I think Mervyn had no idea, and never would have, what interest meant. It was just to be interested. . . .

So the house was put up for sale. Naturally there was some kind of financial crisis in the country, and although we sold it after a time it was at a loss of far more than we could have envisaged, but that follows the pattern.

We put most of our furniture into store, the same familiar but well-lived-in possessions that had survived so many moves. We went with our paintings and some books, our cat and our children, to a studio we had had for many years in Chelsea. A studio which had been found guilty in the First World War, but which had stayed its course until well after the second one. There are not so generous gifts to painters now. It was a studio such as no longer exists, except for people of very large incomes. Somehow or other we all managed to live in it, when the two boys were on holiday from school in Guernsey. We had a kind of little tent within the studio for our daughter, so that in the evenings when she had gone to bed and our friends came to see us she would not be disturbed. It was rather exciting to have a miniature room within a room.

In some ways it was one of the happiest times, apart from Sark. Our only possessions were those which were an integral part of us, books, paints, canvases, chalks, turpentine, and a few necessities, such as a bed and a chair or two, and enough plates and so on to make it possible to eat.

Mr Pye had been accepted and was about to be published, and the writing of the play was taking a great deal of time. Mervyn was placing too much hope in it. Above all things he wanted to prove to himself that he could make money. He wanted to give us all exotic and strange presents. He wanted to *feel* a success. Why did he feel that in a medium less known to him than his own pencils and brushes and pens he could achieve this? I suppose because the fruits of success are more possible in the theatre, if they are a success, than the sale of a painting, a book of poems, or his own books, which had achieved *succès d'estime*, but financially less than any manual

German Boy, 1945

A young Welsh coal-miner, 1938

work could earn. Why did he? Oh why? I've always hated the theatre since those days, the even worse cruelty that can be inflicted by critics on a man who works in silence, and displays himself in public, than the disinterest that a painter receives from the public. What is made in silence, out of passion and craftsmanship, should not be displayed until long after the passion has died away.

*   *   *

Although the lack of possessions was a kind of release, with children growing and needing to stretch their limbs, it was obvious that the five of us couldn't live for ever in a studio meant for one artist or two, in one huge room with a black monster of a stove, pipes of gargantuan proportions, ugly stove and beautiful warmth, and painting and drawing in progress around. It isn't the life for boys, although our daughter was now going to the same nursery school as the two blue-eyed thugs or pinky-orange boys had gone to a decade before.

Mervyn's father had died a year ago, leaving us a big Victorian Gothic house in Wallington, Surrey. In its way it was monstrously ugly, but as is the way with monstrously ugly things or people it was endearing, as is a mongol child to its parents, as all physical defects become endearing when one ceases to notice them and loves the bearer. And that is neither facile nor easy to say.

*   *   *

We went to look at this house, to see if it were possible to become a part of it. Personally, I loved the house, and hated where it was. It was spacious. It had at least twelve or thirteen rooms, with strange mysterious attics where the water tanks had lives of their own. A large garden, a garden where twenty-five years ago Mervyn had played tennis. Tennis parties on the lawn, almost a world of Bertie Wooster, where his parents had lived on their return from China, where his father had built a practice, and a home, far from the world and the aspirations that he had known and groped for. How far removed was this world from the Boxer Rebellion and the medical difficulties of Tientsin!

And yet again, how far removed was this world before the war from the world after the war. To most people this house would have been a castle; and yet, to Mervyn's parents, who were of very moderate means, it was a normal place in which to live and work.

It really was not a matter of a decision for us. It was a matter of when to go, and how to go. No one we knew in Chelsea could believe we were in our right minds if we could banish ourselves to the suburbs. Sark has an elegance about it. Wallington has not. One can be eccentric, but only in a certain kind of way.

★   ★   ★

Arrangements for schooling were made, and one dreadful day all our even more dreadful possessions made their appearance in this strange Gothic pile (and this was long after *Titus Groan* and *Gormenghast* had been so castigated).

The misgivings of possessions are manifold, especially when they have no intrinsic beauty. The thing is perhaps to have less and less, and only the things one wants.

In the seven years that we spent in this Outer Siberia, I can think of only two people to whom we talked. I spoke to hundreds of people, I fetched my daughter and took her to school each day—my sons were at another school—but the aridity was frightening. There was a nothingness, more than the claustrophobia of being surrounded by sea.

We had children's parties for Clare, and one mother on fetching her daughter looked at the paintings and drawings everywhere, and said, 'Oh yes, I dabble too.'

★   ★   ★

The Wit to Woo was finished, and as Mervyn had met Laurence Olivier and knew him slightly he was the first person to whom he thought of sending it for an opinion. His letter in return was not encouraging:

> . . . original and extremely good as is most of the writing I rather fear that the 'Crazy' (horrid word but I can think of no other) theme, is a highly dangerous one, and the audience is apt to get rather irritated by it. I remember we had them stamping out in a rage many times in 'Skin'—a play which was masterly both in its construction and in its writing and packed tight as a drum within its own fold—play convention.
>
> Also the rhythm in your writing together with the sort of verbal and onomatopaeic (spelling?) joking is trickily reminiscent of Fry and I do fear the sensation of its being derivative from both this author and Wilde and falling rather short of matching the content of either.
>
> Forgive me please if this letter steps over the bounds in the way of frankness, but I admire you so much indeed that I cannot but be entirely honest with you.

This was the beginning, only we didn't know it. Or should I say this was the end, only we didn't know it. I think it's almost appalling that human nature does go on hoping, and believing against all odds that everything is for the best in the best of all possible worlds.

I read *Candide* to Mervyn as he was illustrating *Alice in*

Wonderland. A peculiar juxtaposition of fantasy, originality and Gallic coldness and logic.

In the midst of living, working, eating, loving, fighting, a tiny little manifestation of shaking hands began in Mervyn. We treated it as a joke—too much drinking, only he was a moderate drinker, too much work, and that he certainly did to wonderful excess. He began in a small way to tire more easily than usual, to sleep whenever possible, to shake a little.

A wonderful friend of ours, who had known Mervyn since the days when he taught at the Westminster School of Art, saw him in this condition and gave us money to go to Spain for a holiday. The fares, the hotels, and enough to leave for the children whilst we were away if satisfactory arrangements could be made for them.

We thought he was over-tired, strained, we still had a noble overdraft from our foray into Kent, the effort of living, and the effort of working, trying to, oh God knows what.

The world seemed to be a series of cold douches. It did seem to be a time to go away. Spain had always been somewhere that we had both wished to see. Goya was the man and the artist that Mervyn most admired, Velasquez, El Greco, other miracle workers, apart from the world of flamenco, and horribly, perhaps, bullfighting, poverty and wealth.

*   *   *

We did make arrangements for the children, and of course our cats. They were dispersed, happily and adequately, and we left strange suburbia-land for Madrid. For a short space of time our finances, although in our hands, had been put away by another's. There were people since the onset of Mervyn's disease, who used generosity and imagination, and this was the first, and most unforgettable, occasion.

Dry, red, and arid, we landed in a country of small, dark

men. Not the romantic place of singing and carefree laughter.
At least, that is how we saw it. In many ways bleak and
lacking the fantasy of London. But then, why expect to find
what one has left behind?

We had been given introductions by friends, one particularly to Walter Starkie, who lived in Madrid, and was a
Hispanophile. Naturally, before all else we wished to go to the
Prado, to see, it almost seems in the flesh, the paintings,
etchings, cartoons of Goya, the magnificence of Velasquez. El
Greco, the myopic original, whose paintings made Mervyn
write a sonnet to and for him:

> They spire terrific bodies into heaven
> Tall saints enswathen in a frozen flare
> Of twisting draperies that coil through air
> Of dye incredible, in rapture thriven
> And heads set steeply skyward, brittle-carven
> Again the coiling clouds in regions rare;
> Their beauty, ice-like, shrills—and everywhere
> A metal music sounds, cold spirit shriven.
> So drives the acid nail of coloured pain
> Into our venerable wood, earth-rooted,
> And sends the red sap racing through the trees
> Where slugged it lay, now spun with visions looted
> From whirring skies and cold Gethsemanes
> Of bitter light, and all the wounds of Spain.

The Prado was closed to the public for the time that we were
in Madrid, being redecorated, and we thought that fate had
made this decree at that particular moment out of some
dreadful spleen, and we would not see Goya.

We had been asked to Walter Starkie's apartment to meet
him and his wife, and were made encouragingly welcome,
given a great deal of highly knowledgeable information, and

above all an introduction to the curator of the Prado. We arrived with our letter and spent nearly a day there, alone except for an elderly attendant who escorted us, and who clearly loved his canvas protégées. I think his intense devotion to them and his knowledge was one of the most touching things we encountered in Spain. Love always does touch one, watching it in others, whatever or whoever is the recipient.

Despite the wonders the world has to offer, to me the greatest wonder is two people loving each other in their own world. Nevertheless, this isn't the way to see Spain. One has heard of the proud people, the poor, the rich, the beggars, the gypsies, flamenco, caves, bullfighting, Holy Week in Seville, but how can one expect to encompass all within three weeks? Even in one's own country, how does one ever come to terms with the dreadful anachronisms that sway one backwards and forwards?

I cannot write a travelogue of Spain on three weeks' knowledge. I can say we were horrified by the poverty we saw outside Madrid, thrilled by the grandeur and the surrealism of Escorial, frightened and excited by the bull-ring, curious at the extent of the richness of the sea-foods, the octopus, the over-life-size prawns, tired of veal, exhilarated by the genius of castanets and heel tapping so fast that it almost becomes motionless.

We met Lady Lindsay Hogg, who had been an actress called Frances Doble. A beautiful Englishwoman, with a fanatic love of Spain. Mervyn did quite a few drawings of her, which he gave to her. She took us to parts of Madrid which we would never have otherwise seen, and one evening we were asked to meet her and a group of eccentric Americans at the Ritz. Certainly we would never have found our way there—not even to the Ritz in London. We all had dinner at an exclusive restaurant, with very Spanish dishes, and afterwards went on to a small private bull-ring just outside Madrid. A matador called Miguel Osta arrived with his entourage, one member of which brought his guitar. The patron of the inn, which belonged to the bull-ring, a huge man with an enormous paunch, sat on a wooden chair, singing flamenco almost as though one could see his heart, so passionate was the song, or the series of songs that he sang, with tears flowing down his cheeks.

After the singing, the matador staged a bullfight with the wicker bull's head that adorns so many walls in Spain. With immense grace he dedicated the bull to me, and went through the gestures and movements of this barbaric and courageous play. He had with him the ears and the tail of a bull that he had killed that afternoon. How does one ever reach decisions about one's feelings over bullfights? I wish I knew what I felt about everything, but gradually one realizes that one has no definite feelings about anything. I've always hated violence above everything, but watching a bullfight one is lured by its very beauty which encompasses violence to man and beast. But the argument against it is of course that it is man-made, although man also stands a strong chance of physical damage.

After the evening in this obscure and beautiful white-washed bull-ring we were taken home, or rather back to our hotel, in the bullfighter's enormous black car, with all his equipment piled high on the roof. It seemed to me that he had almost transformed himself into the bull, and we charged at the traffic on two wheels, until the moment of truth, when we came to a stop outside our destination, around three in the morning, when one claps for the concierge to unlock the door. I found clapping one's hands for service very feudal.

We were asked to tea by some grandees to whom we had been introduced. I think it was tea as a compliment to us, but it was at eight o'clock at night, and we were admitted to the silent and opulent house by a flunkey wearing white gloves. The courtesy and the formality was from another world, and the aloofness of our host and hostess did not warm us. There was a magnificent collection of Spanish paintings, and of French impressionists. Wealth has the power to awe one, especially when accompanied, and I think it nearly always is, by a withdrawal from the prosaic things of life.

We were led to the dining-room, where an English tea had been prepared. We sat formally and silent, waited on by immaculate white-gloved servants. When the mistress wanted something, or saw that we had need of marmalade or bread, she clapped her hands autocratically, and our needs were attended to like the flick of a serpent's tongue.

We went to Toledo, and saw El Greco's house, his easel, and the skies around which were his paintings. Avila filled Mervyn with horror, at least the convent where St Theresa had lived and prayed away from the world, and where one of her fingers was on display, with a magnificent ring upon it. It seemed a gruesome relic, but then there is in Spain much emphasis on the blood and the suffering of Christ.

*   *   *

We returned to England with various trophies for our children. A veil and roses, and a dainty small lace bag for our daughter's first communion, knives from Toledo for the boys, and a batch of drawings that Mervyn had made. Subjects ranging over many aspects of Spanish life, the ubiquitous priest, the blind lottery sellers, the young army recruits in their far-too-long greatcoats, particularly as they seemed always very short men, donkeys, which are endemic to Spain, and columns of Falangist boys. One or two of these drawings were reproduced in *Encounter*.

*   *   *

Spain had revivified us, and the strange tremors that Mervyn had been heir to were less. Our hope was renewed. Life began again. Teaching at the Central School of Art, becoming more and more immersed in his play, the conflicting reactions to it from people who could influence its coming to life in the theatre.

It had been revised and rewritten, as is the way with people who are perfectionists. Another letter from Laurence Olivier:

2nd Aug. 1951

Dear Mr. Peake—(may I call you Mervyn),

To let you know that 'The Wit to Woo' is not being idled about with. I want you to know that it is being read now by Tennant; I think you should also know that it is on the cards that you are to be a party to the shattering, ear-splitting, smashing up of one of those great old theatrical partnerships.

Vivien seems to like the play more than I don't like it, and so there is nothing to do but to offer it round to other producers than myself—producers of her choosing. Therefore, unless you have wishes to the contrary, as soon as Tennant has read it, it will go to Peter Brook, who is the first producer of her choice; from then on round, if necessary.

I hope you have another copy, so that we can keep this one for this purpose.

Yours, with a stiff upper lip—

Larry.

I suppose we had both become used to the world of waiting, of no decisions, of being postponed. I don't like the world of the theatre behind the scenes. There are too many people involved, too many vested interests. I prefer the solitary world of a poem, or a room in which to paint, and when you have

painted what you are trying to achieve then comes the time
when you have to try to sell it. Only then things become
ugly.

★   ★   ★

The play was one among many things. It strikes me as
inconceivable that one man could do so many things so well,
at the same time, as did Mervyn. The play was being written,
he had been asked by Eyre and Spottiswoode to write a long
short story to be included in an anthology of three stories by
John Wyndham, William Golding and Mervyn Peake, entitled
Sometime Never, and which won a science fiction award some
time later in America. It was called *Boy in Darkness* and was
Titus outside the *Titus* books.

He was illustrating *Alice in Wonderland* for a Swedish
publisher, producing poems, paintings, teaching painting
twice a week, and beginning *Titus Alone*, the third and what
was the last book of what was called a trilogy, but which
would never have ended then if nature had in her aggressive
way not taken possession of all that made him a unique
person.

Later, *Titus Alone* will be explained, but already there were
plans for a fourth book. Nothing so tidy as a trilogy had been
envisaged.

Titus among the

Snows	Fires	Affluence
Mountains	Floods	Debt
Islands	Typhoons	Society
Rivers	Doldrums	
Archipelagos	Famines	
Forests	Pestilences	
Lagoons	Poverty	

Soldiers	Monsters	Pirates
Thieves	Hypocrites	Mermaids
Actors	Madmen	Dreamers
Painters	Bankers	Decadents
Psychiatrists	Angels	Athletes
Labourers	Devils	Invalids
Eccentrics	Mendicants	Blood-Sportsmen
Lepers	Vagrants	
Lotus Eaters		
Shapes	Sounds	Colours
Echoes	Tones	Scents
Textures		

What a book it would have been.

★   ★   ★

The dreams and ideas of *Titus 4* were far away. The dreams of *Titus Alone* were taking shape, with immense difficulty, unlike the preceding two, *Titus Groan* and *Gormenghast*, which must have torn his imagination apart but not his physical being.

It seemed that our holiday in Spain had assuaged the tremors, had calmed the troubled mind. So full of hope are human beings that we were becalmed for a short spell, before life took over again.

It is hard to write of someone else's pain dispassionately. But to watch degeneration, the slow degeneration, both mental and physical, of a brain and of a being is perhaps more painful than the sudden shock of assassination or instant death. If I had to choose the death of someone I loved, if it had to be brutal I would say let it be sudden, don't let it linger until what you are seeing, or whom you are seeing, bears no resemblance to the being you knew.

From now on, it is no use pretending that life had not

changed course. Difficult to say how, but the need for financial success seemed to grow deeper and more urgent. One thing which happened during a summer holiday assuaged some of this urgency.

Mervyn was offered an exhibition in Dublin. He went over to Ireland and stayed with friends in Galway, then wrote to say that he had done a great batch of line drawings which 'are going to be shown to local aesthetes—or rather, horsey Irish women who are very rich and buy signatures—Sickert, John, Innes, etc.'.

In another letter from Ireland he wrote trying to put his ideas of writing and painting into some kind of intellectual order:

(1) To canalize my chaos. To pour it out through the gutters of Gormenghast. To make not only tremendous stories in paint that approximate to the visual images in Gormenghast, but to create arabesques, abstracts, of thrilling colour, worlds on their own, landscapes and roofscapes and skyscrapes peopled with hierophants and lords—the fantastic and the grotesque, and to use paint as though it were meat and drink.

To restore to painting the giant groupings of the old masters—Tintoretto, Goya, Velasquez.

To make studies and cartoons for each canvas. To find myself by ploughing headlong into a genre, and by so doing to evolve a way of painting ANYTHING, from an angel to an apple.

To incorporate within the canvases, that in themselves would be masterly and original, still-lifes, or boys or buildings, and skies based on perception.

He needed three concurrent lives to do all that was simmering, later to boil over, in his restless brain, and his imagination which could find no rest.

I am too rich already, for my eyes
Mint gold, while my heart cries
'O cease!
Is there no rest from richness, and no peace
For me again?'
For gold is pain,
And the edged coins can smart,
And beauty's metal weighs upon the heart.

How can I spend this coinage when it floods
So ceaselessly between the lids,
And gluts my vaults with bright
Shillings of sharp delight
Whose every penny is coloured money?

Storm, harvest, flood or snow
Over the generous country as I go
And gather helplessly,
New wealth from all I see
In every spendthrift thing—
O then I long to spring
Through the charged air, a wastrel, with not one
Farthing to weigh me down,
But hollow! foot to crown
To prance immune among vast alchemies,
To prance! and laugh! my heart and throat and eyes
Emptied of all
Their golden gall.

★   ★   ★

The exhibition opened in Dublin, and I had letters about it, but little mention of any financial benefit. The date and time of his return was fixed. It was to be a night flight, so that his return to Wallington would be in the early hours of the morning.

I had gone to bed, knowing and longing for his return.

When one is suddenly awakened at night, there is always a sense of unreality, so that in the morning it is difficult to know if what has happened is dream or actuality.

This night I was awakened, the light by the bed, and the slow lids lifting, to see Mervyn standing there. He asked me to close my eyes which had, with so much difficulty, only a second ago opened. It was a simple concession. I closed them, and heard a crackling sound, the sound that crisp paper makes, together with a shuffling sound of someone moving quietly. It seemed to continue endlessly, but in that state of half-awareness it was an infinity of sound until I was asked to re-open my eyes.

They were dulled by sleep but they opened, and were only with difficulty able to grasp what they thought they saw. It looked as though the bed was covered with white waves, an endless sea of paper, which when I sat up undulated slowly like gentle froth. What I saw is still like a dream. The bed *was* covered with white waves, a sea of £5 notes. The crisp white notes, which gave one a feeling of enormous affluence, covered the bed. Surely no other paper money has ever had such magic. Money from the sale of drawings in Dublin. Is it sad that it gave me a sense of relief, when I think back to the heart-burn that the first sale of a drawing gave me? I think it is sad, but now we had three children, and three months' holiday from teaching at the Central School of Art with no money coming in.

It is difficult to remember how many £5 notes there were, but there seemed to be enough to get through those arid months ahead. We put them in a drawer, and there was a feeling of benediction in their whiteness and crispness.

It was almost possible to understand a little the feelings of a miser, except that this money was for using.

*   *   *

We played tennis of a kind, in the garden, and quoits, and cricket with the boys and some of their friends. We went to swimming pools. I painted, and was to have an exhibition in the autumn. *The Wit to Woo* had been finally dropped by the Oliviers.

Ziegfield Theatre,
New York.

My dear Mervyn,

Thank you so much for your delightful letter of the 9thish ultish.

I am afraid our ideas regarding 'The Wit to Woo' came to a natural standstill when the only three producers that we could see handling the job well, reluctantly turned it down all one after another, and the answer to your question as to how things stand. . . . 'Still', is the rather brutal, but simple one.

I am awfully sad about this. We have tried to get the thing going, but Vivien I know would not consider doing it under any other direction than that which we have already sought in vain.

Our time in New York has been intense in every conceivable way.

We look forward so much to seeing you later in the year.

Ever,
Larry O.

It had been sent to Anthony Quayle, who wrote from the Stratford-on-Avon Memorial Theatre:

January 14th 1952.

My dear Mervyn,

I am very sorry not to have written before and humbly apologize. I have now read 'The Wit to Woo' twice, and find it absolutely fascinating. I am sure it could be a very big success. I think that Vivien would be quite excellent in it, and I think that Michael Redgrave would be wonderful as Percy Trellis. Please let us keep in touch with it. I would really love to produce it—if I were a manager I would love to buy it. Unfortunately, I cannot give you any clear idea of when I shall be free. At the moment my horizon seems to be cluttered with a lot of plans—none of which may materialize. But please remember that I should be very thrilled to produce the play for you if you need a producer.

Should Vivien wish to forgo her option on it I think I could probably find a way to another very good management putting it on, though that again is a bit conjectural. Anyhow, let me hear from you. I would love to know how things develop.

Best wishes—
Tony.

*   *   *

There were other things happening, though, to lessen the disappointments which seemed to be endless with his play.

Commercial television had started around this time, and Mervyn went with an idea to the head of the children's programmes of A.T.V. A book which he had written and illustrated called *Letters from a Lost Uncle*, published after the end of the war, seemed almost a 'natural' to be adapted.

This time, the answer was yes, and a fairly quick yes. Renewed hope and vigour accompanied the affirmative.

It was to be a series of twelve programmes. Mervyn was to do the drawings from the original, mainly wash and heavy line, over which the camera would play, and the text would be spoken by an actor as the camera moved over the pictures. It was a weekly serial, and he had to do at least twelve very large

'Head floats about me . . .', 1957

Drawings in Madrid
1956

drawings each week, and take them up to the television studio in time for rehearsal. Once, having arrived at Victoria with his large portfolio, when he was already on the bus towards the studio he found he had left them in the train. He jumped off the bus, and rushed back to the station. In a whirl and a panic he made for the lost property office. A week's work! There was no sign of them, nothing and nobody could help. He had to return home, phone the studios, explain what had happened, and stay up night and day until he had worked all over again on the same drawings.

Financially, it was probably the largest amount of money that he had received, but we were still badly in debt from the house in Kent, so that half of everything which came in went directly to help pay off our stupidity in becoming certainly 'landed' but perhaps not gentry.

The programme was apparently highly rated in opinion polls, but it didn't lead to anything further, which, considering the strain of the work, was perhaps a good thing.

*   *   *

One evening, Mervyn received a phone call from a man whom he knew only slightly. A group of his friends, who were all specialists in one way or another, had decided to make up a group to go to Yugoslavia. They wanted Mervyn to go as an artist—the others were an archaeologist, a historian, a geologist, a naturalist, a photographer, a writer (though Mervyn could have done for that too). They planned to do a television programme seen through all these different eyes. It was an original idea, and he decided to go. The term of teaching was over. I think the trip was partly sponsored, or helped financially in some way, otherwise it would not have been possible for him to have gone. The only essential articles for travelling were materials for working with. No oils, but an infinite supply of paper, water-colours, pens and pencils, *conte*, quick and sudden for the quick and sudden sight or thought. Apart from these it was very rudimentary, almost elementary in that it was suggested that essentials at that time to be taken to Yugoslavia were soap and lavatory paper.

It was an exciting prospect, to be going to a completely unknown country with people of such diverse talents and with very little knowledge of what lay in store. Alas, what letters I received have been lost, but I can remember some incidents which were related to me on the return home. I have also a batch of drawings done under conditions of varying degrees of difficulty. A handsome, magnificent old man, bearded and long-haired, a prophet, threatened Mervyn with a knife, on seeing himself being drawn. Both escaped with their lives, and Mervyn with his drawings. Nuns on a boat, sailing down the Adriatic; peasants, who gave him and one other member of the group the kind of hospitality that meant that they themselves might go without for weeks to come, generosity akin to madness, and the lack of linguistic communication stultifying all means of gratitude, except by gesture and sign.

The articles already mentioned as being essential equipment certainly proved to be so. There was one story, which is funny, I think. Approaching the end of the journey, it was decided to spend a night in the best hotel in Zagreb. No one had had a bath for the past three weeks, and the need for one had become a matter of some necessity.

Mervyn found a bathroom, and filled the bath with hot water, having remembered to put in the plug. He lay in the blissful warmth, dreaming dreams, his clothing arbitrarily discarded around the floor. With his toe he unhooked the plug, after an hour of meditation, and lay with closed eyes whilst the water gently seeped away. It was after a little time that he opened his eyes, and saw to his astonishment his clothes floating like ship-wrecked mariners around him. The bathroom had many facilities, but *not* one for disposing of the water. He went into the passage in a towel, and met a friendly house-maid. By gesture he took her to the bathroom to disclose the damage. Her reaction was one of immediate laughter, and shaking of head and hand, as if to a child who has misbehaved but with whom one is not irredeemably angry. I'm not quite sure of the sequel.

There was little to buy in Yugoslavia at that time, but a bottle of Slivovitz was brought back, and a doll in national costume for our daughter, which began a great collection of dolls in national dress.

As is the way with many projects, the visit to Yugoslavia did not materialize as had been envisaged. It was a pity, because the idea had been so good, to see one place through so many different eyes and minds. There was a small television programme, but on a very minor scale. Mervyn was interviewed on children's television, and several of his drawings shown, but the main idea had been jettisoned.

★   ★   ★

So once more there was a return to the struggle.

Mervyn sent *The Wit to Woo* to John Clements, with his wife Kay Hammond in mind to play the only woman's part in it. They were very intrigued by it, and a good deal of correspondence passed and hope revived once more.

If the play had been the only project at this time, we both might have given up hope in every direction, but now, looking through all the ideas, projects, and actual finished achievements, I am overwhelmed by the proliferation.

Mervyn had begun on the third book of the *Titus Groan* series, as yet untitled, and during the Christmas holidays in 1954 he went to stay at a pub in Dedham to enable him to write with less disturbance than he would have had at home. The tremors in his hands had returned. They were still only slight, but enough to make writing, which he always did in long-hand, more tiring. He found concentration more difficult, and returned home having written with far more difficulty than he had in the first two books.

He had been commissioned by the Swedish Radio, who published books in English, to illustrate *The Adventures of Tom Thumb*, and a year later, *The Further Adventures of Tom Thumb*. They were published very attractively in miniature form, which is perhaps appropriate to the subject.

From all the activity and the amount of work done, our finances should not have been in the parlous state which seemed to be habitual. We were still paying for our lost sojourn in Kent, and apart from that book illustration could scarcely be called lucrative, particularly when practised by someone who was a perfectionist, and not easily satisfied with his own work. I did a few book jackets, which, if one's livelihood depended on them, would provide very few luxuries in life.

I was painting every day, in two attics at the top of the house, where my cats followed and sat on the piles of paper which littered every working room. I exhibited in the London Group, in the Woman's International, and in various other mixed exhibitions; and I was working for a one-man show later that year.

I always seem to have been able to paint when there is intense life surrounding me, despite the eternal meals, the fights of one's children, and the constant demands of domesticity.

It is now, with more time and less friction, that I find it harder. I miss Mervyn. He was a fair critic, and honest. Sometimes, I hated what he said, and would fight against it, but knew that he nearly always probed to the essential heart of a painting or a drawing.

In those attic rooms, the surrounding suburb disappeared, and I entered the world of my own making, and the familiar smell of turpentine. My painting was changing and had changed a great deal since the early days of my marriage, when it was unrestrainedly romantic, as I was myself. I certainly knew a great deal more technically, and began to use different materials and to experiment with shapes and colours, but I have never been able to divorce myself aesthetically, to decide between life and painting. My mainspring has always been the heart and not the head, but with more knowledge the heart can be controlled.

I painted a great deal from my children—using their play and their turmoil, boys on stilts, handstands, somersaulting, dressed up in Indian war-dress, trying to achieve the rhythm of their movements in simplified form.

*   *   *

It seems incredible that we were able to part-exchange our Wolseley Hornet car, which had by now very little left inside to make it a going concern, for a wooden shooting-brake which to our children was a revelation of beauty, even after the mushrooms started growing on the inside of the roof.

We went for picnics to the country and sea, and Mervyn, Clare, and I slept in it, with the boys in a tent outside. I never could equate the driving of a car with Mervyn, but for all the excitement and wrong turnings, we saw a good deal more of England than we should have done if he or I had been more of a map reader.

Our garden in Wallington was very large, too large for us to dig and delve ourselves. By some means we found a man who was willing to work in it for six months in exchange for our shooting-brake, which had proved more expensive than we had imagined it would. We knew or thought we knew his name, but not his address—but it seemed unimportant. At the end of the six months he claimed our 'dreamland', as Fabian had called the car, which was as it should be, as both sides had agreed in writing to this rather strange form of payment. What we had not agreed was that all our garden tools should also be included. We found an empty shed, but never again heard of our gardener or his car.

*   *   *

Not having heard about the play for some time, Mervyn must have written to John Clements, for he wrote in reply:

My dear Mervyn

. . . I gave the play to Robert Hamer, who, as you probably know, is one of the really top film directors in this country. He directed among other things 'Kind Hearts and Coronets'.

. . . He is wildly enthusiastic about 'The Wit to Woo', but says he couldn't do it as his next one because there is too little time to prepare it for film purposes. But it is something that he and I would very much like to discuss with you for a future date if it interests you. The delay in writing to you about it has been that Hamer was a long time over it—insisted that he wouldn't be rushed in savouring writing of such quality—and so on. . . .

Yours,
John.

Perhaps we both had now begun to realize that disappointments and setbacks in the world of the theatre were almost more relentless than in the world of painting and writing, although we both had experienced the normal lot of artists or writers in the heart-burning rejections and, perhaps even worse, indifference.

Alice in Wonderland, which Mervyn had been originally
commissioned to illustrate by a Swedish publisher in 1946,
had been accepted by Alan Wingate, in England, and came out
in 1954. Naturally, there was a reserve on many people's parts
to accept illustrations other than Tenniel's, but the drawings
were well reviewed on the whole.

A letter came from Graham Greene in response to the
book:

10th Sept., 1954.

Dear Mervyn,

How very kind of you indeed to send me Alice's
Adventures in Wonderland. I have always liked your
illustrations for this enormously. You are the first person
who has been able to illustrate the book satisfactorily since
Tenniel, though I still argue as I think I argued with you
years ago that your Alice is a little bit too much of a gamin.
But here they seem to have eliminated her nearly altogether.
I look in vain at first glance for a full length of her. I do wish
they had given you better paper.

Yours,
Graham.

Yet another book came out with drawings, called *Figures of
Speech*, published by Gollancz. It is as the title indicates. There
is no text, and it was intended for moments of light-
heartedness when people could guess at the figures of speech
upon which the drawings played. I think they are very funny,
but to some people they are facetiously so. As far as I can
remember this book was also remaindered. Not a new
experience, but always one that hurts anew, and perhaps hurts
the publishers even more in a different way.

★   ★   ★

We had a friend living with us at this time, named Aaron Judah, who had a room at the top of the house, which he fitted up with gadgets of Heath Robinson ingenuity. He had the room nominally, in exchange for sitting in, when needed, and sometimes fetching Clare from school, if I had been in town and couldn't get back in time.

He was a writer, and just then had an idea for a play which he had worked out, and wished to collaborate in, with Mervyn writing and he supplying the technical workings. I must admit that I was not sanguine at the prospect of the disappointments ahead, but the theatre attracted Mervyn greatly, and he was also interested in the theme, which perhaps had its genesis in *Oblomov*. He had always been fascinated by the one or two individuals of great talent whom he had known who had nevertheless decided against using their natural gifts, whether through indolence or cynicism, and devoted their lives to nothingness on a grand scale. This was roughly the theme of *Mr Loftus*, or its alternative title *And a House of Air*.

So began another marathon of patience. The play was written, far more quickly than was *The Wit to Woo*, and it started on its rounds. Its life, rather like its theme, has been lazy.

One of the first people to whom it was sent for a reaction was Kenneth Tynan:

Dear Mr. Peake,

I apologise for my delays in reading and returning 'Mr. Loftus'. I can see in it some fine pointed writing, and a lot of quite unforced pathos, plus a lovely part for a bravura actor to sink his teeth into. What slightly worries me is what might be called a foothold in reality. Your characters weave some splendid verbal wreathes for themselves, but seem to be figures in a pageant rather than people in a play. Also I found the motivation a bit obscure at times: I wasn't quite clear why Flora left Loftus: but perhaps this was due to hasty reading. On the whole while I admire your verbal virtuosity enormously, 'Loftus' isn't really my kind of play. I hope you'll go ahead, get it produced, and prove me wrong. And let's meet again soon, when I get back from Moscow.

Yours,
Kenneth Tynan.

★   ★   ★

Titus Alone had begun, to a slow start. It was perhaps more difficult to be outside the world which had been created as a world within a world than to be in a world which was probably closer to this one, and yet alien. There was too much—the world is too much with us. People have said that Mervyn lived in an ivory tower, or that his books are an escape from life. I think they are an extension, full of humour and compassion: the extremes that are so much a part of life, the quirks and the norms, and *Titus Alone* hints more by its veracity than many a book, factually correct.

There was still two days a week teaching life-drawing at the Central School of Art, which at least brought in bread and margarine. I think Mervyn enjoyed teaching, or, at least, trying to communicate what he felt was the essence of drawing. He had enormous sympathy with people on the edge, as students are.

He was able to use the lithography room at the Central, and experimented in the medium, which excited him very much. He had been commissioned to illustrate *Bleak House*, and did several lithographs, poor Jo, Skimpole, Lady Dashwood, etc. A very evocative set of drawings was produced, only for it to be discovered that the publisher who had commissioned them had disintegrated, so that no book was forthcoming. It is impossible to imagine anything so straightforward as a book being published without complication, but still less so that a play can be written, and within a certain time limit, produced.

Another letter came from John Clements about *The Wit to Woo*:

My dear Mervyn,

I am delighted to have a script of 'The Wit to Woo' always at my elbow.

Katie and I are still desperately anxious to do it in the theatre, and one of these days—if of course we are not forestalled, I am determined to bring that about.

So don't for Heavens sake let anyone else have it without giving us a snap refusal!

In the near future my whole organization is to undergo many changes and when they happen it may make it much more possible for me to come to you with a definite proposition. The making of a TV film would not in any way affect that.

In fact in my view it might easily enhance its chances in the theatre rather than the reverse.

My best wishes to you both from both of us—

Yours,

John.

How could one help but feel a certain hope? Why did Mervyn place so much in it, when his own media had not in themselves brought respite from worry? Up to a certain age, it may be right and proper for a writer or a painter to struggle, not only for recognition but for a certain financial easing, but after forty a man should be able to work without the constant strain that damages the mainspring. There is no one to blame, but perhaps ourselves, in that money had never been the reason for doing anything. But this play was one thing where

Mervyn saw likelihood of the kind of financial reward that he had never envisaged with drawing or painting or poetry. It was becoming an ogre, equating success with money. And yet Mervyn often told me of Cézanne who, after he had been painting a portrait over a period of years and was asked how he felt about it, replied, 'I am not displeased with the left elbow.' Cézanne, I think, was not too financially embarrassed, but to both of us it was a wonderful disdain for the world. Only the world was creeping in.

★   ★   ★

I have no letter, but somewhere the Clements had to drop their option on the play. I know they wished to do it, but the theatre must be harsher even than the Bond Street galleries. It really was *not* our world, but the dreadful devil was beating Mervyn, and he must have sent it to Peter Hall at the Arts Theatre, from whom he received this reply:

The Arts Theatre   26th March, 1955.

Dear Mr. Peake,

Herewith your script of 'The Wit to Woo'. I have had no chance to read it with any close attention, but I skimmed through it last night, and I must say I found it wonderful. So, please, if the Clements don't want to do it, may I have the script back so that we can consider doing it here?

In any case I would very much like to have a long talk about 'And a House of Air' (Mr. Loftus). I think your plays have the most enormous possibilities and I would very much like to do one of them.

Perhaps you would let me know when you come back to England.

With best wishes for your trip.

Yours sincerely,
Peter Hall.

Disillusion never set in on Mervyn's side, although I had far more reservations now with anything to do with the theatre. For me, the silent worlds of painting and writing had an intrinsic truth, whatever happened once they had left their birthplace.

I think it was the only thing I could not share with completely in the making. I was becoming afraid of what was happening to Mervyn. He was becoming more ill. The tremors in his hands and in his legs were more pronounced. He tired too easily. What used to be easy became more difficult. The theatre remained the promised land which he longed for, in some way he felt to prove himself, as a man who could make money, to give presents to his family. The dreadful power of money: it is demoralizing without enough, demoralizing with too much.

*　　　*　　　*

Our eldest son had become greatly interested in drumming, and through holding jobs, and newspaper rounds, had bought himself a drum-set. He had friends who played other instruments, so that in the evenings the house rocked to the sounds of a group. It even reached the attic where I painted—Titus was not so Alone as he might have wished to be.

Titus Alone was growing more impatient to be written, and one holiday Mervyn went over to Sark to try to find the serenity which he now craved. I had letters from him telling me of the progress.

. . . the weather bleaches my soul. It's like a furnace, but I am thriving on it, and am writing at top gear. THANK YOU sweet one. What you say about Titus 3 helps me. Titus 3 is for you as they are all for you. . . . My brain is clearing day by day. With a strong healthy brain one can make studies—and when you have more time from chores and less fatigue we will make progress together.

God bless my darling—you are deep in my heart.

★   ★   ★

He must have had to return from Sark, which had always, since his very early days, held something especial for him, but whilst he was there this time the B.B.C. were broadcasting an adaptation of his book *Mr Pye*, which was set on the island.

I went to the rehearsals, and saw at first hand the production of a play. The music had been written by Malcolm Arnold, and the characters coming alive, in front of so cold a thing as a microphone, was a minor revelation. Mervyn didn't hear the play, but the rest of us listened in our various ways, and apart from the barriers I was developing against the theatre I found it rather wonderful to hear and even to see, through sound, the characters alive, the people he had created, that one knew.

A year earlier *Titus Groan* had been adapted for the Third Programme. Mervyn had done the adaptation, which was a formidable task, as a book of 200,000 words had to be condensed into one hour's listening. It should not have been condensed so drastically. But even so, the actors became the characters and it seemed as though the world of Gormenghast had found itself, living here and now—the people that we knew, just speaking, more real than any politician with his platitudes.

A book called *More Prayers and Graces* was published by Gollancz in 1957. It was a follow-on to an earlier book called *Prayers and Graces*, which seems to have had the biggest sales of any book that Mervyn had done drawings for. There had been an outright payment, so there were no royalties. Likewise with the second book, so although both books sold well,

probably better than most that Mervyn had illustrated, that
was financially all there was.

*   *   *

Whatever happened to *The Wit to Woo* after Peter Hall's
letter I have neither recollection nor letters, until one came:

Jan. 8th 1957.
Dear Mr. Peake,
    I have read these plays once; which is not enough. But
enough to find them intriguing, disturbing and exciting.
    Will you please give me more time to read them again, get
'others' to do so, and then let you know what can be done.
                    Kind regards,
                        Yours sincerely,
                            Michael Codron.

This was no longer enthusiasm without prospect. Through
Mervyn's agent it became not just enthusiasm, but a concrete
proposal. Contracts were signed, and the paraphernalia of the
theatre slowly creaked into motion. Michael Codron was a
young producer, and he intended to put it on at the Arts
Theatre in London, with Peter Wood directing.

It was hardly credible. The play had been begun seven years
ago, and had already lived a life that few people could hope for
themselves. The illustrious of the theatre had toyed with it,
and rejected it, but somebody loved it, and its seven years
gestation was at last in labour.

The cast was chosen, and after that rehearsals began.
Mervyn went to as many as he could, and often came home
late, excited and expectant, full of regeneration. It is a pity that
he didn't design the sets himself, but I suppose he would not
have had the time to do so with the multifarious work in other
directions.

It was exciting for him, like the dumb suddenly being able to speak. To hear his words which he had known for so long being heard, and in most cases, given the meaning that he had strived for.

We both went up to the Arts Theatre and I met the cast. Certainly, they all seemed enthusiastic, and how could one fail to like them after so many years of waiting?

We went to the dress rehearsal, and it was touching for me, as I had not seen or heard it on stage before, to hear words that I had known so long being spoken with the wit and understanding with which they had been engendered, although many critics were later to disagree with that.

The first night was 12 March 1957, and through the imaginative generosity of an old friend, Laura Beckingsale, who had been present at Mervyn's birth forty-six years ago in China, we spent the night at the Royal Court Hotel in Sloane Square. We had had experience of private views, and of books being published, but never of such a soul-baring experience as a play, where you can see and hear and be infiltrated by the comment and the mood.

I had a dinner jacket made for Mervyn as a present, and we both took some form of tranquillizers. Neither of us could help the other, except by the negative things that one always says at moments of stress. Once at the Arts Theatre it seemed less momentous, as there were many friends to give the sense that we were not entirely alone in the world. John Clements and Kay Hammond were there, which seemed to both of us a generous gesture.

The theatre was full, and it appeared as though the years of waiting might be rewarded. It was a silly thought, as the audience had in it so many people who would like it to be a success.

Nevertheless, there was a reception for it which seemed to give point to the waiting. People had laughed, had been amused; and not, I think, only because they were friends and relations. It would take an even smaller theatre than the Arts to fill it with partisans.

Having seen the actors afterwards, and all the excitement which first nights carry, we had a feeling that something was going right.

We were taken out for a sumptuous dinner by relations, at Pruniers, and never has lobster tasted so sweet. A return to the hotel, and a deep sleep, to awaken to the almost outworn cliché of the morning reviews.

They were neither good nor bad, but mostly condescending and ungenerous. How easily and quickly can a man be disposed of!

*   *   *

We packed our bags, but did not run. We returned to Wallington, and from this awful date life has changed.

It cannot be laid at any door, but disappointment, built up by hope for too long, can damage a brain already too prolific.

Mervyn went to bed when we got home, and became delirious. It was as though everything that he had been holding on to had disintegrated. I sent for the doctor who gave him tranquillizers, but who was unable to diagnose any physical trouble.

For the next few days he languished, and the symptoms of tremors in hands and legs became more and more manifest.

One day his memory went completely, and he had hallucinations. My two sons took my daughter out all day, and I phoned a doctor in London who came down to see Mervyn.

He diagnosed a complete breakdown, and made an appointment with a neurologist for the following day.

Somehow or other we must have got up to London to the

hospital, and it was decided that he should go immediately to a hospital and have treatment. Even at that time, I felt it was a physical illness—what is known as Parkinson's Disease, because I had seen an old friend with almost identical symptoms—although there seemed also to be every reason for a mental breakdown. The play was forgotten, the reviews which came in were now a matter of indifference. A friend drove Mervyn and me to Virginia Water Hospital, where he was admitted, and I had to sign forms to allow him to be given electrical treatment. I had never seen male nurses before. I had never seen mad people before. How incredibly worse it must have been for Mervyn. His first letter to me said:

I have almost lost my identity—I long for your white arms around my neck. I am afraid of something subtle. It is the smell of the place—its miles and miles of corridors—the expression on the faces—some of whom have been here for years.

I will never write about mad people again—I am in a kind of dream—or nightmare, and I yearn for your touch.

Maeve! Never! Never again! It has done something to me. I have played too much around the edge of madness— oh I could cry to be free.

I could write a book about an illness which robbed my husband of dignity, of coherent thought, of all his creative powers, and left him an emptiness of tragedy. We have all gone through the extremes of bitterness in watching a citadel fall by slow and tortuous degrees, but even now, at this time, there was still a little left of the life which we had shared.

*   *   *

It was an arduous time. I had the three children, and two or three times a week I went to Virginia Water, after taking my daughter to school and making arrangements for her to be collected in the afternoon. Mervyn was being given electrical treatment, which he feared as a child fears darkness. He would ring me two or three times a day begging me to fetch him home.

I thought that the treatment he was receiving was for his good, so I had to try to calm him and tell him that what was being done was for his good. It was as heart-rending as leaving one's child with strangers.

He did write some poems, and also painted and drew whilst he was there:

> Out of the overlapping
> Leaves of my brain came tapping. . . .
> Tapping . . . a voice that is not mine alone:
> Nor can the woodpecker
> Claim it as his own: the flicker
> Deep in the foliage belongs to neither
> Birds, men or dreams.
>
> It is as far away as childhood seems.

Titus Alone was neglected, and the fate of *The Wit to Woo* had been decided. It ran for two or three weeks at the Arts Theatre, and came off with no further offers. In all, Mervyn received £17 for it.

*   *   *

As he seemed to progress he came home at weekends, and brought drawings he had done, poems he had written. Most of them have now been published, although at the time I sent them to various periodicals and they were rejected. Most of his poems then were nothing to do with his environment, which from his first letter to me had a nightmare quality, but were

Drawings in Madrid
1956

Drawings in Madrid
1956

lyrical and full of a nostalgic lost beauty. This is only one which seemed to come straight from what he was experiencing:

> Heads float about me; come and go, absorb me;
> Terrify me that they deny the nightmare
> That they should be, defy me;
> And all the secrecy; the horror
> Of truth, of this intrinsic truth
> Drifting, ah God, along the corridors
> Of the world; hearing the metal
> Clang; and the rolling wheels.
> Heads float about me haunted
> By solitary sorrows.

It is almost too painful for me to re-read his letters from this time. All, full of hope and projects, ideas for books and paintings, and through all a love which sustained the forebodings.

As he seemed to improve a little, he began to write *Titus Alone* again. It was not easy, as he had been having electrical treatment which affected the memory and made clear thinking impossible.

After about nine months of treatment for a nervous breakdown Mervyn was discharged from the hospital. It was indicated that there was nothing further they could do, as in fact he had the early symptoms of Parkinson's Disease.

The Central School of Art had kept his job open for him all this time, which was almost more than one could expect, but it alleviated one of the foremost worries which was, naturally, financial. We had never been able to straighten our finances since our foolish foray into Kent.

During this first time in hospital, there was unbelievable generosity from friends and relations. His brother, in a most

wonderful letter, sent him £1,000 to help clear the overdraft.
We couldn't believe it when we opened the envelope and saw
such a sum. There was hope, and faith, and charity.

*   *   *

The summer holidays came, and we decided to go with the
children to Sark. It did seem as though the dark days were
over. It was a wonderful time. The island always seemed to
have the effect of a magic wand. The miracles that one
expected in childhood almost came to pass. This holiday had a
healing quality. To climb down to bays, opulently curved and
golden, where there was neither sight nor sound from other
humans, except distant shapes and echoes of voices, was the
peace and the excitement we all craved. Watching a school of
porpoises, discovering caves which may well have hidden
treasure trove. There are many bays in Sark, and each has a
different mood. The grey stony bays, austere and cold, and the
bays with rockpools in which our daughter sat, screaming
with joy. Watching trawlers and fishing boats, hearing the
sea-gulls, their voices harsh, and matching the shrillness of the
child. Cormorants and puffins. Picnics and games, and
crossness on the return home, because whichever bay one goes
to there is a steep climb back to the top, and even the
exhilaration of doing what one wants cannot always preclude
the quarrels of children and their parents.

*   *   *

So the various terms started again, and we all went back to
our own occupations. Mervyn once again started his teaching,
and at the same time he was offered an exhibition of line
drawings at the Waddington Galleries, who had now moved
from Dublin to London. *Titus Alone* was progressing, but
slowly.

How could one fail to notice the slowing down once more, both physically and mentally, and the hand, once so steady, unable to control pen or pencil with its former ease? It was lucky that he had a drawer full of line drawings which could be exhibited, as he could never have made any especially for it.

As the weeks progressed, so it was manifest that medical advice should again be sought. He was admitted to a neurological hospital to undergo tests of all kinds, and the private view of his exhibition took place during this sojourn, although he was allowed up to come to it. He sold several drawings, which at least was a boost to his morale, and I have just come across a very excellent review of the exhibition in a paper called *Freedom*, which is an anarchist newssheet. There must have been other reviews, but they are lost, and anarchy prevails.

One learns the big things in life sometimes in small ways. I had asked to see a doctor at the hospital, to know as far as anyone could know what lay ahead. I was told that the doctor attending him was busy, but if I would wait in the hall I could see him on his way out—almost as though I was about to ask him to tea, not as though I wished to know something which would affect all our lives.

A dreadful feeling of insignificance overcame me as I waited. Was it complete lack of imagination on the doctor's part that he told me the most devastating news that I could hear of my husband, standing in a hall, with the never-ending stream of people who pass and re-pass one almost somnambulistically in all hospitals?

He said, 'Your husband has premature senility.'

He was then forty-six years old.

*   *   *

He returned home with pills, and with perhaps a little hope, as he never knew the possibilities of his cruel disease.

Christmas came and went, and he had a sense of great urgency in completing *Titus Alone*. It was now impossible to write at home. We had heard that often writers, or anyone seeking peace, could go to Aylesford Priory, a monastery in Kent, and live and work there, without necessarily being a Catholic, or taking part in any of the religious services. So we fixed for him to go there, to try to write without the rigours of a family round him.

He was still able to work, but there was an appalling restlessness, night and day, which I was afraid would disturb the other guests, which later proved to be true.

I did have some letters from him:

My own Special beauty queen!

Today (and its only 5 p.m.) I have got on like a house on fire (9 pages) and I am going on this evening.

It is a beautiful 12th century Priory, set on a square with a big green in the centre. There is a library, but its full of religious books. There is also a 'trinket' shop, so I can get you and Clare something. There's not much to appeal to les garçons, but I'll try.

I've driven myself to work and I'll have something to show you. . . .

Am really enjoying and profiting by the break—Women are allowed too, if you wanted to come—it ain't half monastic. However I have a tame radiator. This really has been a great success thanks to you, dear one. I am writing well and steadily.

God Bless you all—I love you all, even the children.

Mervyn told me later that he had very controversial talks about painting and religion, and other aspects of life (if there are any), with the Prior.

I had a phone call one day, from the Priory, asking if I could fetch him home as he wasn't well and, as I had feared, was disturbing the other people. He couldn't sleep at nights, and was in the habit of pacing his room, and suffered quite obviously from loss of memory.

*   *   *

He came home to Wallington, but at least with *Titus Alone* almost completed. He wrote everything he ever did in long-hand, but on account of the tremors in his hand the writing had become almost incomprehensible. I think I was the only person who could decipher a great deal of what was written, so I decided to type it, with one finger. It's astonishing how quickly one can race along in so handicapped a fashion. I was able to refer to Mervyn when his writing became too difficult to understand.

It went to the publishers and was accepted in principle, although they felt at the time the writing was uneven—which, given the circumstances under which it was written, seemed a reasonable conclusion. It was as though Mervyn was no longer master of his own work. He wished to resist the deletions which were made, and some of which I agreed with, but his brain was no longer able to grope and, sickened as I was at the thought of anyone touching what he had done, it was, or seemed to be, a question of necessity.

Titus Alone was published in 1959, and received on the whole good reviews although it was naturally compared with its two predecessors, not unfavourably, but because it had entered a different world, more questioningly.

*   *   *

In the summer of 1959 a letter came from the B.B.C. Television Studios:

. . . I am wondering if it would perhaps be possible to do something on the programme 'Monitor', in connection with the forthcoming publication of 'Titus Alone'. We find it very difficult to handle novels as a rule, as one is usually discussing something quite unknown to the audience, and impossible to SHOW to them, in the sense that a picture or a piece of music can be shown. However, I remember seeing a few years ago some sketches you had done for 'Titus Groan' of Steerpike, Fuchsia, and I believe Swelter; and I had thought that if you had done, or could do similar sketches of 'Titus Alone' of some of the characters and situations, we might be able to organize a discussion around these. Alternatively, we might be able to expand the situation to take in the other sides of your work, as painter, illustrator, poet, etc.

As you can see, I'm thinking in a bit of a void at present. IF the idea appeals to you at all, I wonder if I could come down to Wallington some time for a couple of hours to discuss possibilities. . . .

I look forward to hearing your reactions.

David Jones.

It was a wonderful stimulus, but I felt almost certain that it would be beyond Mervyn. He had never wished to speak in public: his writing and painting had always spoken for him, but now his speech was beginning to slur and he could not think quickly. If he was asked a direct question about his work his thoughts could not assemble themselves.

A very nice young man came and spent several hours with us in Wallington, discussing the various ways in which the programme could be envisaged. I think he understood that Mervyn himself would be unable to speak, which was the integral part of the idea.

We received a letter a few days later:

. . . I have discussed the idea of filming at your house and studio with Peter Newington who produces 'Monitor'. He likes the idea in principle, but feels we must see how the sound recordings turn out before we make a final decision to go ahead with the story. We've found in the past that the success of a story like this depends entirely on how much you yourself can tell us about your work, and your attitudes to painting, writing etc., by way of commentary. To describe your work at second hand through the words of a narrator immediately lessens the impact and makes the thing less truthful, and where possible we try to avoid this. I'm sure, however, that we should be able to get some good material if I come down with a tape-recorder beforehand, and we really take our time over it. . . .

*   *   *

It would have been an impossible task to make the programme, and this was the case.

How Mervyn continued to be able to teach is a minor miracle. He had the journey to London, and then to the Central School from Victoria Station. I've always been very grateful to Morris Kesselman, who was head of the drawing department, for keeping him on when it seemed that he was no longer able to impart very much knowledge to his students.

We were wanting to leave Wallington for many reasons, not the least being the exhaustion he felt in making the journey to London twice a week. Our house was a Victorian Gothic white elephant, and for it we had been offered £1,000 five years previously. It was now more valuable, with the land, for redevelopment. We were offered a price which to us was unheard of, £8,000. We had never envisaged money in those terms. It meant that we could look for a house in London with real and not pretend money.

We looked at one house in Chelsea which even for us was too dilapidated, and then only at one other, which seemed right in every way. A small garden for cats to bask in with a walnut tree, which in London is rare, and a huge bay tree in the front, big enough to enrich the stews of all our friends for years to come.

★   ★   ★

It was almost like a release from prison to leave Wallington, despite the spaciousness of house and garden. I cannot say that any of our houses have been graciously appointed. They would not pass a good taste test, if only because the furniture has not been renewed, but the books and the paintings which I think of as the only things that I could not bear to be without were ever changing.

Everything seemed to go fairly easily, except that we nearly lost the house on account of neglecting to sign a document, but our neglect did not have too devastating an effect. We were able to make arrangements to move. We left quite an amount of antiquated sofas and chairs in the house, and we were told later that tramps made it their rendezvous until prised out by authority.

We had no regrets, and I know that our sons certainly had none; only my daughter, who had many friends, was apprehensive of London, the unknown.

I was preparing for an exhibition at the Woodstock Gallery, just off Bond Street. The upheaval of a move didn't help one's creative powers, although I had been painting until the time of the move, and I had most of the pictures ready.

We moved with our three cats and two children. The two eldest were no longer children. Sebastian had left home to work his way around Scandinavia, which in itself, from what he has recounted, could make an adventure story. Fabian was

at the Chelsea School of Art. Clare was still at school in
Wallington, and came home for weekends.

The cats went under the bath, and didn't reappear until the
hurly-burly of trudging feet subsided in the evening, and they
emerged to seek food and drink in unfamiliar places.

★   ★   ★

The house assembled itself fairly quickly. The same familiar
objects. It was as though we were for ever talking to ourselves.
The three vertebrae of a whale, which had been washed ashore
twenty or more years ago in Sark, were three of the most
important pieces of furnishing. The whale was dead, and
Mervyn had found it lying, how sadly so, in one of the bays.
He removed three of the vertebrae, and some of the ribs,
which he left in a cave to be cleansed for a year. The ribs were
too awkward to carry to England, but the vertebrae—then
whitened by the sun—were more easily transported. He wrote
a long narrative poem called 'A Reverie of Bone'. Some of the
lines in it were perhaps engendered by this whale, though
changed in form to a steed.

> . . . I ponder
> On sun-lit spires and in my reverie find
> The arc-ribbed courser, and his mount to be
> Whiter than sexless lilies and how slender
>
> The spleenful hands can turn:
>
> O ribs of light! Bright flight, yours are such stairs
> As wail at midnight when the sand meanders
> Through your cold rings that sieve the desert gale.

Never far from poetry, and yet growing away from it. Of
every form of human expression, poetry moved Mervyn

more than any other. He read it so beautifully, too. His voice was gentle, and he often read it aloud. He could quote, before his illness, poems from all periods. Love poems, funny poems, and the hymns of his childhood, as with the poems ancient and modern.

*   *   *

The private view of my exhibition came, and a few pictures were sold. A little time later I was offered a job as 'artist in residence' at a University in Indiana. Even if I had wished to take it, it would have been impossible to leave Mervyn, and I couldn't have done so.

In 1960 he had been commissioned by the Folio Society to illustrate Balzac's *Droll Stories*. We were both apprehensive as to whether he would be able to control his tremors, but he accepted the commission as we needed the money.

It was the first book that he had illustrated where he could not even read the text. He could read, but no longer fully comprehend what he saw on the page. I read all the stories for him, and chose the passages which I felt he would be able to see in his own idiosyncratic way.

It was a kind of nightmare. I was with him each day as he floundered, trying to draw what would have been second nature to him, a gift for his humour and his power of insight into another writer's mind, although illustration has often been belittled, particularly now. If he was at one with the author, it was not only interpretative but creative.

Somehow or other the drawings were achieved, with brush and water colour. Three colours were used, and I think the Folio Society was satisfied with them. At any rate they produced a book of great attraction.

Life had become almost impossible. His tremors precluded most normal activities. His walking was nearly non-existent, although he still dragged himself to the art school, and the nights were such that one could no longer envisage sleeping.

A school friend of mine, whose husband had Parkinson's Disease, told me of an operation that her husband had had, and to whom the benefits were immense.

It was obvious that life could not go on as it was. I wanted a miracle.

I went to see my doctor to ask him if he approved of the operation. In theory he did, but it seemed that there was not enough knowledge of the after-effects. The brain, and this particular brain. An undiscovered world, even in this scientific age.

Mervyn was ill with despair, and a longing for someone to piece him together again. I spoke to him of the operation, and to him it seemed like manna. We do clutch at straws. We went to see the neurological surgeon, who agreed that an operation could be beneficial. That the tremors and the malaise should be eased but, I think, we were given no assurances of complete success. It was left to me to make the decision. I decided that things could not be worse than they were (how little I knew), and arrangements were made for him to go into the hospital as a private patient. National health meant a long delay, and the money from Balzac's *Droll Stories* paid for the fees and the room.

Whilst the operation was in progress his brother was with me, and of all strange things we went to a cinema in Victoria and saw a film called *Pollyanna*, none of which either he or I saw with our eyes. Perhaps a church would have been better, but the darkness in a cinema seemed to calm the fears and the dreadful thoughts which penetrated one's own brains.

I saw Mervyn the next day, and his hand was still, his leg was still. His speech was impaired but this, I was told, was a normal reaction to such a shock.

*   *   *

It was my eldest son's twenty-first birthday within a week of the operation. I felt he must have his day, and so we had a party at home, with close friends and relations. Sebastian was saddened by his father's absence, and at the same time I was hoping that Mervyn would within weeks or months be able to resume a life which had been so rudely interrupted.

He was in the hospital for about two weeks, and on coming home he was noticeably calmer, with his physical disabilities greatly improved, and yet the speech was still slurred and his thoughts still slow and confused. It was a matter of time, we were told again, before his brain would clear, so delicate it is. I always think of the beginning of *Titus Alone* when I think of his brain, unique.

To North, South, East and West it was not long before his landmarks fled him.

It was not to be long before *his* landmarks fled him, but slowly and remorselessly. The signposts were becoming harder to read, the mist was descending, but with the frailty of a gauze curtain between the audience and the player.

*   *   *

He spent his days trying to recapture the felicity of drawing, but finding it more difficult, although his hand was steadier.

Many years ago, in Sark, he had written a long narrative poem called *The Rhyme of the Flying Bomb*, which had been written almost in one burst of writing, day and night.

This poem had been lost for years, but one day, on sorting all the multifarious papers in his cupboards, it appeared almost as suddenly as a ship in a fog.

There seemed to be little need for revision. It was sent out and accepted by Dent, who wished Mervyn to do drawings for it. When I thought of the enormous difficulty of his drawings for Balzac, I must say my heart sank, but the publishers were very anxious that he should produce not just a poem but drawings to complement the text.

It was unbelievable. The ease with which he had worked in the past, ideas growing upon ideas, cartoons for drawings being made, for all the books he had illustrated, not with ease, but with fluency and amplitude. And now, the brain could not grasp ideas long enough to hold them and turn them into visual life. Once again, I tried to work out where the illustrations (if that is what they were) should go, and I sat with him, until we were both exhausted, trying to make the salient picture. Seeing them in the book, I doubt if anyone could know the pain with which those drawings were imbued.

The book was published in 1962. There were very few reviews, and after a certain interval it took its place with the several other books which had been remaindered.

Two years later a radio programme made from it was broadcast on the Third Programme, with most evocative music by Tristram Carey, and touching performances by Marius Goring as the sailor, and Marjorie Westbury as the baby. This, strangely enough, had wonderful notices.

*   *   *

That was the last book, although I have tragic notes for the beginning of a fourth *Titus*—the gropings of a man, wishing to write something to surpass anything he had already done; a huge vision, and nothing to allow it to manifest itself.

There was an exhibition of his drawings in the Portobello Road, to which he went, and was still able to talk moderately coherently, but there were less and less times when he could meet people. If we went out, it was usually thought that he was drunk or drugged, and offence was often taken. I longed to shelter him, and I bear resentment of the intelligent ones who turned their backs on him, thinking he was insulting them. There is pain in seeing so gentle a man cold-shouldered.

Nothing was right or could be so ever again. And yet does one ever give up hoping? We went to yet another specialist, who diagnosed encephalitis, which often occurs with Parkinson's Disease. Too late, his opinion was that there should have been no operation, but how can anyone know? The implications were told to me, and we went home where the television was full-steam. The tears which were flooding my eyelids had to be stemmed until my daughter was in bed.

★   ★   ★

I do not wish to write further of an illness that left a man bereft in mind, but I wished to write this book for a man, unique and alone.

> Rather than a little pain, I would be thief
> To the organ-chords of grief
> That toll through me
> With a burial glory.
>
> Wherefore my searching dust
> If not to breathe the Gust
> Of every quarter
> Before I scatter,
>
> And to divine
> The lit or hooded Ghost, and take for mine
> The double pulse; so come
> Forth from your midnight tomb.
>
> Cold grief
> I would be thief
> Of you,
> Until my bones breed hemlock through and through.

'Hallo . . . Hallo . . . Are you there? Oh, are you there? Darling, are you there?'

The line was there . . . The possibilities of communication were there, but he was not there.

'Hallo . . . Hallo, I MUST go on saying it. I want to see you. I want to speak to you. I want you to answer me . . . I want life to be as it used to be. Darling, I'm wilting from the need of you.'

The silence remained, but the line which had been connected for thirty years was frail, and only a few unintelligible sounds could be heard. Despair gave way to the hope which always lay in my mind.

'Darling . . . I haven't seen you for twelve years. . . . Nearly a third of our life-time together. Answer me. . . . Say something, tell me.'

The silence remained. A crackling of sound. . . . Noises which were incomprehensible. Silence alone is better than incomprehension.

'Where are you? Where have you gone? I can see you, and I can touch you, but YOU have gone. I am coming to see you. Each time before I see you, I flower . . . Each time I have seen you, I die.'

Silence . . . Always the silence of a foreign language. Unbelievable that what had been rich, funny, vibrant, had become vacant.

'I am coming to see you. I long to. I have forgotten all now, but the past. The intense joy of it. The madness and the love. I will be with you today.'

There was no sound, but a series of sounds that I have heard but do not understand. Sounds from a world so far away. Is it an empty world . . . As desolate as I think it is, or is it peopled with visions? A world exclusive to you? Somewhere, may I share a little of that world?

The silence was now so white, . . . so untrammelled that speaking could do nothing but violate it.

There was a journey. There was fear that hope was unfounded. There were people. There was no silence. There was nothing, and there was hope clinging like a wet garment, so close to me.

The red buses . . . Strings of them . . . Not silent . . . Took me. There is the waiting and there is never silence. There are the black conductors, and the Cockney conductors, and the Irish conductors. Laughs sometimes, the lusty wit of the office cleaners. The pushing in the North End Road, the burdens of string bags full of cut-price detergents, vegetables, and sometimes even flowers, and I am making my way to you. . . . Full of hope, with sweets for you. I see you, my dark man, and my lover, full of aspiration. . . . Full of hope. I've forgotten about God. Once he was part of our universe, but he has gone, and the thin line has gone, and there is nothing left but what I know of you. Dark man . . . Funny man . . . Gentle man. Man that made life something new each day. Where are you? Please tell me where you have gone.

You said, 'Each day we live is a glass room.' It is, and it is so easily shattered. Every time when I see you, the glass is in one piece. Each time I leave you it is shattered.

Quickly, I want to see you. Slowly the door is unlocked. The niceties of life are fulfilled. 'Good morning,' to the white-coated man. 'How cold it is. What a lovely day. The crocuses are coming up.' The squirrels are darting jerkily across the drive. 'Good morning,' again. Pleasant people who do not know who they have in their possession, so lost and so alone are you.

I go down the cold stairs, and sometimes you have heard my voice, from above, as I say my platitudes. There is a

shuffling. I am afraid you are going to fall. I'm always afraid
for you. Sometimes there is no sound, and I open your door,
to your room, but no longer to you.

Quiet empty room. Quiet empty man. Your eyes look, and
do not see. Your ears hear, and do not hear. Your mouth
opens and closes and says nothing. Your hands hold a pencil,
and let it fall. Your feet move, but do not walk.

Then suddenly the eyes focus, and they smile. Your voice
speaks, and I understand, then it is all gone again. You try to
lift a chocolate from the table, and it falls.

I show you your books—that you have written, and which
are you, but you don't see them. I read to you the wise words
of the men who judge them, but those words fall upon stony
ground. You have gone away, and I can't find the way with
you.

I want the vision of you, as you were. Are you *you*? or have
you gone?

We sit silently, and then you are restless. You want to move
and cannot. You want to speak and cannot, and the silence no
longer has peace in it. The beautiful silence.

I give you a pencil, and I prop a sketch-book on your knee.
The pencil falls, and the book drops off your knee.

Sometimes, I make a feeble joke, which used to make our
children laugh when they were very small. You do and can
still laugh. 'Mary Rose sat on a pin. Mary Rose.'

A squirrel comes nervously in sharp little movements to
stand with its hands crossed outside your window. I throw
crumbs to it, and quick as a pickpocket they have disappeared,
before the pigeons or the sea-gulls or the sparrows have a
chance to battle for them.

Such small happenings now. So little to divert you. Now it
is time to go. When I leave you, I say 'Goodbye', but goodbye
was said many years ago, before we knew we were saying it.

And now you sit amongst others, who sit because they are

old. With their pasts known to themselves alone. Is it patience or tiredness which makes them so still? Are they empty of everything? Their eyes seem to be. Are their hearts too?

You look almost like them, and I want to say that you are not. But in the presence of such silent silence, I cannot think of you as any different from the other tired people.

You have gone. I long to see you again.

MERVYN PEAKE

A bibliography of his principal works

Captain Slaughterboard drops Anchor, London, Country Life, 1939

Ride a Cock-Horse and Other Nursery Rhymes, London, Chatto and Windus, 1940

Shapes and Sounds, London, Chatto and Windus, 1941

Rhymes without Reason, London, Eyre and Spottiswoode, 1944

Titus Groan, London, Eyre and Spottiswoode, 1946

Craft of the Lead Pencil, London, Wingate, 1946

Letters from a Lost Uncle from Polar Regions, London, Eyre and Spottiswoode, 1948

Drawings of Mervyn Peake, London, Grey Walls Press, 1949

The Glassblowers, London, Eyre and Spottiswoode, 1950

Gormenghast, London, Eyre and Spottiswoode, 1950

Mr Pye, London, Heinemann, 1953

Figures of Speech, London, Gollancz, 1954

Titus Alone, London, Eyre and Spottiswoode, 1959

The Rhyme of the Flying Bomb, London, Dent, 1962

Poems and Drawings, London, Keepsake Press, 1965

A Reverie of Bone, London, Rota, 1967

Other books illustrated by him

Carroll (L.): *Hunting of the Snark*, London, Chatto and Windus, 1941

Joad (C. E. M.): *Adventures of the Young Soldier*, London, Faber and Faber, 1943

Crisp (Q.): *All This and Bevin Too*, London, Nicholson and Watson, 1943

Coleridge (S. T.): *The Rime of the Ancient Mariner*, London, Chatto and Windus, 1943

Laing (A. M.): *Prayers and Graces*, London, Gollancz, 1944

Hole (C.): *Witchcraft in England*, London, Batsford, 1945

Grimm (J.) and (W. C.): *Household Tales*, London, Eyre and Spottiswoode, 1946

Collis (M. S.): *Quest for Sita*, London, Faber and Faber, 1946

Carroll (L.): *Alice's Adventures in Wonderland, etc.*, Stockholm, Zephyr, 1946

Stevenson (R. L.): *Dr Jekyll and Mr Hyde*, London, Folio Society, 1948

Stevenson (R. L.): *Treasure Island*, London, Eyre and Spottiswoode, 1949

Haynes (D. K.): *Thou Shalt Not Suffer a Witch*, London, Methuen, 1949

Wyss (J. D.): *The Swiss Family Robinson*, London, Heirloom Library, 1950

Drake (H. B.): *The Book of Lyonne*, London, Falcon, 1952

Palmer (E. C.): *The Young Blackbird*, London, Wingate, 1953

Austin (P. B.): *The Wonderful Life . . . of Tom Thumb* (2 vols.), Stockholm, Radio Sweden, 1954/55

Sander (A.): *Men: a Dialogue between Women*, London, Cresset, 1955

Drake (H. B.): *Oxford English Course for Secondary Schools, Book 1*, London, Oxford University Press, 1957

Laing (A. M.): *More Prayers and Graces*, London, Gollancz, 1957

Judah (A.): *The Pot of Gold and two other tales*, London, Faber and Faber, 1959

Balzac (H. de): *Droll Stories*, London, Folio Society, 1961

His Principal Exhibitions

Exhibited for first and last time at R.A.	April 1931
	(aged 20)
Soho Group, Regal Restaurant—Soho	1931
The Twenties Group, Werthern Gallery	1932 and 1933
Sark Group at newly opened modern art gallery in Sark	1933
Sark Group, Cooling Galleries (London)	1934
R.B.A.	1935
Leger Galleries	1936
Calmann Gallery	1938
Leicester Galleries	1939
Satirical Drawings of our Time, Delius Giese Gallery	1939
Drawings sent to America during the war for exhibition	1942
Paintings of 'Glassblowers' exhibited at National Gallery during the war (now in Birmingham Art Gallery)	1943
Adams Gallery	1946
Arcade Gallery	1946
Waddington Galleries	approx. 1956
Collectors Gallery, Portobello Road	approx. 1957
Collectors Gallery, Portobello Road	approx. 1958
Upper Grosvenor Galleries	approx. 1967

Drawing from *The Hunting of the Snark* presented to the Queen for Prince Charles

Drawings in Private Collections in England, Ireland, Scotland and U.S.A.

Drawings in Victoria and Albert Museum

Painting in Imperial War Museum (of R.A.F. officers, commissioned by War Office)

Sets and costumes designed for *The Insect Play* by the Brothers
   Capek for the Little Theatre, 1936

Exhibition of diaries and manuscripts, Westminster City
   Public Library, 1968

Posthumous exhibition at his school, Eltham College, of
   diaries, paintings, manuscripts, etc., 1969

Exhibition at Swansea University, 1970

Sebastian Peake

A CHILD OF BLISS

Growing Up With Mervyn Peake

For most of my life, I have had the omni-present influence of Mervyn Peake as poet, playwright, illustrator and writer all about me, physically and metaphysically. In writing A CHILD OF BLISS, I have tried to give tangible examples of my father as a man, not just as I have always held him to be, superman.

Work freely and madly and you will make progress
– Paul Gauguin

The aims of life are the best defence against death
– Primo Levi

PHOTOGRAPHS

PROLOGUE

The intense love that I have had for my parents, with its resultant anguish and emotional ramifications, lives on for me. Although my father died in 1968 and my mother in 1983, the all-pervading atmosphere of their influence still envelops me, like a wonderful but harmless leprosy. I wish they would go away sometimes and leave me alone. Their own glamorous early life together, like a dream idyll, was something from which I felt totally excluded, and the frequent violent attacks I made on my father as a child and as a youth, swinging my fists and grappling him to the floor, were just the physical manifestations of my profound jealousy.

Throughout my life, my parents have had the greatest effect upon me. Wherever I was, I would write to them, whether as a child at school (as this book will show) or later, as an adult. My letters and cards were a varied lot, but I later discovered that they had been kept, a discovery that meant much to me. Their letters to me I kept, too.

My mother's collection of my correspondence included postcards and letters, notes from all over Europe, written as a young adult during the four years I lived and worked there, and during my trips to Africa and America, the Middle East and every part of the British Isles. My father wrote very infrequently. One of his rare letter shows his parental concern. After the disaster of my 'formal education', after failing all my GCE exams at the third attempt, he wrote a letter to me, just before I left the tutorial establishment in St Marychurch, near Torquay, where I was studying in 1957.

He begins with an experience that I had told him

about, when I had gone to see a great friend of mine in Jersey during the previous holiday, and had had the door shut in my face by the friend's mother. Oliver's father was at the time a minister in the French Government and was very unhappy about his son's academic progress. He and I shared the same tutors and they felt my influence to blame for the state of affairs, hence the mother's reaction. Though this was not an easy letter for me, my father went on to write to me as an equal, as one would to someone of the same age, using expressions like 'one can feel rather a "nut" if one is shut out'.

He continued:

>...*When you get home I am anxious that no time is wasted in regard to your work. We may not have your English results but in the meanwhile, while waiting for them, we must work out the best kind of plan for your future. You have so much to catch up on. The Allan experiment [Torquay tutors] was a ghastly and expensive failure. I can feel in your letter through what you say and how you say it, that you are reaching a stage that is more adult and interesting. Conquer your temper and you can become a most interesting and attractive chap. Make up your mind that you are a real student of life -*
>
> *You have some fine qualities and I am often most happy about you. But then there are other times when you give way to another kind of mood. Also you have been really bad over such things as "forgetting" your Geography exam. That was a blow.*

He went on to write that my mother had had a bad attack of laryngitis, and asked me to say when I'd be returning home.

He concluded:

We all send our love and hope you are happy. This letter
is not supposed to be a lecture, but I think it best to say
what is on my mind. Love

from Dad

That letter may not convey much of Mervyn
Peake the artist, but Mervyn Peake the father is there. The father of a
son whose life must have perplexed, worried and occasionally hurt the
father. My memories of growing up as his son will show, I believe, that
he had cause for concern, and at the same time, how much he mattered
to me.

Another letter that it is fitting to quote now arose
from a very different and terrible set of circumstances. After the onset
of the awful diseases from which he suffered and subsequently died,
he was sent for electrical shock treatment to an institution in Virginia
Water, and in many heart-rending letters to my mother, pleaded for
these experiences to stop. Not only in physical, but terrible mental
pain, he cried out in these letters for the horror of Parkinson's Disease
and encephalitis to be cured. Yet in 1963 he found time to write to me,
and said in the note:

SEB

Dear Sebby: Just a note to thank you for your letter &
your news. I miss you also - old chap, and long to see you all
again. My longing is to sit in our sitting room, or in the
garden - the 5 of us all together.

I am most interested about the (Van 1940) and how you drove it from Wimbledon.

How is your drawing. <u>That,</u> I look forward to - too.

I miss my father greatly, for he was an artist with unparalleled talents in many fields of the arts, and not only that, for he was also a man with a fine sense of humour who loved practical jokes; he played the mandolin and recorder well; he was an athlete - his high jump record at his public school remained unbroken for 25 years; he could belch from A to Z in one breath; speak Chinese; ride across La Coupee in Sark on his bike before the Germans built the concrete and railing bridge, with one foot on the saddle and one on the handlebars; he could paint, draw, and illustrate. And he could write, philosophically and with understated ease of the conflict between nature and man, these words:

> To live at all is miracle enough
> the doom of nations is another thing
> Here in my hammering blood pulse is my proof
> Let every painter and poet sing
> And all the sons of music ply their trade
> Machines are weaker than a beetle's wing
>
> Flung out of sunlight into Cosmic shade
> Come what come may the imagination's heart
> is constellation high and can't be weighed
>
> Nor greed nor fear can tear our faith apart
> When every heart-beat hammers over the proof
> That life itself is miracle enough.

I will begin my story overleaf. The illustration of despair that it sometimes provides was based on my craving for moments of familial happiness to continue unaltered, with me secure within the family. I always had with me, however far from my family, the memory of my mother's breast, of my father's stories, and the <u>feel</u> of home, which gave me an inimitable, poignant, indefinable sense of one's own private corner of love, kept alone for oneself, that secret thing.

CHAPTER 1

HAMLETS AND VILLAGES
IN SUSSEX-BY-THE-SEA

– Arundel Castle and the languid Arun

My life began in Littlehampton in Sussex, on the seventh of January, 1940 at three fifty in the morning, in the company of my paternal grandfather, who was a doctor, and a nurse. "It's a boy, Maeve", is the first recorded remark made about me, made by my grandfather who delivered me. Later, he planted a tree in his garden to commemorate my birth. Apparently I was a healthy boy with no birth marks. I cried a lot. I was in the nursing home for three days and my father, Mervyn Peake, brought me home. He had been told to stay away from the birth itself, because of his habit of fainting when confronted with anything slightly medical.

This first house which I lived in for some six months, was in a hamlet called Lower Warningcamp, near Arundel in Sussex, so-called because the Romans built lookout towers and encampments there. My parents had moved from Maida Vale from a fear of air-raids several months before I was born. Of this period, I remember nothing except those flashing, dream-like sequences when you think you remember things, but which are only the retrospective memories of hindsight, deceptions created by current reassessments of what you **feel** your earliest life was like. During the first few months of my life, my father worked on *Titus Groan*, but of course I knew nothing about it.

If I am aware of anything in the first year or so, it is the beautiful woman who looked down at me when I was being fed. Breast-fed by my mother, I was put to bed in a small bedroom but always slept badly. My father was so often away in the army, and it saddened my mother that my first tooth, and so on, were experiences shared only by post. Soon after we moved again, one of the many uprootings that punctuated my childhood. This move was to nearby Burpham where my grandfather lived. My parents took a flint cottage adjacent to his, a fourteenth-century group of tiny buildings later converted into one dwelling. Even then the place was still quite small, but since for some while only my mother and I lived there, there was enough room for us, though as a painter and sculptress my mother had her works all around the house, together with my father's paintings. It was a house with art stored in every room.

Whilst my father was away in the army, my mother would take me to Arundel once a week, on the back of her bicycle, and I travelled in a small metal seat just under the saddle. The three miles from the cottage were flat except for one or two small hills, but with the shopping done, the return journey was more difficult. I was left in the small seat all the time, and if I try hard, I can feel the wobbling of the frame of the bike as the shopping at one end in a basket and me at the other made the going quite hard for her.

It was at the age of two that I was no longer alone: my brother Fabian was born. In the summer of 1942 the sun shone in that way that people always seem to remember of their own youth and childhood, and from those summer mornings I can still hear the chirruping of the birds just outside my window. Rays of sunlight warmed up the bedroom and lit up my toys in the early mornings. These were my intimate toys, which then seemed so peculiarly one's own, but are often so ordinary and unoriginal when seen in later life.

My first memories of my father date from this time. He was still in the army and working on illustrated books - *The Rime of the Ancient Mariner* was one. I can see him now, as he takes off his army cap and puts his arms around my mother's waist. Then he would put his cap on my head. Except for the promotion to Captain made in order to facilitate his freedom of movement in Germany in the weeks

Baby, 1940

just after the War, my father was a sapper throughout his years in the army. As I grew up, with an awareness of the absence of my father around me, he was working, on rare moments of leave, on *Titus Groan*. When he came home to Burpham I was about three and a half, and as he came into sight just over the brow of the chalk sided road and down the few hundred yards leading to our cottage, his cap was my target. Somehow, although the whole man was my father, it was his cap that made me like him. I am sure he could easily have taken it off earlier, rules notwithstanding, but I must have shown such visible happiness the first time he placed it on my head, tipping it back so it almost drowned my skull, that on every subsequent and appropriately expectant moment he did the same. It could not have been a more ordinary thing, but he seemed a general, this private. He had made me a marvellous car, for even from the earliest age cars were a delight for me, a fact he rapidly realised. I would zoom down the garden path with his cap on my head in my grey bullet car and encircle my parents.

From this earliest point in my memory of my father, when the prisms of talented light, talented shade, and talented dark that coloured his life worked their magic into my consciousness, beaches, in their emptiness the opposite of the complicated artistic horizons that were his, played the fullest of parts. From Burpham the windy road to Littlehampton would be about five miles. When he came on leave, my parents and I would ride to the coast, me sitting in a basket over the front wheel of his bike or behind the saddle of hers, and I would sense the wobbling of the frame with wonder. My mother's bike had been bought by my father as a surprise when he had left her at the end of a leave. She loved it. En route to the beach, powered it seemed by the force of love and dependence, the bicycles would at first sail down the initial little hill, over which I had earlier seen the cap approaching, and I would hear the woosh of air in my mother's golden hair, stretched out in the wind and following two feet behind her head. There were smells of cows, smells of fields, the murky, dank smell of the River Arun and its adjacent meadows, reeds and grass. We sailed by towards the harder bit of the journey, the main south coast road. We only had to travel the very short distance between the evocative Arundel Station, with its awful, poignant partings and blissful arrivals, and the Littlehampton turn, opposite a convent. From the main road the road was fairly flat and sometimes my parents would have a race. There were only very occasionally vehicles of any kind; a slow, horse pulled hay cart in summer, or an old tractor whose driver would greet the passing cyclists and their little passenger, with the open, uncluttered greeting of an earlier way of life.

Now we came to a cluster of houses. This hamlet, Lyminster, was soon past, then over the level crossing and a half mile or so later, there was the seaside town of Littlehampton. If they had ridden enough and my little legs, folded up for the last four or five miles, had long since gone to sleep, they would drive straight to the beach, another half mile or so. If both parties, pushers and charge, could face it, they would turn right at the shops, past the railway station, over the bridge across the mouth of the Arun, and ride along the banks of the river to where it joined the sea. There were rolling dunes which stretched as far as the eye could see on the shore side and merged into the horizon beyond Climping. Out of my wickerwork cage, with its soporific effect on my legs and knees, I would hobble like a new-born fawn and gradually increase my strength before wildly tearing off along this long, open nothingness of golden sand which seemed limitless to me. I used to like pretending I was lost or abandoned, forgotten. Off I'd fly, my legs weaving out, with the beat of the heart, and the knowledge of my parents' **thereness**, away to a further point of the beach by the river. I knew that they would always wait for me, and that I would always come back.

This was where I learnt 'skimmy', at which my father was very adept. On still days he would pick up stones, for at

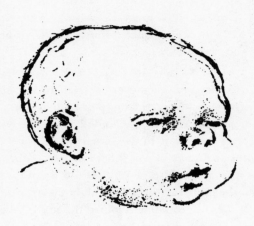

Baby, 1940

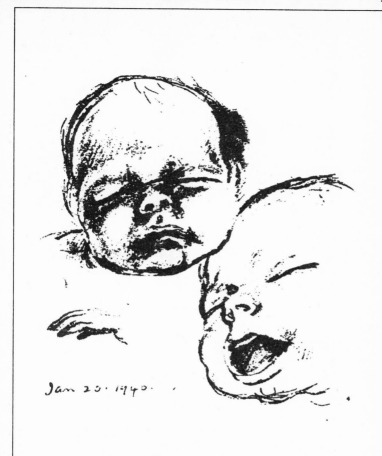

Jan 25. 1940.

Artist's son, 1940

high tide the beach is stony, and selecting them meticulously, would let the stones skim the surface of the water. He taught me the selecting of the best stones, not too heavy or light, flat like a doubloon. He could sometimes count up to twenty five times as they rose slightly and landed again on the surface of the water. At first I could only manage a plonk or two, my arm inadequate for the bent aim and the powerful throw needed. Little by little as I grew up I found I could skim as well as he could, but my record still lags behind his. Sometimes we would all go right down to the sea, a long way from the bicycles and clothes and we would sit in the pools and make great scarves of seaweed, dark brown and damp, like massive flat tongues with odd holes in them. My parents would drape each other in these strange wet shapes and cover me up like a tiny Robinson Crusoe, imprisoned with weed on my head, around my shoulders, across my arms and legs. Here my father, who had made a collection of stones on the way down to the sea, would build a tower of stones for me to aim at with others that were to hand. When I had knocked them over, one of us would rebuild the tower and the next one aim and so on. We would sometimes stay on the beach the whole afternoon until the sea would advance towards us, the tide having turned. Then, slowly, we would shuffle backwards on our bottoms, trying to be more successful than Canute.

At the end of the day, we would bicycle home along the river beside the golf course, through the town, past the railway crossing, and how I longed for the express to pass, but it never did. We returned down the hill, at the top of which the great fairy tale castle loomed above Arundel, and home to Burpham.

The beautiful flint walls of Sussex, especially the one surrounding our cottage in Burpham, or the one round my grandfather's house in the same village, played a part in our lives, as they were   solid things, strangely shaped silver grey stone erections meant to last. I sat on them daily and never slipped, because of the gritty concrete top, rounded and secure, and I would dangle my legs over the edge, being careful not to cut my bare legs on the jagged flints which jutted out from the wall proper.

There must have been awful farewells at the gate or the local station when my father went off again after just a few days. Bedtime was marvellous when my father was home because it meant his reading stories to me, my father who had one of the greatest imaginations possible. Of course, like many children at the time, I heard the Beatrix Potter evergreens read to me; but it was the classics that came alive through my father. My father loved *Treasure Island* especially, and as he could quote passages by heart, later, when I could read, I would test him. I would read the first word or two, 'Squire Trelawney, Dr. Livesey and the rest of these gentlemen...' and he would then go on and on, faultlessly, with the story for pages if I had wanted. My mother would stick to the text much more than my father. Sometimes, whatever he was reading, he would go off on flights of his imagination, unable to stop himself. So Peter Rabbit might start off in Mr. McGregor's garden, and would end up on the beach with lots of local Sark or Kent or Chelsea friends, frying sausages over a roaring fire; or he would set out on all kinds of marvellous wanderings that would be quite at a tangent to his usual life. My father would make me a sort of tent out of the sheets and blankets and I would be snuggled up in it listening to strange stories of exotically named pirates of the Spanish Main or the South Seas or Jamaica, and shiver with fright. These great wild men, scabbards dangling to the ground, trailing sabres of blood-curdling sharpness, knives and blunderbusses, pistols and arms of all sorts, stalked my bedroom long after he'd said goodnight. With the wind sometimes outside howling, I imagined the voices of Blind Pew or his own Captain Slaughterboard, about whom C.S. Lewis wrote, in a letter to my father: 'How many parents have received doctors' bills for these children's disturbance I will never know, but other children's books pale into insignificance compared with yours.' I grew up knowing traditional bedtime stories very well, but interwoven with unique, strange and sometimes mad episodes: always exciting, always original.

The earliest sounds in life that one remembers are contained in a shroud of mist from which only slowly does the prosaic meaning emerge. An early dawn sound was the clink of the milk bottles arriving at the front doorstep, then mumbling in the next room, muffled sounds, unclear. In Burpham when my father was away in the army and before my brother was born, and even until he was a year or two old, I would open my eyes slowly on sunny days as the light advanced and hear the bird outside. Now that sound remains in my mind, the bird on a particular branch. From its perch, and of course there must have been many of them, it directed me by its call to the day coming. My reveille. Then about 7.30 a.m. or a little later, my mother would creep in and ask if I would like to 'climb in' with her. When my father was on leave, I would join them both and cuddle up in the middle and be in the deepest sea of contentment imaginable. I would mention my bird and we would listen for it. It would sing and when I was old enough, I would say that it was my 'early friend' and, like my Dinky toy cars, lined up so I could see them on waking along the window ledge, its sound has lasted my lifetime.

My father loved practical jokes. Later in the war, we lived for a short while in a billet in Blackpool. One morning my parents, together for the weekend as he was stationed nearby, awoke to find a huge wardrobe falling towards them and were unable to prevent its crashing down onto the floor. On lifting it up again, they watched as I calmly stepped out through the open door: I'd gone in unawares and not being able to get out, I pushed forwards against the door, causing it to fall. During this very weekend after I was asleep, they were to entertain a friend in the dining room. They were to meet downstairs and my mother, who was to follow my father downstairs after getting me to sleep - there were no cots and so I was put in the bottom drawer of the chest of drawers with a sheet and blankets covering me - was to come down a few minutes later. Meanwhile my father, wanting to play a trick on the other two, and remembering my activities, got into a large linen cupboard in the dining room while no-one else was there, and awaited their arrival. At last he heard sounds of chairs being pulled back and people sitting down, at which he sprang out making wild, monkey-like sounds, all the while sticking out his tongue. It was, however, two very shocked old ladies who saw this mad apparition leaping from the sideboard, and after they had somewhat composed themselves, he apologized by saying that he thought that they had been his wife and his best friend. As there was no-one else in the dining room, he only added to his apparent madness.

In the main, my early years were spent in Sussex. With the real possibility of a German invasion, the famous pitchfork and sickle brigades of the Home Guard proliferated, but it was the coming of the American Army down to the Sussex coast that gave us a greater sense of security than the old boys could, however noble their spirit. On most days, platoons would march past and often I would be sitting on the flint wall watching them, held by my mother. She was not only very attractive but always dressed with an idiosyncratic taste that caused her to be noticed, especially by homesick soldiers. One day an American soldier broke ranks and from behind his back gave my mother two pairs of black silk stockings, and gave me one of the most memorable gifts of my life. This was a khaki coloured Scout car, with moving gun turrets and lovely fat, round rubber sand tyres. This present, which I played with all the time, racing it up and along, over and under everything that had a surface, was my pride and joy and its loss in a move caused me real and unmitigated anguish which lasted for years.

Sadly, we never saw that soldier again for soon after we left the area, evacuated from danger. In those summer days before evacuation, the village hummed with sounds of agelessness, the church bell, the birds swooping and singing, the cattle on the surrounding hills, all the peace and tranquility of English village life. My brother and I had our evening bath outside in the long zinc tub. We had no inside bathroom or electricity: just a cold water tap. The bath would be filled and refilled and we'd splash naked in and out on the grass. I'd zoom my scout car around the edge of the bath and my little brother of one would gurgle, splash and shriek. My grandfather's house, just adjacent, built in the 1920's, had a sweeping drive to the front door through a little avenue of lilac and lavender bushes, the smell of which lingers in my memory. Some time after he retired (from the medical missionary service to different foreign missions and compounds in Tien'tsin, Peking, Kuling and Hangchow and different parts of China), a fire damaged the house: the roof was burnt and much of the house as well, since the roof was made of Reed Thatch. The red tiled roof that replaced it was an attractive enough substitute, but it was not the roof but the doctor's surgery that was most fascinating to me. In the hospital that he had built in Tien'tsin for cataract patients, he had kept photographs of all the awful afflictions that his patients suffered. These he kept still, and some were quite horrific. It took a strong stomach to see these medical records. He also had a five pound gallstone that he had removed from a dying Chinese patient, which is still used as a paperweight somewhere in the family. I wonder how these must have affected my father and his growing imagination.

The beauty of the shapes in chalk on the Downs, the myriad different forms in the flint rock, constitute much of this earliest part of my consciousness, as well as the Arun river, which was nearly the cause of my end before I'd quite begun. One day, my parents had hired a rowing boat and had set off, with Fabian and me, on a gloriously sunny afternoon during a weekend's leave. After rowing for half an hour or so upstream, my father decided that he wanted to take a photograph of his sons. He asked me to step onto the boat's rear seat, which I did, and as he left his seat to get a better angle from which to take the photo, I fell into the river. The Arun is particularly fast running, and although my father dived straight in after me, being fully clothed he could not really swim, but could only flail and wallow hopelessly. I can still hear the gurgling of the water as it swept me away and as I started to lose consciousness. Tragedy beckoned: during the whole afternoon when they had in turn floated and oared their way along the river, they had neither met nor seen anyone else. Then, as their panic reached its height, for I was presumed lost, two professional scullers came swiftly round the bend in the river and seeing the confusion, dived in and I was saved. I had to be given respiratory attention to regain consciousness, but I survived because of those masters of timing.

Sometimes my parents would go for walks together. When they did, and I accompanied them, pushed as a small child, later holding hands and running and skipping beside them, there was always fun with stones or twigs, branches or boughs. Using a stick as a kind of golf club my father would make small, round, stones scurry off along the lane for me to chase after and retrieve. He would bend twigs supply into strange shapes or choosing fallen branches in autumn, after storms or high winds, would put the V of the branch up above his forehead and say that he was a stag - a wild one, and would come after me or my mother, baying and whinneying. He told me a story once on one of these walks, when I was perhaps seven or eight, about the appalling end that befell enemies of certain North American Indian tribes, whereby the outstretched legs of the victim were strapped to either branch of a taut, forked bough. The rope holding back their captive was cut, the branches would fly apart, and the victim would then be ripped in half. When walking along cliffs, my father would sometimes pretend to slip at the very edge of a precipice and scare my mother senseless, then spring back on to the path unharmed.

When we lived in Sussex, one of their favourites was The Lepers' Path. They would often keep to the route taken by my grandfather who had shown them it originally. It snaked along the lee of the South Downs and from afar looked like a white knife wound which had gouged out a path from the grass that covered the chalk. They would talk of his work, his book, paintings, drawings, his poems, his plays, and invent wonderful names together that would be added to the short lists they regularly made, of candidates for inclusion in his works. On these walks Flay, Swelter, Prunesquallor, and other exotic, idiosyncratic onomatopoeic names were invented for my father's characters. They would try out sounds to see if they suited the characters' nature, and jettison hundreds in the process. They would arrive back at the Burpham cottage exhausted from imaginings, but with a dossier of new ideas for my father to work on.

When my brother and I would go off to the beaches on summer days, we would run ahead of our parents, whom we would ask to follow on, five minutes later. On Sark, there were no motorized vehicles except the rare tractor. We could tear down the middle of any of the roads and not worry about anything. Usually we would race as fast as possible up to the windmill and hide inside. They would then either walk past or ride past, and by the slight raising of their voices in feigned pretence that they didn't know where we were, we would jump out shrieking, "Here we are, you didn't know we were here, did you?!"

On his way back overland from China when he was eleven years old, my father had got off the Trans Siberian Express at Omsk, where the station was some way outside the town. It was midwinter and the landscape was pure white. Snow covered everything, even the line, before the snow plough attached to the front of the two engines had cleared a path. He had been expressly asked by his parents not to leave the train, but had climbed down from the carriage because he wanted to feel the snow. As he was only a small boy and the carriage being very far above the ground, there was a big jump from the lowest stepping board onto the snow below. Not only was this deep, but the temperature very much below zero, and the approaching darkness of late afternoon all made this exploit very dangerous. All he wanted to do was to play in the snow, unaware that the train was taking on water from the tower which was situated some way from the station proper. The train having filled up with the required amount of water, a great hissing and opening up of the boilers took place, and the great long express from Vladivostok to Paris started very slowly to move forward. My grandparents had by now noticed my father's disappearance from their compartment and had sent for the guard to help them find him. Although the train had begun to move and my father was still several feet below the still open carriage door, Dr. Peake could, by holding onto one of the handles at the side of the door, ease his free hand down far enough to grab his son. By now my father was running alongside the train in the snow, but was pulled to safety and back into the train. This story of his getting off the train in Siberian mid-winter was always used, by my parents, as the tale *par excellence* of what would have happened, **if**...?

Several years later when we lived at Smarden in Kent, my father, brother and I would go sometimes to the level crossing in Headcorn, a town nearby, and would watch the expresses rush by, with their steam whistles and pure grace as they thundered past, making the earth tremble and vibrate with their power and speed. This reminds me of *Gormenghast*, though the 'Thing' that features throughout the book is not necessarily anything mechanical; it could be fleeting love or an eagle, a rocket or that beautiful moment in life when for a tiny space of time one fools oneself into believing that transsubstantiation is understandable. The Mallard engine was like that, as it flew past at 100 m.p.h.; beautiful and shaped like the most perfect of bullets that could shoot dead straight into eternity. This exotic and powerful engine, pulling prosaic-looking carriages behind it, was only seen once at our level crossing vantage point, but it left a mark in all our imaginations that lasted long, long after its last tiny carriage had disappeared into the distance of mid-Kent.

Travelling on trains with me involved my parents with a child that seemed permanently to be screaming. Once, during a journey which lasted 17 hours, I allegedly screamed from when the train set off from Arundel Station all the way to Blackpool. This journey involved several changes and during the last long, slow part I was comforted by a soldier who could see the weariness in my mother, and putting me on his knee sang songs for hours while the blacked-out train ambled at snail's pace towards Lancashire. When my parents were first engaged and wanting privacy, my father would do a drawing of a totally authentic looking madman sticking his tongue out and making a wild face. If anyone looked as though they wanted to join them in the compartment he would place this drawing against the window. Apparently it always worked, for even if the drawing didn't do the trick, the fact that the person holding it to the window had gone to such lengths to keep others at bay was taken to imply the same state of mind as the figure depicted.

Before I was born, my father travelled for more than a year up and down daily between Wallington and Victoria after he'd got a job teaching at the Royal Academy School, and would practice his craft of drawing on the crowded trains. At that time, the early 1930's, most businessmen still wore the bowler hat and striped dark suit, and Wallington was the very essence of *petit bourgeois* sobriety. But people didn't mind being drawn, and would often ask him if they could keep the results. In this way, many hundreds of his studies of people 'caught', as my mother noted in her book, in the act of living, were given away. These drawings, now sometimes fetching thousands of pounds each, are a regular feature of fine art sales, and in several instances form little collections – hoarded and put up for sale decades later.

Only occasionally did I express myself through the art chosen by my parents. When I was fifteen I gave my mother a pen and ink drawing of myself that she kept in the hall with the other paintings and drawings. This drawing captured, I'm told, the downward angle of my face and the sense of loneliness that seemed to emanate from me, which I have tried to expunge from my being. It always seems to return, like a wrinkled old person's lines which partly disappear when they roar with laughter, only for the deep lines of age to return. Sometimes I would grin broadly for long periods to force my face to look happy or lighthearted, but the skin would seem to force the natural shape back to the image that comes over in this drawing.

When I was about seven years old, I produced three watercolours for my parents – all were quite large, about three feet by two feet. One was of strange beasts at sea, a great sailing ship with flying pigs and baboons, long necked giraffe-like animals cavorting in the heinous currents, and I think I was seen as a sort of potential prodigy. The second was of a gypsy washerwoman in scarves, hanging up her washing on a line with a tiny, dwarflike apparition at her side; and the third equally bizarre, with bounding figures wildly floating and darting in space about the Earth. All three pictures were framed and placed in my parents' bedrooms in every house we lived in, for they were done especially for them and I think they really loved this present from me. A sort of self portrait figures in one corner of one of these three pictures, where a small child appears to be floating above the choppy blue sea and is obviously loving the abstract world around it. As they were executed when I was so young and as I did no more work in the conventional art sense, painting or drawing, for the next eight or ten years, these three pictures meant a lot to my mother. But they were efforts that had no predecessors as yardsticks against which to judge progress and, for a decade, no successors.

Nevertheless, if I created few works of art, I figured in many. Portraits of children were ubiquitous in the Peake household. Every wall had paintings or drawings on them – of myself, Fabian, or later our sister Clare, cousins, even children of friends. These drawings, some in the fine, dextrous line of pencil, some

As Jim in Treasure Island *– overhearing the murderous plot.*

gouache, some water colour, all brought to their subjects life, held in that second of play or concentration that my father would see, catch and put down. Sometimes a canvas was placed on an easel and I would pose for long periods. There would be breaks, when he would say, 'You can have a rest' from the prone position I was in, and these would be enough for him to get back into the mood for another quarter- or half-hour session, when, behind the canvas, the unseen energy was again applied to the new work. Finally, he would emerge and I would be allowed to rest and 'have a look' at myself as Jim in *Treasure Island*, a Dickens urchin or a character from *Swiss Family Robinson*.

• • •

I was drawn, painted, sketched and 'gouache'd' many, many times, and I always loved the results. I became a leaping athletic hero with pistols in both hands up the rigging in the 'Hispaniola', or hiding in an apple barrel listening to the murderous plot nearby. My mother would read the book being illustrated at the time and my father would paint or draw, while I stood, or sat at the pine table, sometimes in costume, sometimes naked, sometimes dagger or sword in hand, but always in action of one sort or another.

He drew me many times as I was about to go back to the detested boarding school, and always caught that look or glance that was my mood at the time. I have so many of these drawings and paintings and I can go back to the room, the atmosphere and time when they were done. I can relive the smell and feel of the occasion, its uniqueness, and although I didn't know it, the sheer power of these images taken from the written word and put so powerfully on paper. I can't say that I always relished the idea of posing as much as I did, but in the main the atmosphere was workmanlike and easy, almost as though I was an apprentice to my father's wishes.

There would always be picture frames around the house. There was a collection of discarded ones, found at the Royal College or Central Schools, Chelsea or the Slade, old, often rather tatty, hardly ever new. New frames came much later and not until the mid-1960's did the famous Sark fishermen series of the mid-1930's, or any of the subsequent oils have decent frames. The many thousands of drawings were kept in a specially made artist's drawers. These drawers, very shallow but quite deep, held his most beautiful illustrations. The *Ancient Mariner* drawings, commissioned by Chatto and Windus and for which he received £10 and now valued in excess of £10,000 each; the drawings for *Treasure Island, Bleak House, Quest for Sita, The Hunting of the Snark*, all were kept in this unusual cabinet and followed us in all our moves. Many of his oil paintings are still unframed. Hundreds of drawings also remain in their original protective wrappers, as he was simply so prolific. After his death in 1968 my mother spent what was then a large amount of money framing 30 or 40 major oils and several hundred drawings, illustrations and water colours, bringing them to even greater life. I remember a marvellous game once, where he and I skipped and danced through the Sark house, him with a large wooden frame, and me with a smaller one resting on our right shoulder, being held in place by our right hand, and hopping from one side of the lower part of the frame to the other, with our feet sometimes on the inside and then on the outer sides of the frame. Making wild Red Indian whoops, we went upstairs and down, out into the garden, round the duck pond and in and out of the bunker until we had had enough. Once my father put the front cover of a *Picture Post* magazine into a frame under glass. It showed a beautiful girl, but he blacked out a tooth or two, then took it to show the vicar's wife who greatly admired my father's talents. He had 'touched up' this beauty so well that the photo appeared to be an oil, and her apparent need of a dentist was so convincing that the vicar's wife couldn't understand why his subject had let my father paint her with her mouth open.

Pencils were everywhere, in tins or jars, boxes or drawers. Especially prevalent were the 3B kind, soft and supple, giving smooth, full lines. I remember hearing sharpening of pencils long before I knew what it meant: a kind of tiny scraping, clipping sound that came out of the workrooms - it was **his** sound. Later, when more aware of his craft and the utensils used, I would watch quietly while he would take the used pencils out of their receptacles, sharpen each one and put them all back, base first, into the jam jars, ready for use. He must have had hundreds. Not as many as fountain pens, however, which he lost frequently. My mother would replace the pens, usually good ones, Shaeffer, Parker, Conway Stewart or Watermans, and when she could afford it, gold ones which he loved. I remember once hearing her say, "But Mervyn, that is the seventeenth gold pen you've lost. Couldn't you look after them better, darling, and not lose them?"

CHAPTER 2

CHELSEA IN THE DAYS
OF THE ARTISTS

– Dylan Thomas sometimes takes me
to kindergarten

At the end of the war, in 1944, we moved to Chelsea. From this time there is a well known story in the family, one retold in my mother's book on her life with my father, *A World Away*, of the lions which, my brother was convinced, were looking at him from behind the curtains at his window. It began, his conviction, at the same time as a private vendetta against my parents by a fanatic who lived nearby in Chelsea, who had taken a real dislike to one of my father's paintings. Disturbing incidents had happened and these took place just outside my brother's bedroom. One night my parents had Graham Greene in for the evening, and they played a game of practical tricks in which people's names were picked out from the telephone directories, who were then telephoned to be the unfortunate recipients of their wit. Suddenly, a terrifying scream went up, emanating from Fabian's room. He had seen lions and they were coming for him, he was sure. He was so beside himself with fear that the practical jokes were abandoned and my mother stayed for a long time with him, trying to calm him before he went back to sleep. They remained for years, these nightmares about the lions, and the family always felt that the *malfaiteuse* did actually do something involving strange costumes or masks outside his window, that he took for a pride of lions.

Our Chelsea house was a small Regency one painted charmingly, with a carved oak door and painted ceramic panels inset on the outside front wall. It was just off the King's Road. There was one main sitting room, a small kitchen off the main room and two small bedrooms above. At the time, 1945, my father was busy revising *Titus Groan*, one of his now famous books which he had begun in the Army and was due for publication later the same year. Peter Ustinov lived almost next door, Carol Reed next to him, and in a building across the road, Augustus John had a studio. I used to go to visit the painter sometimes with both my parents, sometimes just my father. There was a lovely bread shop, which sold cakes and did cream teas, just yards from his studio entrance, and I can bring back vividly those pre-boutique days when the King's Road really had an atmosphere of artistic and literary activity about it. Dylan Thomas, a friend of the family, would sometimes hold my hand and take me to kindergarten at the end of the road, and one day *Picture Post* did a feature on it in their magazine, but to my childish annoyance my brother got into the piece and not me. A few days later, I ran away in the milk break, and on knocking at our front door a few hundred yards away and finding no-one in, I wandered about, finally being brought home by Dylan Thomas, on whose knee I sat outside our front door until my parents arrived home.

Dylan Thomas was not a very important part of my father's life, but one day in 1946, when asked to give a lecture at a fairly august institute in the West End, he asked my father if he could borrow one of his suits. My father obligingly lent him two to see which one fitted, but he never saw either again. One was of lovely brown corduroy, a style I've always liked myself, and to make up for the disappearance of his, I have had several in my time. They always remind me of that incident.

During a lull in the bombing, and after an all-clear signal had been given, my parents took me to the cinema in the King's Road. The Odeon, now a shop, was near the corner of Sydney Street, and I had passed it many times while being taken for walks. Once I was walking down the King's Road holding Dylan Thomas's hand and I had asked him if he would take me to the cinema. He refused in a very gentle way, the probable reason being a lack of funds, The Chelsea Potter or The Markham Arms having taken the last of his usually very meagre resources. On this day, however, I was taken, and inside what excitement! It was the first showing of *Dumbo*, the elephant who sails and gracefully glides around the air currents. I was enthralled by it: dreaming of Dumbo, talking of him, living it all over and over again. I had a special friend at this time, a cockney boy from a street or two away from where we were living. He heard about Dumbo so often from me, as we ran and dashed about the bomb craters near the embankment, that one day he failed to meet me at our usual rendezvous. I found out later that Dumbo had split us: he couldn't take my love for this sentimental Disney creature.

I would be taken sometimes to Peter Jones in Sloane Square where, in 1944, my father had an exhibition of paintings, to have tea in the restaurant on the fifth floor overlooking the trees in the Square below. I would always feel very proud of my attractive mother, elegant and quietly glamorous, with golden hair down to her waist, and hazel eyes. When as a joke my father or brother called them brown, she would feign pain and whisper that they were wasp gold. They were lovely and I got used at quite a young age to the daily glances and compliments she received.

On V.E. night I was taken – as a great treat – to see the lights, dancing, rejoicing and celebrations of that memorable day. We had a space on one of the benches booked for the family and we watched, cheered and clapped as all the army, navy, air force, nursing and bands of every regiment, colour and part of the Services marched past. Planes flew overhead, floodlights flashed and the evening finished with great moving tears as laughter-filled patriotic songs were sung.

1.
*With my mother at
Warningcamp in Sussex,
Summer 1940*

2.
*Held by my grandfather
Dr. Ernest Peake,
who delivered me, 1940*

3.
With my father
at Warningcamp, 1940

4.
*A portrait
at the age of one,
January 1941*

5.
*Wearing my father's
army cap,
Summer 1941*

6.
*With my father, outside the cottage
at 94, Wepham, March 1942*

7.
The Peake family boating on the River Arun,
in 1944 – the episode when I nearly drowned took place very
soon after this photograph was taken

8.
My brother
Fabian in
Picture Post
1945

9.
On Sark with
Armand the gardener

10.
On Sark with
Judy the donkey

11.
My father on Sark, 1946

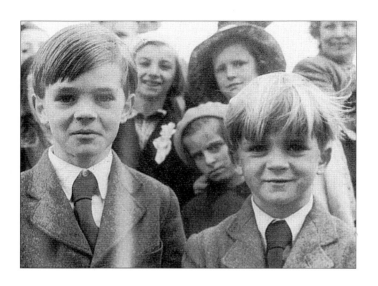

12.
*My brother and I on Sark, dressed for the visit
of Princess Elizabeth*

13.
*With Fabian, dressed as clowns for the
Sark Carnival, July 1948*

14.
The Peake family at Le Grand Greve, Sark, 1947

15.
The family with Louis Macneice and his wife, Sark 1948

16.
Taken by my mother on Sark

17.
*With my mother, as I was about to leave
for my catholic boarding school*

18.
Family group, Sark

19.
Le Chalet, Sark – before

20.
Le Chalet, Sark – after

21.
Clare and my father at Smarden, 1951

22.
Smarden

23.
Smarden

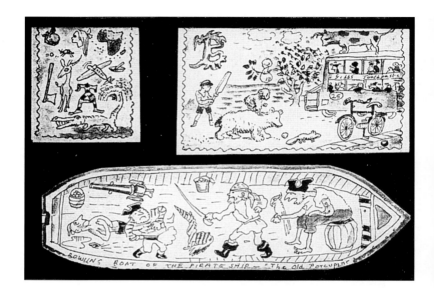

24.
*Drawings from the autograph book
that my father gave me*

CHAPTER 3

SARK C.I. – A BOYHOOD IDYLL ON A GRANITE ROCK

– Days of sun and stormy seas
and sad, sad partings

Then in 1946 something happened that was very important in all our lives: we moved to Sark, in the Channel Islands. Moving was a frequent part of the Peakes' life. I lived with my parents, and latterly my mother, in nine different houses, flats, rooms or studios, but the moves seem to have been comparatively easy affairs because my parents had very few possessions. The table, a few chairs, a bookcase or two, that was about all. The main complication involved in any of the many moves was the number of paintings and drawings, since they were very precious and easily damaged. My trunk, with 'S. Peake' beautifully inscribed on it by my father, for my first time away from home, when I was sent away to school, would be used for my few possessions: my Dinky toy car collection, my clothes, shoes, books. This trunk, so much part of the lot of the child sent off to boarding school, I have still. Our moves were ordered, quiet affairs, because apart from the paintings, we had no Georgian tables or porcelain that could come to grief. What was of worth, not perhaps according to the accepted yardstick of inherited or purchased wealth, were those objects peculiar to the Peakes.

My father was not a great reader, but possessed many books, and one aspect of these many moves was the many tea chests, containing the hundreds of books that weighed a ton, as any remover will vouch. The bookcases, whether primitive structures of bricks and planks, or later, the usual wooden kind, contained many wonderful first editions. The magnificent *Don Quixote*, illustrated by Doré, that my parents were given, containing whole block plates etched in memorable black against the sombre dark quality of the

'Jim' in Treasure Island

writing, was the weight of 50 paperbacks.

Later some Pan paperbacks joined the hardback collection. My father had designed the pipe motif, and had to choose between the ten pounds offered for the drawing, or a royalty on each use of the design. At the time, during the war, paper was scarce and it was not thought that a paperback edition could be sustained. In the circumstances, my father followed the advice of a friend and took the flat fee. As there were about four 'Pans' on each book published and as it became an incredibly successful imprint, my father would have been rich indeed. Wisdom after the event.

Graham Greene sent my parents a copy of most of his books as they were published, often signed, and these formed and remain a very important part of my late parents' mutual collection. They were catholic in their taste, Dickens being a great favourite, as well as R.L. Stevenson, James Joyce, Flaubert and Zola. Books were all around me and I was taught early on the worth of books. My parents collected books for the pleasure of having them in the house and as a reminder of how they had been moved or influenced by the writing.

Apart from his own illustrated books, which I read or had read to me, my taste for literature until the age of 18 or so did tend to veer towards the easiest of forms. The adventures of Blyton's 'Five' held me in its summer of yesteryear atmosphere, tinged as it was with tolerable criminality at the edges. Apart from these, famous war books, *The White Rabbit, The Dam Busters, Colditz*, gripped me and I read every one, advancing my knowledge of other literature not one jot. The stuff of youth, easy, prosaic, but so exciting at the time. My godfather gave me a leather bound copy of *The Forsyte Saga* on my twelfth birthday, a kind, well meant and surely perceptive gift. It remains in its virgin state today. If only I had had the brains to see that Thackeray and Blyton can both be devoured, not one or the other; the easy 'other' being my route. I gave myself a crash course in reading to replace my literary ignorance from about 18 onwards, and read Chekhov, Pushkin,

Tolstoy, Gogol and Dostoyevsky like a man possessed, day and night and at every opportunity, followed by my favourite Americans: Faulkener, Thomas Wolfe, Walt Waltman, all of Salinger, twice, all of F. Scott Fitzgerald, and in the easiness of its fine popular writing, Steinbeck. I hope this was due to my parent's influence.

Graham Greene I loved, his travels not only with his aunt, his alcoholic priests, his crooks and tarts, but most of all the sweating descriptive powers of Africa and Central America. Later I admired Heinrich Boll, Thomas Mann, Gunther Grass and that wonderful poet and perceptive human Heinrich Heine. All these so different, but all so powerful in atmosphere. What would life have been like without them? Surely far emptier? Many of these were presents from my parents. I was not asked to read by my father or mother. All that was ever done was suggesting that I might 'find something' in such and such a writer. How right they were to choose that path for me, initially to smile gracefully or accept the recommendation knowing I wouldn't probably do anything about it, but for it to have been obvious, later, that their choices were right Forcing me or ignoring me in the field of reading would not have led to the catholic love of, say, Marques, Borges, Baschevis Singer, Primo Levi or Anthony Burgess: favourites in my current world.

The abundance of books that my parents possessed made up in some way for a lack of other possessions. My parents' kitchens had no gadgets, except for a tin opener, and the Aga installed by the previous owner of one of their many houses. The scrubbed table, bought at a jumble sale for ten shillings in Sark in the mid-1940's, was the focal point of a very simple kitchen in whichever house one was in. A simple wooden draining board, a sideboard and much later a refrigerator, cutlery and some silver left to my mother on her parents' death were the accoutrements of family life, which as in so many houses took place around mother's kitchen.

The kitchen revolved round the table and chairs

and the talk there was of artists, of shape and form, of light and shade, of colour, of personality. Would you save the cat or a Rembrandt if a fire broke out? My mother the cat, my father the painting. And for me too, the choice of the painting, for me the 'living' masterpiece. This luxurious and hypothetically inane question exercised my mind many times. The scrubbed pine table, white from a thousand scrubbings, was used from the distance of my earliest memory until just before my mother's death four decades later. The legs that wobbled, the grooves in the top where the wood was worn down, the uneven opening of the drawers at either end, the personality of it, the thousand meals had on it, even its ignorance of its part in a family history took it far above the dignity of a noble Sheraton. There was no sophistication to it, no style, nothing beyond utilitarian, but it was unique and wonderful.

My mother had a penchant for simple earthenware vases rather like a pitcher, which could have been used for milk or water or, in Latin countries, wine. Brown, with a yellowish rim, these vases, of which there were several, always contained my mother's favourite daffodils or lilies. In the Spring and early Summer when the car-free lanes of Sark would be teeming with buzzing life and the hedgerows came out of hibernation and into a thousand stirrings of green, we would dash along the stone lanes and pick wild flowers to take home, and in the Autumn hunt blackberries for jam or wolfing there and then. The house would then be alive with the smells we had brought back and the wafting of the golden and yellow and white daffodils would be everywhere. They are now my favourites, and when they are placed around the room, I can shut my eyes and feel Sark again.

Breakfast with my parents was always boiled eggs, doorstep fried bread and 'Post Toasties', my father's word for any cereal, which derived from his boyhood in China. He, his brother and their parents lived for a while in the American compound in Kuling, and an American who also lived there always ate a brand, unknown to us, called Post Toasties. My father took a great liking to them and forever afterwards called cornflakes Post Toasties, Weetabix Post Toasties, even porridge Post Toasties.

My father was not much of an eater, but he loved everything my mother made and always complimented her on her efforts. Breakfast, after the Post Toasties, meant great pieces of fried bread or toast – and when on Sark my father loved the appearance of butter, which came in moulds in the shape of buildings, giving impressions of Sark Castle or other edifices, usually the Dame's house, La Seignerie, or Le Manoir, a fine stone Georgian house nearby. This golden coloured butter set in the moulds and delivered to the individual customer's houses direct from the farms, was ladled out of the dish with sad sighs, as the lovely designs were scooped away. We all sat around the famous table eating toast and talking excitedly of local events or the forthcoming episode of what at the time held us all entranced, Dick Barton Special Agent. Then off to the local little tiny school - 'Smallest in Great Britain' - my mother and I would go, and my father if he was with us would go to his workroom to write, illustrate or paint. My mother would clear up – she was extremely tidy – and afterwards would go to her own room to paint.

The house we moved to on Sark had been the H.Q. of the occupying German forces and they had painted the place in a camouflaged grey, had taken away all features like balconies and porticoes and toolsheds and had made the place feel unlike any home. After my parents had acquired the house on a 99 year lease at £80 per annum, the place was painted white and all the features replaced. Our first night was one devoid of furniture, but paintings were, of course, everywhere.

I loved this house with its great garden, the small pond, in which we put the ducks given to my father by the local vicar as a quid pro quo for a drawing my father did for him, and an underground bunker the Germans had dug in the garden in case of invasion.

      When we arrived, the Sark house still had signs in German on the doors, and all around were other signs of the occupation: there was the flooded bunker which we used for boating and catching frogs; there were the lookout posts, the rusted armaments, the evidence on the tree nearby, from which, according to unfounded local gossip, people had been hanged for alleged collaboration. All over the islands, for I knew them all very well later in life, were piquant reminders of the Germans. Yet there was something about this legacy, in its concrete form, that was attractive to me - its solidity. These relics are everywhere still – 50 years later. Their potential as hiding places and the games that we could play on top of, inside, and at the back of these shapeless monuments of power meant that they held a fascination for us. Not so the concentration camp. My father visited Belsen a few weeks after liberation, with the inmates all still in their huts, many dying of typhus. He drew them, spoke to them and wrote the most eloquent and moving poems about some of the dying that have ever been written. This one I cannot forget:

Belsen, 1945

> *If seeing her an hour before her last*
> *Weak cough into all blackness I could yet*
> *Be held by chalk-white walls, and by the great*
> *Ash coloured bed,*
> *And the pillows hardly creased*
> *By the lightness of her little jerking head -*
> *If such can be a painter's ecstasy,*

(Her limbs like pipes, her head a porcelain skull)

Then where is mercy?

And what irony?

Is this my calling, for my schooled eyes see

The ghost of a great painting, line and hue

In this doomed girl of tallow?

O anguish! has the world so white a yellow

As the pernicious and transparent mist

That like a whiff of Belsen in her cheeks

Detaches her by but a breath from linen

In that congested and yet empty world

Of plaster, cotton and a little marl?

Than whiteness what is there more terrible?

There lay the gall

On the dead mouth of the world

And at death's centre a torn garden trembled

In which her eyes like great hearts of black water

Shone in their wells of bone,

Brimmed to the well-heads of the coughing girl,

Pleading through history in that white garden;

And very close, upon the small head's cheekbones,

As upon ridges in an icy dew

Burned the sharp roses.

My father's experiences in Belsen, a place set in the flat forest region of northern Germany, remained in his conscious and subconscious mind from that visit until he died. When the condemned war criminal Peter Back saw my father at the cell door, he jumped up and saluted my father, and after the sketches had been recorded, he saluted and said, "*Danke schon*". He was hanged some hours later, an event to which my father was invited to attend. The senior S.S. wardress had to be punched and kicked to make her stand for the British Officer taking my father around the camp. When he had drawn this woman, who had come with Rudolph Höss, last Commandant of Auschwitz, to complete the *Endlosung* of the Jews, she approached my father and spat all over his face before being thrown back onto her bunk. She was a murderess from the most awful place in history and her physical prowess made her quite capable of killing my father. In *Titus Alone* (which has a mood fundamentally different from *Titus Groan* and *Gormenghast*) the evil man Veil and the faceless millions staring expressionlessly from the windows in the factory are both testaments to his experience of Belsen.

Expunging complicated feelings of guilt about the way in which my father had accepted his visit to Belsen, when he could have turned away on being dropped at the gate on that dark day in 1945, was almost an obsession with me for over 20 years. When the extent of the atrocities became known to me, I read avidly anything I could on the subject. Borrowing books from the library, buying books, talking to people who had been incarcerated, all I felt I had to do to try to ameliorate in some distorted way the lot that I knew to be that of the inmates, and of my father visiting them, treading across the human excrement everywhere, seeing the S.S. guards pulling the skin and bones across the rough ground, hearing the skulls of the dead cracking on the stones, the shaking of the nearly dead in the communal pits; the heaps upon heaps of cadavers and the near skeletons and the vomiting by the former captors as they scraped bodies from the teeth of the bulldozers' scoops. How can his experience of the camp not have created an eternal helplessness of the soul?

I soon found out, however, that it is one thing to have been there, and to have lived in the atmosphere of total war, and quite another to be able to go to visit these places now: however well intentioned my visits were essentially an emotional kind of voyeurism. I feel very ambivalent about my father's work at Belsen because my admiration for his total genius does not excuse the circumstance of his visit. Is he the greater talent, still misunderstood by many who should be ashamed of their ignorance, because he suffered and later died as a result of seeing manifest the antithesis of joy, love and beauty, or is he the bigger for *Titus*, the *Ancient Mariner* drawings, the idiosyncratic depth of painful, intuitive and explosive observation? I don't know.

Between 25-30,000 died in Belsen, ten times that amount in Chelm and Sobibor. Even a small camp on the Baltic near Gdansk-Stutthof, with its meandering small gauge lines ending up in a clearing in a wood and the Alsatian dog house (the first building seen upon entering the compound) still intact, witnessed terrible numbers of deaths. Treblinka in Eastern Poland, is built a few feet above the marshes, with its pretend railway station and clock. Even more overwhelming is the massive and bloodcurdling Auschwitz. The scaffolds are still there, the wall against which many more were shot than died in Belsen, the never-ending lines of huts – making me feel as though the thousands upon thousands of shaved heads were looking down on me, the visitor. There one sees photographs taken just before the death march to the gas chamber. The newly canonised Maximilian Kolbe, who took the place of a gypsy family and died in their stead, was gassed in the chambers that now one can walk through.

I shook before I saw the dreadful name Oswiecim coming into view when I drove across Poland a few years ago. It was, I felt, as though I was walking where I had no place to be – and this before I even arrived in the town. In an article in a magazine I had seen the most chilling photograph of the rails leading up to the main entrance to Birkenau, the women's part of Auschwitz. It had been taken in an early morning mist, and the finality of that line and its entrance under the great black wooden tower, shook me completely. Years later, when I walked along that track deliberating at 6 a.m. on a freezing day, the death-like poignancy of the place was hideous, despite my being the only person in the whole camp.

I felt that I had to write my own poetry, capturing my own feelings about concentration camps.

Treblinka, Eastern Poland

On the eastern side of nowhere
twelve hundred miles from home
the marshes of the hinterland
obscure the Polish soil.

Reeds and wetlands are all there is to see
of the million souls that met their fate
passing under the hour still clock.

The 'transit' station, leading
nowhere, the facade that fooled the lot
now houses one lonely guide
in the 'station masters' hut.

Bergen-Belsen KZ

He'd seen her shattered smile
and put it down in ink.

I saw a heart rending look, but
from a photograph.

The silence of the heath, the proof
with mass graves.

The gypsies plaque and Belgium's pure
simplicity, 'Matria Belgiae'.

Ann Frank stared out at us as
Modern British soldiers cried:

The bastards!

Kramer from Auschwitz came, and others too,
to smash the weak, and feeble.

Or is it in all of us
that desire to destroy?

       The Poles encourage visits by children and foreigners and I agree. I think in some ways we should be obliged to visit these places where the grossest of violent acts took place. In one camp though, some school-children came sauntering towards me, chewing gum, smoking and singing pop songs. I found it difficult to grasp their unawareness as they strolled around what was to them just another old boring museum. Walking in Treblinka I tripped, and, looking down at the skeleton of a hare, prostrate, staring up at me in its death state, I froze. At Chelm camp in central Poland, in a mile square clearing in the forest, all that remains is the electrified entrance gate stating that in the space of only 18 months, 300,000 people died, including tens of thousands of Czech children and old people. There was a woman arranging some paltry flowers at the stone mausoleum a couple of hundred yards into the camp, whom I asked for information.

She spoke no German, except a few words, and I spoke no Polish. French was no good either, so in a combination of sign language and her very elementary German, she explained that if I would like to kneel down she would show me something. I did so, and there just half an inch or so below the surface were the bones of some of the children buried. 25,000 were shot, gassed or knifed to death on their arrival and because the mass graves filled up so quickly and there were so many, the bodies just got higher and higher in the pits, until just the small amount of earth covered them. She put a selection of arm and leg bones into my hand and made the knifing gesture across her throat. I dropped the bones almost at once. I felt completely unclean touching them. This woman had lived in the camp for the entire period of its existence and was in charge of washing the clothes taken from the victims just before their death. Then those pathetic garments were bundled into sacks and taken by horse and cart to the railway station about three miles away and sent to Germany.

All these camps that I had felt compelled to visit had the same chilling feel to them, whether small, medium or large, in woods or hills or on marshes, in high ground or in valleys. Usually they are silent places and should be visited, for even empty and laid flat, grassed over as in many cases, they exert such a power that only those with no imagination could fail to be profoundly moved and embarrassed by mankind's evil.

• • •

Sark had at the time about 360 people, most of whom were indigenous, patois-speakers: "un shoulder de boeuf", "un leg de mouton" they would say in the butcher's. The strange and very pronounced, rather South African accent of Sark I have always loved, and recently I gave a lecture to a Californian audience in a Sarkese accent, as the subject of my talk was *Mr Pye*, one of my father's books written on and about Sark. My audience was baffled.

It was a splendid place to grow up in. In the high summer my mother would pack a lunch and we would go on various bicycles off to some of our favourite haunts: beaches, cliff tops, the lovely and dangerous Venus Pool on Little Sark with its dark depths invisible below the lure of its blue and shimmering surface.

In the mid-1930's, when my father lived on Sark in an artists' colony, breeding cormorants, painting like a man possessed and drawing until the lead had worn down to the fingers holding the pencil, he found a whale. At least he was told of the whale, which had been carried out of its normal path in the Atlantic, and had somehow become parted from its fellow travellers and landed up on Grand Greve beach. Very few local people liked the idea of going very near the putrifying remains of the grounded mammal, but my father, with handkerchief at nostrils, went to examine it. There were a few other brave souls prepared to go up to the carcass and between them they collected some of the whale's larger vertebrae as mementoes. These bones were dried out and scraped of all appended flesh and a small collection of them kept. Throughout their life together my parents treasured these beautifully shaped bones, which had so delighted my father. They travelled with us when we moved and now, long after my parents' death, they still grace the fireplaces or mantlepieces of my home and those of my brother and sister. Their shapes can be seen as a horse's head, a gargoyle, a ship, or strange flying objects, modern in the extreme and yet ancient like China, strange emblems of power. My father was fascinated by the idea of bones from a whale who lost its way in the great ocean and who ended its life on a beach in the Channel Islands, finally dismembered for the unique shapes formed along its back.

Bones had a perennial fascination for my father. He once bought a skull and many other bones from a museum which was closing down, and he and I would often find yet more bones on walks – bones of rabbits or other dead animals. We would make them into invented skeletons, then half bury them in out of the way places and tell my mother that we had found a body. She wouldn't always come and see, so I would have to pretend to be going for a walk, thereby accidentally coming across the dead body my father and I had planted earlier. Half covered with leaves, it looked very authentic indeed, and we would invent some famous murder or violent happening that had occurred, and deem ourselves the discoverers. I don't know if she believed us, but as the skull was real and the tibias and fibulas from the same museum, the cattle, sheep and rabbit bones suitably ordered, all looked authentic enough. But the most lovely of all were the large collection of those whale bones, which at first numbered twenty or so and which were sometimes arranged in a snaking line, progressively getting smaller as they wound across the sitting room, starting at the fireplace. During the many moves, most somehow disappeared.

Once, on finding a dead rat in a lane, my father drew it, seeing a dignity in the rodent. Here was its unpleasant grey colour, its awful tail immobile, stretching out so far from its flanks, but this rat which now hangs on a wall in my house has grace, for my father caught the life in its death, the helpless paws caught in an innocent supplicatory gesture, as though they were gripping something. His drawing even brought out the rat's own individuality in its position on the path. I wonder if its being dead made it more attractive to him. Rats were endemic in Belsen: perhaps this later drawing somehow showed the rat as the dying Jews he had seen there.

On wild days on Sark my brother, my father and I, dressed in sou'westers, wellington boots and macs, would all leave the house, and walk up past the windmill - a defunct and small Sancho Panza magnet - along the stony roads to Grand Greve. This bay, against which on wild days the sea would rage, was a wonderful sight when viewed from 300 feet up. The isthmus linking Big and Little Sark, called

Dead rat, Burpham

Sebastian, Circa 1951

La Coupee, had on one side this usually sheltered beach, and on the other – 300 feet below – the amethyst and topaz beach. On the wildest of days, if my father wasn't working, we would descend the zig-zag path downwards, through the bushes at the top, treading carefully on the muddy steps, for rain on these chosen days of wildness often accompanied the discomfort. Nearer the bottom of the cliff, the only concession to the modern life were about twenty poorly constructed concrete steps, the final one was about two feet above the shingle, from which we both would make a yell as our feet struck the stones and sand of the beach. We would head off to the left of the beach, for here we could see the violent meeting of the five currents at their most powerful. Great sea horses and spray ten, fifteen feet high, would dance in a foaming clash aiming into the dark sky. Ever changing the shape was for a split second recorded in the eye, but then would evaporate almost immediately, to be replaced by another permutation. We would perch on hard granite rocks, as near to the seas as possible, almost on the edge of drowning, as the sea rose higher, and the chasm closed between the rock we were sitting on and the beach, until a great leap through the foam found us on terra firma again. All over the island, from the northern point at L'Eperquerie, with the rocks tapering little by little into the sea, to the southern tip by the tin mines by Venus Pool, the seas pounded Sark like no other place I have known. Every time my father took me out, from the primordial days of January when storms would lash the tiny island, to summer days, as when I was eight and my father, Louis MacNiece and others explored the caves and cliffs, rocks and caverns, with a background of the softest of lappings of tiny voices – the meterological perfection of 'calm'; on all occasions the darkness of the banked depths around Sark always suggested power to us. A power which is caught both in *Moby Dick* and in the gripping poem my father wrote about the terrible retribution wrought on the mutineers, *The Touch o'The Ash.*

As a child, I was always an adequate swimmer, but

a show off too. I would wait for an audience, then run like mad down to the sea and stay underwater, counting up until I felt the entire world would be waiting with bated breath for me to surface. I could often quite frighten myself, however, especially in fairly high seas, when I would go out so far that I lost sight of where I had started from. This was all in the cause of being noticed, but on laboriously swimming back, a task sometimes made harder by an outgoing and strong tide, it would prove to have been virtually useless, as no-one had even noticed my efforts. This and many other similar childish endeavours I think I must, in part, have inherited. Even in later life, my mother would dance wonderfully on our famous table to flamenco music at the end of her parties, as she always liked to encourage other people to dance. She would attend parties with magnificent great feather boas around her neck and click castanets she had been given in Spain. The guests would clap and cheer her and she would yell back, "Olé!".

In his earliest days on Sark my father would take enormous risks that were commented on far and wide. He would climb sheer rock faces and suspend himself above caverns and once, caught by a large octopus while exploring a cave, emerged with its tendrils securely locked around his right leg. After prising the creature off him by clubbing and knifing it, my father displayed the hundreds of suction marks as signs of virility and daring. Riding on his bicycle, standing on the saddle or the handle bars, one foot on each, was another of his tricks, a hazardous one, as I found to my cost on trying to emulate it. He too was a good swimmer and we would swim together in Dixcart Bay and try to clap hands underwater, to no audible avail.

From my bedroom I could see the French coast on clear days, but I could also see the ferry the 'Sarnia', quite clearly sometimes, although it was often several miles out. From my bedroom, from the warmth, security and inviolability of my home, what seemed the terrible heavings, plungings, even the final movements of the ship in violent storms, made me feel for the poor passengers, who would later include me. From my vantage point I would have a feeling, so common in children, when the tingling sensation of knowing that one's own safety is in a way at the expense of others gives one the most glorious of temptations towards unwitting smugness. There but for the grace of God, and on the stormy sea people are being terribly ill, they're afraid, they long for journey's end, but I am safe, I am secure and there they are, stiff upper lip perhaps, as the 'Sarnia' went out of sight past the North East of the island. It was a false security though, because I knew that I lived on an island, that there were no aeroplanes, no bridges to the mainland, no firm stones across the deep, dark water. I knew that one day I would have to cross it, and that it would be rough. I was right - the day I had to go to Guernsey for the first time was very stormy. Later in 1949, in my last term at Les Vauxblets, I crossed from Weymouth to St Peter Port in a severe storm, a force eleven gale, and the journey took two days instead of six hours. I had had a bunk reserved in a cabin with another person and it was in the bowels of the ship. Giants of the deep hammered against the porthole from which nothing could be seen in the darkness of Weymouth. As it left the harbour, before even reaching the open water, the ship had lurched over at such an angle that all the crockery was thrown across the small restaurant and smashed. "The journey," said the Captain, "will take somewhat longer than is normal and our expected arrival time cannot be given. All seats on the ship have been secured where possible; it is advised to hold the sides of your bunk, if you have one, for stability." The storm of that January night, and the parting at Waterloo Station from my parents, which seemed like a century before, will never leave me. We had to stay outside St Peter Port for eight hours because we could not dock. When the 'Sarnia' was finally tied up, I cried with relief.

My mother captured, in many oil paintings, the storm bedraggled lanes and byways of the island; after particularly bad ones, she would take out pencil and paper and draw or paint the trees wildly lurching away from the winds. Storms during my time on

Sark seemed ubiquitous, exciting and dramatic, but were most comfortably observed from behind my curtain on the first floor of my home. My father and my mother always saw things in terms of their artistic content. An old man's face, a giraffe or antelope, a ballet dancer or frog, a map of Kent or a shape like France - anything had in it the potential to arouse the artist. If you look at clouds, you can see a thousand shapes, my parents would tell me. And they're there. Who could guess what that shape reminded one of? Often, when looking into the sky, my father would try to guess the shape that my mother had seen in it, and my brother or I would try as well. Just as one can tap out, on a desk or on a table, a favourite song and ask for the tune to be guessed at, so it was with the clouds: "Just like Mrs Somebody's hat, just like the butcher's nose or the parish priest's head", we would reply.

The main island of Sark held in its tiny grasp the Robert Louis Stevenson power of the gorse heathland and the high adventure of summer's idyll. On some days, sandwiches rolled up in our towels, our swimming costumes on under the short grey trousers we wore, my brother and I would set off for the 'Hole in the rock' above one of the beaches and throw stones the 50 feet down onto the empty stony strand below, while seagulls, the buzzing of flies and the heady smell of gorse and fern surrounded us, before the steep and precipitous climb down. Once, carried away by strong winds Fabian was swept out by the powerful current and, like myself at an earlier stage, was rescued. He, like me, had lost consciousness, and the presence of a medical friend who was with us on this whole family day out, saved him. These outings were mostly with my parents' friends. The poet Louis MacNeice and his wife stayed once and took us on walks. He later sent a short poem about his stay and dedicated it to the 'blue eyed thugs', as he christened my brother and myself.

• • •

I am afraid the countryside in its technical specific sense, as a place made up of species identified with scientific detachment, did not figure in our lives – and as far as I can remember I never was taught to differentiate between types of tree, bird, crop or mineral. My father could quote from books verbatim, could recite complete poems if given only the first line from the works of Shelley or Wordsworth, De la Mare or Byron, but wouldn't know the latin name of a species of common tree. On the other hand, he could, just by my showing a square inch of paint from one of my parent's large collection of art books, tell me the painter. I would place a piece of paper right across a reproduction of a Picasso or a Monet, a Chagal or a Constable, even old masters - the tip of a finger from a Van Dyck or Vermeer - all were known to him by the minutest of details. Trees as clinically defined plants did not figure very highly up the agenda of priorities. But trees in the sense of shape, like clouds: that was another thing. My father's inexhaustible imagination could make a burnt-out tree stump in Kent, or the ancient oaks in a wood near Salisbury, into things with the most eerie and frightening primaeval malevolence about them, could make them into living, dancing creatures in a thousand descriptions of their beauty, ugliness, majesty and sheer powerfulness, giving them an instant life. Trees blown down by storms affected him the same way. The centuries of gales made sure that a walk along La Segneurie road from the cross-roads on the middle of the island, to the northern tip, took one past gnarled, broken, weather-beaten and ancient trees, which gave him shapes of huddling men and women trying to keep out the inevitable fate of eventual, ageing death.

Each summer the annual fete was held, when all the islanders were invited to the main field in the centre of the island. They had fancy dress parades, egg and spoon races, the sack race, running races, tombolas and prizes. My father had made a tray with

Fabian, Circa 1947

a glass glued to it, which I held aloft and would suddenly tip towards people, who were convinced that the glass filled with water would fall off, bruising and drenching them. As it was, the glass attached to the tray just spilt a little water, but stayed on the tray. My brother wore a clown's costume, painted cheeks and eyes, with a top hat and stick he looked like one of the Bertram Mills's professionals.

The main event of the day for children was a slow bicycle race which I entered one year. The reward was a hamper of sweets, and as sweets were rationed, these Aero bars, Mars bars, and assorted chocolates were far more of a luxury and rarity than they are now. The starting pistol rang out and forgetting or being mesmerised by winning, I tore off at a mad speed, easily beating the other competitors with their strange slowness. Why the 'slow' part of the race didn't make an impression I don't know, but once I was declared the 'last' by the judge and the peals of laughter that greeted my arrival had really struck me, I found that even my parents' explanations were quite incomprehensible. I arrived first so I had won; now it seemed you arrived first so you were **last**. These ideas taxed brain power to an extent that both hunted and haunted. 'You're first so you're last' remained etched graphically, poignantly, and very emotionally on my mind for years, as the humiliation was so painfully public.

On Wednesdays the great event of the week took place in the hall. Next to the churchyard this green painted and faded corrugated iron building was also the Island Parliament or Chief Pleas and would be also the venue for occasional dances. The horsedrawn black ambulance was housed nearby, and here the St John's Ambulance man would occasionally practice bandaging arms and legs. This high spot was the weekly film with the trailers, cartoon or B films. In the late 1940's, the secondary crime films were sometimes so poor, with their ham actors and transparent plots and chases, that they became comedies. The laughter from the hall was deafening as the actor on film

was saying deathless lines: 'take that you cur' or 'I'll get you for that
Smith', as everyone reacted in feigned shock, guffawing and squealing
whinneys of sarcastic mirth.

When the lights went off and the turning of the reel
for the big film audibly announced its imminence, a hush would come
over the sixpenny section for, as Alan de Cartaret, a local friend of
mine, would always say to any main film at all to be shown there, it was
'supposed to be good' in a broad Sarkese dialect. My favourites were
the Will Hay films which made me cry with laughter, but the old
ukelele player George Formby, Charlie Chaplin and the early Tarzan
of Johnny Weismuller held us all in their grip. It was the pure
Hollywood enchantment of Deanna Durbin that really bowled me
over. Captivated, head over heels in unrequited love, transported to
heaven on the backs of soaring, melifluous but sentimental violins, she
captured the whole of me. Dreaming of her, dazzled by her naive and
openly sweet nature, I saw no sugary transience here, just the pull of
the first woman I fell in love with.

To get to the hall from our house we could leave
through a hedge at the back of the garden, across the side of the large
field next to it and through the graveyard by the church. On summer
evenings when the light was still up, this part of the walk was easy. In
winter, howling gales would often cross the island and add to the sound
of the branches creaking and cracking in the trees. The blowing gusts
of January nights through the graveyard were bad enough on the way
to the film. **After** a Lon Chaney thriller, an Edgar Allan Poe adaptation
or a Dickens masterpiece, the return across the graveyard was that
particular horror come true. As there were no lights on Sark, it was
straight out of the hall and a few muttered goodbyes, see you next
week, or tomorrow or whatever, then the walk became a 'Whistling in
the Dark' mad dash. Sometimes I had to take a younger boy or girl back
over to Little Sark. After dropping them off I was on my own, I would
race like one possessed on the return journey up the other side of the

Coupee, racing along the straight road, with only the wild whistling of the telegraph wires above for company. I would get to the crossroads, and still flat out, pass the doctor's house on one side and the two teachers' bungalow on the other. Our gate, a wide cross bar style, was set back 15 feet from the lane and pulling back the black metal securing arm, I rushed up the gravel drive and into the house. All the way back, voices I thought I heard would say "I'm just behind you" or "Not long now until I catch you." Tingling, my blood streaming through my veins, I felt the spirit of boyhood eager for adventure: "Jim Hawkins, a hero from *Treasure Island,* wouldn't have quaked", I used to say to myself, "stop breathing for a second", which I would then do, and pain would course through the young body, living at its highest pitch of excitement.

We had a donkey which came with the house, called Judy. She was grey and quite large. I loved her, but I thought she could do more than just stand around, either in the house, which caused great amusement to visitors, or outside the front window: I felt she could be put to more enterprising purposes. The man from whom we leased the house had some traps and even though I was not yet eight, I put my idea to him, that I harness the animal to one of these, and take trippers on rides round the island. There was a group of carriages always ready for hire at the top of the harbour hill. It was an idea that worked, for at the end of the first day I'd given five rides at sixpence each, and half a crown in 1947 was quite a bit of money.

We hadn't long been on Sark when I started nagging my parents to take me to Herm, and finally I did go on a day trip to see Shell Beach, the famous sheltered bay that collects all the drifting molluscs ebbing their way south eastwards, carried by the Gulf Stream. In the event my parents didn't take me; I was taken by some Sarkese friends. We went on a 20 foot long wooden boat, completely open, with cross benches and a rear seat for the passengers and powered by a small mid-engine.

Donkey, Sark, 1949

The day had started off slightly breezy and although there was a slight swell on the sea over from Sark, the wind became quite strong as we left on the return journey in our little open boat. About half way back, the grey clouds became thunderous and the first drops of rain fell on us. We did not have long to wait before the full wrath of heaven was unleashed and the seas began to swell. Although only a few miles, the journey took two hours and towards the end I began to panic, so I stood up on top of the engine housing, which was in the middle of the boat, and in a voice of real fear began to shout "Jesus save us, Jesus save us". In sight of Sark the engine started to splutter and one of the most terrifying hours of my life ended eventually as the little boat limped into Creux by the skill of the pilot. I have been haunted by the apparently tiny gulf between the boat reaching harbour and capsizing ever since.

Our style of living on Sark was relaxed but unnerved others unused to it. Judy the donkey walked about the house shocking the midwife brought in for the birth of my sister Clare. When Leon Goosens, who played his oboe in our sitting room, came to stay, Judy, who had found the front door open, passed the open sitting room door and walked upstairs into the bedroom, where my mother was nursing a three day old daughter. The temporary nurse, Mrs Kilfoyle, who my father christened Tinfoil, found this too much, packed her bags and was gone by the same evening. This wasn't the first time the animal had made an appearance, as two days before the birth while her back was turned to the open door as she was discussing arrangements with the local doctor, Judy had ambled in and bitten her ear. She shrieked, which probably didn't do my mother in labour upstairs much good.

Armand the Moroccan gardener loved to rake the gravel path until symmetrical lines stretched from the gate to the larger area in front of the house. The donkey would tramp about and undo the painstaking work and Armand would rake it again. Once on a walk

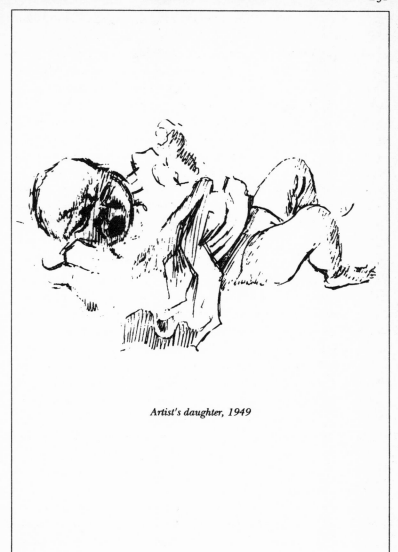

Artist's daughter, 1949

across the island, he found a beautiful pair of tortoiseshell glasses which he tried on and saw nothing through them, his eyesight being very good, but he persevered until he'd ruined his eyes, but could wear these symbols, as he saw them, of the well-to-do. Sometimes he would take my brother and I to Grand Greve, the largest beach, and we would amble along the mile or so with one of us carrying the packed lunch my mother had prepared. Moist egg and cress sandwiches under damp muslin, tomatoes, some oranges and maybe a banana, on the carless island with hidden coves and beaches, gorse and fern, bracken and stumpy dried grass at the cliff tops above the beaches made the clamber down the simple paths adventures all those days ago. Grand Greve had 645 very rudimentary steps which we counted every time, zig-zagging downwards towards the sand. At low tide a tall single triangular shaped rock was exposed on one side of the beach. We'd climb up it and wait for the tide to come in, hopping in and racing back inshore when it was a few feet deep.

The day was marked by giant S or F marks made by big toes in the soft yellow sand, by races to the rock pools, by nibbles of lunch before climbing the big rock again, by counting cormorants and watching the lights come on in St Peter Port across the sea as dusk fell and later by packing up our sandy things for the slow walk home. We were very happy, kicking stones along the top of the beach, before reaching the hundreds of steps which had to be climbed, eyeing the crying gulls floating and wheeling across the sky above. This precious time epitomised the pleasures of my boyhood with its timelessness and freedom from care.

The sizzling wheaty smell of Horlicks evokes the cold days of winter time in the Sark school, with cup in hand before the treat of the day: schools radio or Uncle Mac. Little desks roughly gouged and damaged by predecessors before the war: the Guilles, Perres, the de Carterets, Lanyons and Bakers; the patois still very much extant, these went hand in hand with outsiders from a different

Fabian, Circa 1947

culture. Listening to Uncle Mac, which seems now so naive, was the great radio treat of the Western world, the miracle of the sound 'all the way from London' as we were often reminded, was not a thing to miss. Our own aptly-named Pye radio had a battery about the size of one found in a small car of today, and had to be recharged weekly at the bicycle shop at the top of the harbour hill, or else the far more exciting Dick Barton – Special Agent would be missed. With Jock or Snowy just about to grab the villain around the neck in a cliff-hanging ending in a Scottish glen, the evocative music necessitated the battery being fully charged even if for three years or so a mile one way and the same back was the price to be paid in energy.

In 1947 a really wild and lasting winter started about November and lasted until March 1948. Snow came and stayed and obliterated a great deal of the landscape for weeks on end. To begin with it was very exciting and snowmen were made in the school yard; to begin with Horlicks was served hotter than usual and the log fires roared in the tiny school. But as there was no change in the weather by December, the electricity was cut off due to the generator failing at the little power station at the top of the harbour hill, attitudes changed fairly quickly. The lasting snow meant no let up in the temperatures' low level. Ice clogged the rain pipes and drains, and the rain water barrels were frozen over. The power was off in the school so we were sent home early on in this famous bleak winter; and people soon wished for the Spring, a thaw and an end to what had begun as a heaven-sent childrens' novelty. My father had come back to Sark for Christmas from his teaching in England and one day, unknown to my brother or I, he got up very early. Using lots of blocks of ice which he had formed by using casings and boxes as moulds, he built an igloo with carved entrance tunnel and domed main room. Leaving out one block of ice just above the end adjacent to the main body of the thing, he installed in its place a picture of an eskimo looking out, and when we were called to come and see his handiwork there was this grinning eskimo to greet us. With our cherished gauntlets on, wellington boots, scarves wrapping us up, we tore out of the house, down the tunnel and into the little house where some blankets had been laid across the ground over the earth he had cleared of snow.

It took a long time for the ice and snow to melt that winter and that last little pile of ice which marked the final end of the igloo stays as a poignant memory of all that I so longed for and loved about what it was to have a father who could do that for us. "This is where my igloo was," I would say to people when they would come to stay, or to friends or locals who came to the house. "It lasted weeks and weeks," I'd say. "My dad made it."

Archery, an ancient and dignified art, had taken a hold of my father about the summer of 1948, and he brought back from London a whole set of bows, arrows and lovely canvas-covered targets in bright colours of red for the bull's eye, blue and white for other scores. This canvas held a tightly packed straw body to the board and in summer my parents used the garden for archery practice. They had long slender quivers and bows of different shapes and sizes in yew and ash. They loved the singing sound of the arrow, the silence just before and after the shot, the simplicity of the act of firing

Once to see, I suppose, what would happen, my father fired directly above him with the largest yew bow, pulling the gut to full force and letting fly the arrow, which sailed into the sunlight to descend at a murderous pace a foot or two away from my brother standing nearby.

At the time, and, I wonder, did I ever behave differently, I needed so much attention that people would sometimes in later life despair of me. As a boy an *idee fixe* would seize me: I remember wanting a dog, I would not give up, for weeks, the chant of "I want a dog", "I want a dog", which would echo around the house in Sark until, just accidentally like an arrow that had landed on my head, the chant might stop. My father's method of silencing me at this time remains engrained; and that was to put my head just between his knees and hold me there for a long, long time. Snuffed out, my current demand would be forgotten in my relief on being released, only to start again when I judged the atmosphere right. I must have been an awful experience for my parents, for the 'hairbrush' on the hand or backside I received from my mother when my father was back in London was a frequent punishment. I would go up to my parents' bedroom and really get whacked, but I loved my mother very much, and I think her knowledge of this love meant that she couldn't produce the cold, dispassionate presence needed to mete out physical punishment in its most effective form.

When I was about nine my father gave me an unbirthday present: a bow of my own. He already had his bow and my mother had hers. We would stand some way from the target and try to hit the bull's eye. The grass grew quite long at the sides of the very large garden on Sark and in that very hot summer, when flies and insects, birds and the quacking of our ducks on the little man-made pond in the garden, all expostulated their freedom of movement and life, the arrows sailed with various intensities of sound in the direction of the target. I loved that bow, but the only difficulty was that after particularly athletic strainings to create maximum velocity, the gut would snap out from its nick at the top of the bow and limply hang down and the bow would regain the semi-straight shape. My father would then deftly place the bow against his left knee, press forward and re-attach the string. Whenever I tried, the bow would shoot off at an angle, because my knee was nowhere near the grip at half way mark, so it spun awry. One day I was so angry with not being able to restring my present that I threw away the bow as far as I could and it landed in undergrowth. I ran around the garden screaming that this bow was stupid and "I'm glad it's lost". I didn't know if it was or not, for my parents, probably having had enough of me and archery for the day had gone off somewhere else. Later, after leaving, I'm sure, a small trail of destruction all over the place, I went to look for the bow. I hunted and hunted, but as I was in such a temper when I threw it away, now I couldn't find my unbirthday present. I shouted and screamed for assistance; none was forthcoming. I screamed again and again. Other people were doing their own things. My brother with his tribe of Sioux attacking the cavalry behind the windmill or catching fish in the translucent waters of the old Creux harbour built in Napoleon's time. At any rate I had to find it myself, but I didn't. My noise continued. There must have been a point when another string broke, that of the nerve leading to my parents' patience with me. My father took hold of me, put my head between his legs, and despite entreaties, cries of help and supplication, there I remained. Whether the claustrophobia from which I suffer still began on that high summer day I don't know, but I can imagine my head placed in the same position and feel again the blackness of physical control, and my inability to do a thing about it. I was released, but not before I was blue in the face, frightened and humiliated. Quite right too, for I had caused the day to shatter. I found my bow eventually, but never fired it with the same keenness again.

My father knew many people destined for the top of their own tree. A constant friend was Dr. Gordon Smith, an academic with a unique command of Chinese culture and history and a great advocate of my father's many talents. He was a great support in the early days: days of *The Moccus*, a collaborative book project worked on for many years but never published. During the years when *Titus* was being written he was a good critic and friend, supportive and helpful. In later years this influence waned and they geographically and in spirit drifted apart. During my early life in Sark, he would come over to stay and he would take either myself or my brother and I for dare-devil walks and show the exact spots where he and my father nearly came to grief a decade earlier. He was the most marvellous story teller and wove magnificently intricate stories, so that at the end, spellbound, we could have been in the Congo, the Nile

Road to Little Sark, 1948

Clare, Sark, 1949

Delta, or the Gobi, for all my brother or I knew. He had an educated soft voice with inflections that held one gripped at salient points, but it was in the telling of ghost stories that he showed his full talent. We had no electricity for the first two years in Sark, and at night, when the wind howled, he would keep a particularly gruesome and cold story for the time the light had gone, then when huddled around the Aladdin oil stove, he would begin his story. The hair on our heads standing on end, he would sometimes cut off the story in mid-stream and ask, "Who's that?" about a noise the wind had made. This petrified us even more, then he would continue, reaching the denouement slowly, deliberately, culminating sometimes in an unexpected wild shriek. We would be practically beside ourselves with frozen fear at this point, at which he would say, "Time for bed now, boys," as though asking if we would like another cup of tea. Even into our late teenage years, when he used to stay in our Wallington house, he would tell stories, sometimes even not flinching from addressing lots of our friends - up to ten or twelve sometimes. Gordon Smith, or Goatie as he was always known - a nickname my father had given him - drifted out of our lives after Wallington. That was really when my father began the beginnings of his illnesses: he could not cope, I think, with watching the disintegration of his best and only real friend.

Of all my father's paintings my favourite shows me the day of the rentree, and a sadness permeates the picture: the hopeless, helpless look of the boy not ripe for ejection from the bosom of the family, from a peace that I must have so tried to disrupt. This painting, haunting as it is and depicting a dark mood of solitary incomprehension, poses questions when I look at it now, perfectly observed and executed

In Kenneth Grahame's masterpiece *The Wind in the Willows*, the apogee of homesickness, the hatred of the forced separation brought about for whatever reason so poignantly shows the human condition through animal shadows. Mole's rediscovery of his home and his nest and his own place in the world is powerfully put as 'Moley smelt his little hole again': This is the coming home I talk of, and always remember.

With my trunk packed at the door, the wait for the carriage going to the harbour, Armand at hand to say farewell, the cat Chlöe haring up and down the palm tree, the Khaki Campbell ducks quacking on the little pond and the look on my mother's face was always too much for me. My brother's phlegmatic "Oh blow" when the moment of farewell came, was so much braver, philosophical and strong, I caved in to something too big to be contemplated. Down the hill, the creaking wheels over the gravel lanes, along the avenue with its corrugated iron shops to the Carrafour and the descent past the running streams on either side of the harbour hill and the sea. This journey towards another world was like a last journey. On days of rough seas my fear became palpable. I could hardly get on the boat for fear of the unknown, I would grip the handles when on board and ask Jesus to save me, to bring me to some sort of equanimity, to be in control, to try to be calm enough to stand alone, but not frightened or afraid. No one was ever any real help, I tried to be brave, to pretend I wasn't in a type of pain which I still feel acutely, but somehow it never worked.

The wonderful days of boyhood and the lack of responsibility gave the illusion, real at this age of innocence, that nothing was answerable for or to. Heady days in the beating winds that crowd the rocky lanes and hedgerows of Sark. How I loved the wind, watching the 'sea horses' as my father called them, that others were sailing on. Often they were calm, but it seemed the balance was in favour of the rough ride. I hated every minute of being away from home, I was only seven years old when I first went away to boarding school, and each parting was like being pulled off a rock, as though the limpet I felt I was should not be prised off. However I was, for the first time, and my packing done, my trunk painted by my father with my name beautifully painted on the outside with counterpoint colour, nearly filled with the necessary pairs of everything arranged inside, I waited in the hall downstairs. I cried with tears that dazzled me. I always hoped for a reprieve, though this ploy never worked.

Down the harbour hill I went with both my parents, if my father was not away teaching in London. The tiny distance from the house to the boat taking me away, not more than three quarters of a mile was like the walk to the gallows. And on the boat, at either Creux harbour if the sea was calm, or La Maseline if rough, the wrench I always dreaded even into late youth took place. When the ropes splashed down into the water, and there came the slow reversing out from the jetty to the open waters where the boat could turn round for it to head off, it was that tug which the hangman gives the feet to make sure the neck is broken that I felt.

No alleviation to my misery was found in being in new surroundings, in places to discover or in new boys to meet. At this time the nooks and crannies of home, the toys, dens, hiding places, the rope ladders up the trees, the dank, watery smell of the bunker the German occupation force had built in the garden of the chalet, these were everything to me.

But I had to go, and I went to school in Guernsey to a college run by Christian brothers, the first half of their title often at odds with their behaviour. Some were sadists, others latent homosexuals or other oddities who didn't do a great deal for my general education in any subject as far as I can remember. Becoming champion at two highly intellectual subjects, weight lifting and roller skating, was about the apex of my achievements.

On being sent away to boarding school at the age of eight, I felt bereft. I quote the short letter below, that I sent before we were granted permission to write home, which was only given after a month into the new term. Pocket money was not allowed, and stamps

Sebastian, Circa 1948

could only be bought from the headmaster, so having stolen the paper and envelope, I finally stole the stamp by going through his study to find one. Then, in September 1948, I wrote to my parents for the first time:

> *Sebastian*
>
> *... Dear Mummy I do do wish you would come O please come mummy come mummy   Seddy*

This letter, from Les Vauxblets College, Guernsey, was followed by others, not always quite so pleading for a return home, but all similar in tone. Once, following the discovery of the arms dump, (of which more later), I did write very excitedly in a happier frame of mind:

> *Les Vauxblets*
>
> *...dear mummy and fay i hope you are well i am bringing some nives and too helmets one for fay and one for me i got them from the gurmen tunels in the tunels it was very smely and a boy went with a candle and set the tunels on fire with love from Sebb*

Gloom descended again, and long before the next half term arrived, I was feeling very lonely and disturbed, living incarcerated in what felt like, and resembles, an impenetrable, dark castle. The pleading continued:

> *dear mummy i am looking forward to seeing you dear mummy i want you to come over and get me at half term i am sending these nots*

and they are called testimon, tales and will you sine them at the

back and send back as soon as you can with lots of love from sebby

Finally, the Christmas holiday was approaching and in my fourth Vauxblets letter to my mother and fay, - Fabian my younger brother - I wrote:

...dear mummy and fay i hope you are well we went to the end of

the island and had a nice time i climbed a big rock there. i am

lokiking forward to Christmas with love from Sebastian

I inherited all my mother's correspondence, letters and writings after she died and amongst them all I found every letter I had ever written her, which she had kept chronologically and had marked them, '1st letter', '2nd letter' and so on. They must have been quite precious to her. For the son of not one but two writers, my handwriting was awful, for I was already eight when the first one was written. Ungrammatical, rather tragic and naive, I used only lower case, misspelt my own nickname, and signed myself in each of the four quoted with a different name. I always felt myself to be very unhappy as a boy, and that perhaps submerged somewhere in my being, there was something stunting my ability to listen and learn. Then, only one year later and just before the last half term before being sent to my next boarding school, I wrote in quite clear writing and in ink - all the previous letters had been in pencil -

Dear mummy and daddy. I hope you are. I am very well thank you

for the parcels you sent me there is only 1 week and 6 days till

half term and then you sead that daddy would send me one of

thoes modeled aeroplanes to play with in the roady room. thre
lites went out on tuesday and Brother Charles told us a gost
story of when he was going on his bike when he sor sparks
comming out of the grave and a figure of a gost coming out of
the gra
pto.
ve

  With love from
  Sebby and fai

(My brother joined me at Les Vauxblets for a couple of terms in the winter of 1949). At the end of the letter I executed a strange drawing before signing myself again underneath.

The drawing is of a ghost-like apparition emerging from a coffin, his arms and legs shackled in awful looking metal clamps which pinion him. From a bubble he is saying 'i am a gost'. The letter ends:

...'from sebby', under that drawing. The words 'from sebby' are incorporated into the body of the coffin, and it is probably this fixation with death and its doings that gave rise to the ubiquitous doodlings of coffins and coffin shaped boxes with the crucifix always embossed on top during the unhappy years of my failed marriage.

I used to be teased about my Christian name and was bullied quite a bit, but I learned early on that surreptitiousness helped to keep me from the major bullies' attention. I picked up the facility of appearing so innocent that even if I were the culprit of an escapade I didn't get the blame.

There was a Spaniard there who used to pick frogs up by their hind legs and with a machete type knife slice them in two to watch the legs continue to squirm after dissection. Later he became

more adventurous and created a primitive type of pistol which I used
to watch him making. One night he went out of the dormitory and shot
a cow to see what would happen; It died later and he was expelled.

Fights in the dormitory between enemies were
arranged for after lights out at 7 p.m. and were quite vicious. When I
couldn't get out of one, as I'd been seen as the culprit in someone's eyes,
then I would do my best, but these nocturnal events rarely involved
me. I was much busier listening to someone or other's crystal set under
the sparse bedclothes.

This order of Catholic educationalists believed in
strict regimes for young boys: the windows were left open at night,
only one blanket was allowed and a 6 a.m. rise was the order of things.
In the mornings the brother on duty would come into the dormitory
clapping his hands loudly (still echoing in my ears to this day) and if
one didn't get up immediately, then, on his return journey down the
line of the double tiered bunks, he would pull all the bedclothes off and
beat the offender. As the windows were left open, even in winter, it
was often freezing and immediately on getting up out of bed, we had
to form two queues fanning out from the first in line just outside the
wash basins. Strict silence was maintained and any noise resulted in
'the shower'. That was the punishment meted out for any minor
infraction. It could have been seen as a special privilege to have a
shower cubicle to oneself, if it hadn't been for the fact that icy cold
water was used, and some of these brothers in Christ would deliberately
take the soap from the dish in the cubicle, drop it on the base of the
shower, then demand its being picked up, and with the culprit's back
to him, would then rain blows on the boy's backside.

Dressed, we marched in lines down to Mass, which
we had every day just to remind us, I suppose, of forgiveness, humility
and love, before the silence of breakfast in the refectory. Talking was
only allowed occasionally, when the high table and the headmaster
and his lackeys ordained. No free-for-all ever ensued, but subdued

mutterings, as fear of far worse treatment than the soap dropping (or the 'chocolate' that I had yet to experience), would be the consequences of the pent up enthusiasm of wild boys from six to fifteen years of age. I don't expect any of the parents of the 180 or so boys during the 1940's at this College would have believed stories of the cruelty and ignorance that went on at this supposed place of education.

I had only been at the place some three weeks when, as a result of not answering a question correctly, I was brought before the class and asked if I would like some chocolate. "Yes Sir", was my fairly greedy reply, at which the chuckling from some of the class should have warned me that chocolate was the one thing I wouldn't be getting. "Hand out, boy", the master said, "Would you like a big piece or a little?" "A small piece, sir," I said, hoping to have caught on a bit to the clue in a sense I'd been given by some of the class. With that the stick he had been holding behind his back came down with a memorable swish on my outstretched hand. This happened not once but six times, with blood drawn from the soft area at the base of the right thumb testifying to its being a 'chocolate' worth having. Boys answering "a big piece" got six on each hand. The boys' pact of silence concerning the punishment I broke on behalf of the new boys of the following year, a disclosure for which I paid dearly, not only from the old timers but from this same sadistic brother. He chose me to grasp Jesus's suffering at Easter by being given holly leaves to wear, next to my skin under my shirt, which he ground into my chest with vigour.

The atmosphere of the place was strangely one of aimlessness. Although classes started on time, and routine marked the day to lights out, the war, (which had only just finished) the occupation of Guernsey throughout the duration; and the fact that tanks and guns left by the Germans were still on the playing fields nine months after liberation, all made for a frustrated feeling of directionless change.

The great drama of the place was supplied by Brother Charles. He was tall, well built, quite handsome and a poor teacher. What he loved most was to take his chosen pupils with him on his trips around the island at night and, leaving after lights out, he would drive them out on secret missions in the Fordson lorry that belonged to the College, and which was usually used for taking the farm produce from the school to St Peter Port on market days. This open backed, three ton lorry had a flat metal floor and 13 inch wooden side boards, and seemed to always be in very good condition. I think it was his pride and joy.

I was still, at about eight and a half years old, a bit too young to have gained favour with him as an older 'chosen one' would do, but as the academic side of things didn't so much impress him and it had come to his attention that I consistently came top at roller skating and weight lifting, I think he must have felt that I had the makings of one of his nocturnal accomplices.

Nothing was ever spoken about what they all did at night, but little by little, finding my way into the inner sanctum of the special group, it came to light that these trips had something to do with taking notes on smuggling round the coast. It must have been in the autumn of 1949, when the leaves from the trees started to make their annual flight into independence and death, that I was first asked if I'd like to join the team. We crept out of the dormitories, Brother Charles having as always given a list of names to the night brothers on dormitory duty so as to let us out, but not without the muffled cries of jealousy from those not allowed to join us, and then, hearts beating, we all met in the back lane beside the school farm.

It was very dark, but he drove only on side lights, and the lorry weaved about the country lanes as we held tight to its sides, since the metal floor was very slippery. After 20 minutes or so we stopped on a cliff above one of the bays. The lights had been doused some time before we arrived at the destination and then with his finger to his lips indicating silence, we followed him down a rough path behind some rocks. After a few minutes he waved his hand for us to crouch down, for he'd seen what we'd come to find. Very dimly visible 100 yards away at the shoreline was a group of dark figures at the edge of the sea, and further away two men in a small boat which was bobbing in the water. My heart was beating and I'm sure the others felt the same excitement as the contraband from the boat was handed to the group on the shore - we were watching smugglers in action.

Our job it seemed was to gather some sort of idea of the amounts of boxes, packets and other objects being handed over. We had to be absolutely still, of course, as to be heard or noticed would have caused at best some sort of attack or aggression, as these smugglers were Breton fishermen bringing in cigarettes and drink, and were risking a great deal in this hazardous trade.

It appears that some 10,000 cigarettes and 50 cases of spirits were handed over that night, for our purposes it seemed was not just to count the contraband, but to report where it subsequently went to. The boat was then pushed out after it was emptied by those on the shore and we heard garbled patois farewells being exchanged. It was time for the men with the goods to start the tedious job of taking all the boxes across the beach and up the cliff path to the waiting van.

Brother Charles had obviously been at this for some time, for he knew where the stuff would arrive, but never when. And so it was that these nightly vigils brought Guernsey and several French fishermen from the Cartaret region of Brittany before the local magistrates in due course.

These hazardous sea journeys of what appeared brave men in hindsight made less than glamorous reading. At the time, cigarettes were in very short supply and in France Gaulois and Gitanes were very cheap and plentiful. Cognac, Cointreau, Benedictine, unavailable things of pre-war luxury, were craved by some in Britain, so a small trade started between France and the Channel Islands in these sought-after items of civilised life. The perpetrators usually got a few weeks inside or were deported if caught, and what then seemed so shady, dangerous and *Treasure Island*-like in its impact on me, was really just small time trading between allies in different parts of the Channel.

The Germans had left in 1945 and in September 1948, when I joined the school and started making those sad journeys away from home, across the stretch from Sark to Saint Peter Port, much of their presence on the islands had disappeared. There were, of course, all the hideouts built into the cliffs and the underground hospital, but of the posters, placards on walls and shop fronts, all these were torn down and burnt very soon after they had left. What had not gone was far more exciting for a boy of nine years old, and formed one of the most adventurous parts of my early life. Brother Charles had discovered, and had kept secret, a cache of hidden German arms. In one cave, guns, pistols, bayonets, swords, emblems, flags, and insignia of every type had been found behind a beautifully disguised, imitation rock, hinged and made to fit exactly in front of the entrance of a cave in a very quiet bay, under an overhanging cliff.

This secret discovery, made by a German speaking islander who had overheard a conversation at the docks just before the occupying forces had left hastily to return to France, was passed on to Brother Charles, who had a knack of being the confidant of many. I'm sure that the Christian Brothers' calling was a hollow life for this swashbuckler who was just like us, a boy at heart.

I had not known initially about this arms find and found out only by a blabbermouth talking, after a friend of his was asked to go and see, but not him. Piqued, he let on to one or two of us, and thereby incurred the full wrath of Bro' Charles. The boy in question who'd given the show away wore the stripe marks on his hands and backsides for days and bandages were needed for the pummelling his body received. He had not let it be known where the cave with the false boulder in front was, as he didn't know, but it made the excitement, now that it was known about, impossible to contain, and the whole thing, even for the select few of Charles' trusties was dropped. This poor fellow then found himself at the receiving end of kicks and blows administered after lights out for preventing this prize 'boys-own' drama from being enacted.

Bro' Charles, like all the others, was called by the shortened form of address, except when a boy was being punished, at which moment it was not allowed to shorten this title even in supplication. This order formed to specialise in the tilling of the soil to emulate Jesus' pastoral and rural image, were outstanding cowherds, butter makers and producers of honey, but as far as I was concerned and judging by the results, were not the cream of the teaching profession.

The temptation was too great for such as Bro' Charles to resist, and it seeped into the daily knowledge of the unsaid that he would like to pick a crew to join him in the lorry in a few days time, to examine the cave. This possibility held captive all our imaginative powers from the first we heard of it.

Intense was the competition within the coterie of 'probables' vying for his favour; sycophancy knew no bounds. My plan, however, was to act as though it didn't matter, as though not to be asked along wouldn't hurt. The question was how to appear uninterested, but also to be asked for this most sought-after sortie. My evolving plan was to ask open, simple questions of the favourite of the bunch likely to go when Charles was not around, like: "Where do you think the cave is?" or "If you are asked what would you most want to get for yourself: a gun, knife, or bayonet?" This particular boy was, however, far too concerned with keeping his mind on the matter at hand, which was to have Bro' Charles constantly aware of his presence, to care about minors' questions.

One evening, the rumour went round that there was to be a meeting to decide the six boys to go. Usually for trips with him Brother Charles would take about 12 or 15 of us, and when it was discovered that only six of us would be picked, my hopes, rightly as it turned out, faded. The day arrived that the six were announced, most of them his closest confidants, not, sadly, including me. They were to leave after lights out and they should each bring a torch. When they got back about eleven p.m. we were all asleep and as none of them who had been were in my dormitory, I had to wait until the morning for the news of the trip. It transpired that it was not an exaggeration; the rumours were true: The cave was indeed full to bursting with armaments of all kinds. The half dozen boys and Bro' Charles had had a job pulling back the imitation boulder, as it had not been opened for some time, and at night darkness made it more difficult. It was absolutely illegal not to declare arms discoveries after the war, and in addition to this the overriding concern for Bro' Charles was the explosive gas inside the cave, for there were gas cannisters there that might be triggered by a boy bringing matches. This fear of explosion shortly had terrible consequences, but for the first foray the boys safely followed Charles.

Those who went there brought back booty which made our impressionable eyes stare: beautifully made daggers with the Iron Cross inlaid in the handles; Luger pistols and leather cartridge holders complete with bullets; sub machine guns; bayonets and ceremonial swords; officers uniforms; helmets and the awful S.S. death's head insignia were all displayed in the dormitories. These articles created such wonderment in the eyes of most of us that the pressure was then unleashed to get either one of the boys (sworn to secrecy) to tell us where the cave was, or to persuade Bro' Charles to take another group.

The days went by. No one would let on, Bro' Charles became quiet and less approachable, and little by little the whole ambiance of the college seemed to change. To those still mad keen to make this journey to get some of the prizes for themselves, hope

began to fade. And then the thing happened that, I suppose, Bro'
Charles had always feared: one of the original six mentioned at a
moment of indiscretion, when showing his Luger to some excited
onlookers, that the cave was to be found on the south west tip of the
island and that the boulder could be prised back only by pulling from
about half way up it on the right hand side facing it.

        This was my moment. I knew the boy whom he
had told, who then confided in me and without waiting any longer the
two of us vowed to creep out that night without permission. We had
a torch each and had to creep out past the night duty master down the
main staircase and through a window by the front door which was
locked, the key being with the night janitor. We had to leave it very
late as at night conversations were in progress often until nine p.m. or
later, with the topic often that about which we now could wait no
longer in discovering for ourselves.

        Of course we had to walk, that was the only way,
and it took one and a half hours to clamber down the rough path to the
beach at the sides of which the caves were to be found. This particular
cave was soon seen in front of which the roundish boulder was to be
found under a windy moonscape and trembling with nerves, cold, fear
and blissful excitement, we heaved at the retaining facsimile and there
before our torchlit eyes was an arsenal for our taking. We had agreed
between ourselves, Taylor and I, that we would not be greedy and
would each take only a representative selection. The cave held a
mountain of weapons and the slightly gassy, greasy smell of this
enclosed space made it also very frightening. Thinking of its original
purpose, I wanted to make my choice and get out back to the college
and bed. Taylor felt the same, and with a Luger, bayonet, dagger,
helmet and ceremonial sword each we left. We pushed back the
boulder and ran, clutching our booty to us closely all the way back
with a couple of breach loaders, back through the window still slightly
ajar, up past the snoring night duty brother and putting the weapons

very quietly beneath our mattresses, we had successfully completed the whole enterprise without being noticed.

A few weeks later tragedy struck. Two boys from the school ignored the warnings about gas and struck matches on entering the cave, so blowing themselves up and with it the dump (which the authorities still didn't know about) and injured several who were still outside. The scandal that broke out over the arms dump and how a Christian Brother from one of the best schools in the Channel Islands could let his pupils see and not report this find, caused him, the school, parents, boys and the authorities the greatest amount of trouble.

The boys had long since hidden their treasures and in my case to this day cannot remember exactly where under the palm tree in our garden in Sark I secreted mine. I feel like Jim in *Treasure Island* when I remember back to those dark nights on the island, when the stuff off dreams was made reality. I'd hidden my treasures there at dusk I remember, before I left for another term at Vauxblets the following day.

Les Vauxblets, now a carpet warehouse, was eventually closed as a school when non-Catholics heavily outnumbered the original Catholics as pupils. It is a dark red building set in fine and extensive grounds with the small shell chapel a place of interest. At Easter we would take it in turns to light candles in the little windows and ledges inside and a priest was on hand to say Mass occasionally so that from outside on autumn days the flickering of the candlelight through the windows from afar made a haunting impression as the light was reflected from off the millions of shells inside. At the little shop not far from the College gates I would spend my 6d a week on condensed milk, which I loved, perforating the small tins with two holes, one opposite the other, and pull hard on the solid liquid from inside. I would have to save up for some time for these tins, but when I'd scraped the money together it would be a great treat going to the shop.

The tuck shop had its opening hours at the school half an hour at lunch time and in the evenings before benediction, a daily event, and I would sometimes, if not saving for the condensed milk, spend it on Aero chocolate.

The result of my time at the Vauxblets was a grounding in teaching at an impressionable age as being a take it or leave it affair with the two extremes of severe physical punishment for even minor infractions, vindictiveness from unfulfilled men who maintained a position somewhere between the lay and the ordained members of their religion and the totally lax attitudes of heroes like Brother Charles, a man for all boys of adventure but not for the history student. At least not for those waverers amongst us, those who find the temptation to fool about, run rings around weaker purveyors of knowledge, and those whose sense of an open opportunity for freedom from scholastic constriction too much to miss. My time there came to an end in 1950, and apart from a short break at home after we had left the Channel Islands for good to settle in Chelsea, my education, so-called, in Sark and Guernsey was over.

CHAPTER 4

CHELSEA

– And my later childhood

In the dark studio again in between houses I spent the winter meeting lots of interesting people, friends of my parents. There was Peter Ustinov who lived up the road, who always said hallo to me; Quentin Crisp and his brightness often seemed nearby. This was just an interlude, for although my father taught at the Westminster School of Art and had exhibited at the Royal Academy, it was his writing that occupied a lot of his time, although poetry-writing, painting and the drawings of all sorts came unhesitatingly from his imaginings. This time in Chelsea was a remaking of friendships and acquaintances after the period spent in Sark.

My brother and I were often asked to go to parties at friends of my parents, who had children of similar ages. Moist sandwiches, egg and cress, thinly sliced cheese, or ham, lettuce and cucumber, under muslin on silver trays, sometimes even staff serving them. The Countess of Moray, a friend of my parents, would ask us to her house in Ebury Street or her other place in Hans Crescent and we would meet Augustus John, Dylan Thomas, Graham Greene or Rodney Ackland; the list went on and on. Later in my boyhood, until I was sixteen or so, I would ask my father to keep the letters of famous people who wrote to him, so I could save them. Because of this, he kept a wonderful letter book for me, into which I pasted the signatures of famous people. In some cases, if the letters were short, he would paste the whole letter. Orson Welles, Alec Guinness, Edith Evans, Laurence Olivier, Stephen Spender, Walter de la Mare, Dylan Thomas, Anthony Quayle: all wrote encouragingly, sometimes ecstatically, of his *Titus* books, or his poems, or both. Without my knowing it, he made a full

Sebastian, Circa 1951

book collection of these names and presented it to me on one of my birthdays. Once I lent it to someone to look at, who cut out Dylan Thomas' signature and later gave it back to someone else, who in turn gave it back to me. Otherwise, it is intact. Under each signature or letter, my father wrote the name, just in case I couldn't read the original. At the time I saw it as a little book for me which he had time to assemble for me. These were just people writing to him, who all admired his work. Only later did I realise that this was something unique and rare; only then did I appreciate the significance of the names which he had collected, not all of whom I knew.

Later, writers like Michael Moorcock, J.G. Ballard, and the poet Michael Horowitz attended the parties given by my parents. The art critic Edwin Mullins; the Oriental specialist of an older generation, John Brophy and his daughter Bridget, were all frequent visitors. In a way, looking at those parties from far off, they left me with a grounding in the language of writers that I can't now do without. I think the atmosphere was generated a great deal by the host and hostess, the ability to listen and to encourage, and the total lack of cleverness, the absence of the gratuitous non sequiturs.

My father had a collection of coats, including a marvellous camel hair one from China. It really was made from camel hide, it smelt, had holes in it and was completely hideous, but was utterly rare. He also had African chiefs' capes, Spanish capes and a great dark blue cape with a brass buckle and pink silk lining. With this on and his lone earring, worn before it became fashionable, my father attracted attention, sometimes indeed provoking aggressive, physical combat and accusations of being homosexual. A more unlikely condition than the last cannot be imagined. I do not know the number of female admirers my father had, but if the line of women I shook hands with recently after a lecture on him is anything to go by, then homosexual he certainly was not. In flowing cape, dark hair brushed back, odd coloured socks, often striding, a handsome, talented young artist, the world of his youth, wherever he was, must have been his oyster. His great array of capes and coats, jerkins and leather jackets, corduroy suits, were all worn with marvellous abandon, as a true original. I emulated him later but much less daringly, being far more conservative, and with a nauseating self-awareness that he did not possess. I wore trench coats which, although worn by Americans, Frenchmen and Italians were still not worn by their originators, the British – or at least the trenchcoat still did not capture the romance that the European brings to it.

　　　　　　　　　I don't think my father had any real enemies. Apart from the mad woman of Chelsea, who put the cheese wire across their front door at throat level, luckily noticed in time, I know of no circumstance in which enmities were made. My father was a taciturn man. As an artist, he knew a lot of the intense feelings that arguments provoked. He knew when the argument was in full swing, that if opposite views prevailed, to join one side or other might lead to physical confrontation, and these often took place in Soho bars, as painters argued different points – bloodied noses, broken arms. Rubens or Delacroix, Matisse or Renoir, Giacometti or Klee: was the fight worth it? He thought not, unless there was real conviction, unless in a way total honour depended on it. From the colourful, spontaneous, histrionic exhibitionism of many of these arguments he fought, you might say, shy. I cannot always maintain his distance. For instance, I maintain that the heroism of the fighters in the Warsaw Ghetto, cooped up in rat-infested sewers, as their city crumbled about them, when they went on and on, as did the partisans in Primo Levi's *If Not Now When?*, this represents some of the greatest acts of exemplary courage in history. On mentioning this to a German friend once, and a Russian on another occasion, and being told that in their opinion the Poles were fools, I would in this case defend my corner to a point at which, if enmity ensued, then that enmity provoked was the concomitant of belief. One of the main reasons for not having had any enemies, I think, was that my father worked best within the family, learning of its workings and thereby knew much more about his wife, children and home than would have been the case if he had gone out to work in the normal way.   He taught life painting and drawing at the Royal Academy Schools, the Central School and other institutions, but at all other times he worked from his own home.   He has always been something of an unknown figure, for all his fame with his *Titus* books, his *Glassblowers* poems, his illustrations of many of the classics, his plays and drawings, oil paintings and talents as a teacher.   This ignorance of him as a man, apart from the establishment's bumbling ineptness in accepting him, instead of ignoring him in their gauche, "We don't know where to place him" excuses, is due in great part to the fact that his huge outpourings took an enormous amount of the short time he had on earth.   When in due course the Aladdin's cave of his genius is opened and the coy and the uncommitted venture in, brave enough to find that they haven't been bitten in the process, they will exclaim: "This Mervyn Peake - of course we have always known about him, always was my favourite illustrator".

I'd like to write about my mother now.   Mother. What a small word to contain the essence of man.   My love of personal apartheid, or, more prosaically put, distance from human involvement, stems in large measure from her.   It wasn't, of course, that the person she was with smelt, or whatever, or even that there was a profoundly off-putting aspect to their nature, but that the close proximity of someone else simply provokes a need for attention.   The problem gets, as it were, out of hand, as in my case, when I feel that I am set apart. The way a guest holds his knife, if at the same time the conversation in progress involved the deepest of examinations of the first few bars of the Fourth Movement of Mahler's Ninth Symphony and their presaging imminent war, should not matter, but it does.   Its mattering, however skilfully argued, lies at a most primitive level of prejudice and cannot, I think, be avoided.   Prejudice it is and remains.   My mother would not say a word about it, but a woman who had made no obvious effort to make the best of herself and was a guest, or had been met at a party or on introduction, did not receive the immediate attention a well dressed female would elicit.

Mummy, and later Mum, could be the only appellations I ever used, although I would have found it pretty hard to say Mummy in company and didn't ever say it from my fifteenth or sixteenth birthday on. If, on Sark I was naughty or had misbehaved - a daily occurrence - she would ask me to go up to her bedroom when my father was away teaching and would whack me with her hairbrush, either on the hand or bottom: it really stung and sometimes she would be so angry I would be given the full treatment: hand and bottom. Off I would go again, apparently contrite and reformed, back to tantalising something or other, someone or other, until the next time I was caught. Earlier I spoke of her dress sense and her predilection for clothes. Very often I would watch her dressing, putting on make-up or choosing the combinations of things to wear. Certain patterns, as we all know do not go together; nor certain combinations of colour or material; but at the point at which the subtlety of dress sense takes over, a point where many allow a cursory 'That'll do' attitude to guide them, there she would begin to seek a rarer harmony. This called for an expert eye; but then she was a painter and was always fashionable in her appearance. She would never leave her room before feeling right. This 'feeling right', really a need to be noticed, to be admired, was very noticeable throughout her life, and she certainly was noticed. When she entered a room, one felt her presence and this, allied with the fine exploitation of her obvious beauty, made many gasp. She was so obviously in a different class. This quality had another side to it, and if she wasn't noticed, then one fairly soon found out. Her tendency to require compliments once led to my father saying, to my brother and I, that we must always be sure that Mummy is not upset and that we should always treat her well and say how nice she looked. He had a little rhyme, the words of which were changed from the nursery rhyme, and went:

> We love little Mummy her coat is so warm
> And if we don't hurt her she'll do us no harm.

I remember singing this fairly frequently during my life, from about the age of eight until my early teenage years. For the most part, it was sufficient to notice the way she was dressed, the food was presented, the things she did for the family, but as with most people. Her humour was charming, and in a way incongruous in a beautiful woman. She had always told us how, as a girl, she would limp on purpose. My desire to be discovered beaten and bloody in a gutter, and at one stage to orchestrate arguments that could lead to fights, was from the same source: insecurity. It is easy to be clever about this need for recognition as being odd or indescribably juvenile in intent, but I would maintain that her method and mine were just our way of doing the same thing that many others do, but in different ways.

At breakfast my mother would place puffed wheat pieces under her top gum so that they stuck to the inside of her top lip and then, opening her mouth, let out a blood-curdling witch's cackle. The puffed wheat would look as though they were filthy old teeth and complete a face now contorted and made as ugly as possible with the shutting of her eye, into a real witch. This witch's cackle, which she often used at unexpected moments, was very realistic and was when I was younger, quite terrifying. A habit to which she was frequently prone was of asking for a number from one to ten, and then going off into her own thoughts. The particular number given then translated the letters from A to J. After switching off after, say, the letter C was given, she would metaphorically disappear leaving us to our own thoughts. Now, years after her premature death, these idiosyncracies seem isolated and divorced from them when they happened almost daily.

She had a range of little tricks to play on us. At meal times she would sometimes hand over our plates after serving the food with just one pea on the plate, or would give us coffee in dolls' house cups and be absolutely serious about it, as the look on her face showed. The others, after having asked permission, would begin to eat, those with normal helpings, while the person with the tiny helping would have to wait. We would then all burst out laughing and she would let the sufferer of the day have their food. One certainly couldn't have got annoyed, even when famished. That would not have been accepted and usually it <u>was</u> great fun. Only when it went on for too long did it pall, although any hint of its irritating us would have caused her to change her mood and she might say "Don't you like my little joke?" "Of course, Mummy." Lots of these sort of things were in her repertoire, like placing things at the very edge of tables so they looked as though they would fall off, or wearing a collapsible top hat and holding a cane as she did a magnificent interpretation of a Marlene Dietrich sexy song in German. My mother spoke German, so the authenticity of the 'Lili Marlene' song or 'Ich bin von kopf biss fuss auf liebe eingestellt' ('Falling in love again') came across wonderfully, as she slowly danced on our famous Sark pine table after lunch and the dishes had been cleared away. She was not an ordinary mother, she was my mother, and had qualities that emerged because they were uniquely hers. My father's catalytic and singular influence gave her the moment and the security to expand from the shy cocoon of an Irish Catholic upbringing into the wholly original woman that she became. She loved my father with a partisan fanaticism with which a genius is sometimes rewarded.

'... Into the sculpture room he came, quick and sudden and dark, and when he left the room they said, "That's Mervyn Peake; he's dying of consumption." For me, at seventeen, someone dying of consumption (even though he was not) had a terrible romance about it!' So begins my mother's book of her life with my father and *A World Away* traces her life with him from that young age to his death in 1968. She ends: 'You have gone. I long to see you again.' Her book, published and written within only a year of his death, is a *tour de force* in its romantic tragedy and is tender and loving, perceptive and quiet, as well as being a controlled display of what human dignity is able to achieve. The display of grief by Wagner's widow at the graveside is surely what my mother felt; so, probably, did many wives of the uniquely talented. Somehow, the prerequisite control was achieved and my mother went on after his death to make sure she did everything she could to advance his reputation. In the 1970's, when his book sales were fairly low, when the discovery had not yet been made of his contribution to illustrate classics, his poetry for the most part unread, she went on and on and in a very solitary way. It is this mission that I see as my life's work as well. One day, when the wider reading public becomes aware of his talents and not just the imaginative and sensitive ten per cent, her work (and my continuation of it) will be vindicated.

Just after I was born I was photographed by my father with Polyphoto, which at that time was a very new method of photography and usually used for baby bubbling and dolled up in party best, propped against cushions, possibly smiling. I was photographed in a series of 100 pictures in all manner of nude relaxation. 'Sebastian at 10 days' this group was called, and he suggested that a black cloth be laid out on the studio floor and that I should just move about freely. Some of the shots show that if he had been interested in the subject he could have been a good photographer. These pictures, and the many many taken by my parents, began a collection of albums which in the end contains snaps and composed photographs that spanned the one taken just after I was born in 1940 through my mother's early years to my records of my sister. Some taken by my mother on Sark at the grand fancy dress competition held in 1948 especially for the then Princess Elizabeth's visit to the island, beautifully capture the exotic apparel designed and put together by my father. I spoke of the day earlier in this story and my waiter to Fabian's clown is a case in point. It was not just an instant composite but brought out the hopes for success in those boys' faces.

My mother had a habit, which unfortunately I have inherited, of gripping the thumbs in the palms of her hands, or pressing different fingers into contortions that brought the white to the surface. A need to cling onto security perhaps, but one I think I make a more conscious effort to eradicate than she did. Trailing my arm outside my bed in hot weather to achieve a coolness, would only be feasible for a second or so, because I always felt that someone was going to come from somewhere and touch or grip my hand. I am not sure if there is a connection between the gripping of my thumb and a feeling of fear at being touched by the unknown other hand, but a feeling persists.

The short stories that she wrote, observations of the way that people behave to each other, often unaware of the effects they have on others, were acutely seen through a gifted eye. These stories, which are unpublished, show how much we are unaware that a change takes place when one person says something to another whose experience of life is different; thus both people, although speaking the same language, hear different things, different meanings, and as Louis MacNeice observed 'Two people with one pulse'. This would have been her goal.

CHAPTER 5

KENT

– A Georgian House amidst
the hops and orchards

Our next house, in Smarden in Kent, a Georgian manor house, had proportions of great beauty, with columns outside, long sash windows and a vast greenhouse to one side. It had a pond with fish and an apple orchard of over an acre. As I was eleven years old and had already lived in six houses, I was getting quite used to moving about with my parents. The nomadic life already lay in my character.

My next school, the local village one, does not impress itself greatly on my memory, perhaps as my short time there was less than a year. Perhaps the most exciting event of our time in Kent was the arrival of the Peake's first car. An engineer friend of my parents made its delivery one day. He had a very pretty daughter, taller than me by a foot, who once, when I met her in our years in Chelsea, used some wildly bad language, which both shocked and fascinated me. Now she accompanied her father when he secretly delivered our car. For my parents to own a car was like me taking a post in pure maths at a university, so when, on the day after I'd arrived home, I was led blindfolded to the garage by a small family group, I was quaking with excitement.

The door was opened to reveal what would now be a collector's piece: a 1936 Wolsey with bonnet temperature gauge, sun roof and wire wheels, and with the engineer, his daughter and my mother and father looking on, I smiled and said "Cor! Terrific, a car!" My father could never hold secrets, but bizarrely thought I could put it from my mind if he **hinted** at something. He had vaguely mentioned a Wolsey, and the idea had been going around in my head like the whirl of dervishes ever since that hint was let loose. At the time, *Fabian of the Yard* and most other British police stories on film featured the chases using the Wolsey 6/80, a mighty, usually black painted powerful car that had, for its time, a most modern and lovely shape. But the Wolsey that arrived was nothing like a 6/80: this was the rural midwife's car, the old gentleman's carriage. Inside my heart gasped in dismay, but outwardly I grinned with boyish pleasure and I hoped I hadn't given the show away.

At the same time, Victoria, the engineer's daughter, made her entrance into my own growing awareness of womens' pull over me. Unfortunately she and her father didn't stay after they had delivered the old romantic car, but left immediately. The impression she made was not so much of her as an actual person, for she was older and I didn't know her, but of the tempting lure of which I'm sure she was unaware; that opposite that seems magnetic.

In the apple orchard, my parents' beloved cat had a hole in one of the bigger trees in which it would sit attempting to snap at, and always miss, the birds perching in the branches above. Chlöe had been with us through five moves and even in Kent at ten years old she still had a long life left, until the last pathetic attempt to climb the stairs in a future house brought her tumbling down, the strength having given out. She died while on her way to the airing cupboard on the first floor, her favourite spot.

Gypsies sometimes parked their caravans at the end of the orchard beyond our land and were often moved on. Occasionally they stayed for a few weeks and the wooden, highly coloured, horse drawn vehicles were visible through the trees in the Spring before the leaves were fully out on the apple trees. Once I went with the wife of the leader of the band of wanderers and some of their children blackberrying in a local wood. The Romany dialect was still very much in use and at the times of hop picking, apple or potato harvesting, they made some cash labouring for local farmers. This blackberrying was on a day off for them, so I joined them. A rather more unpleasant part of that rural afternoon came about when the gypsy woman in question said that she "wanted a shit", lifted up her skirt and did just that. No under garments needed to be removed, she had none. This rather displeasing interlude, from which I stole away, did make me very aware that the gypsies at the bottom of the garden had quite different habits from ours. I don't think a self respecting Romany would lure an innocent from the house to go blackberrying just to shock. It seems that she just was not used to the sanitized ways of others. Her appearance was alarming. She was beefy, with a wild eye and a powerful voice. If at closing time, or even approaching it, she peered through the public bar window (this being before the 'No Travellers' signs were put up), and saw her husband reeling about singing too loudly or in any way misbehaving, she would punch him heftily and drag him out, back to the gaily painted but grubby interiors of their caravan.

There was a very old lady in the village who made things for my mother to give as presents on birthdays and Christmas and Easter holidays, things like jumpers, knitted skirts and gloves. She lived just on the outskirts of the village in an ancient cottage that had no electricity inside, water or lavatory and certainly no bathroom, near a reed inlet which was home to moorhens and coots. She always reminded me of a witch, but was a knitter of the first order. When sent to collect whatever she had finished, I liked to leave quickly. Although she was only an old lady and allegedly harmless, the long long fingers and the black fingernails which completed the ends of her bony arms always caught my breath. One dusk, arriving for a collection I walked up her path, the flickering candle visible through the tiny window at one side of the front door, and I heard whispering coming from the little reed bed opposite. I felt terrified and only stayed a moment or so, thanking her for her lovely work as quickly as I could and wished her goodnight. There was not a sound as I left and I ran home the half a mile or so with my heart pumping. I discovered later that the same gypsies set traps for ducks and other water birds often found in this slightly marshy land.

Like many boys, I was fascinated when crime came to the village. A celebrated murder happened in Smarden in the early 1950's when a local girl was murdered, then discovered some days later by frogmen who dredged the village pond. A local man, himself thought 'odd' by the villagers, was apprehended and was tried for murder, but because of his state of mind he was sent to Broadmoor. In retrospect this is horrifying but it captivated me then. During the dredging, the local village school was shut as the pond was adjacent to it, so we had time off which pleased me even more. This school gave the first public performance of my father's play *The Wit to Woo*, which was later so badly received in London. At the village school the one production that was put on was an immense success. The locals clapped, and at the end I stood up and in a clear penetrating voice announced, "My father wrote that play!" I felt great pride, though now I feel a kind of embarrassment. "That's interesting," some said to me or "I know he did, his name is on the front of the programme," all in an amiable tone and a far cry from the public and humiliating panning the London critics gave it later. In time it was vindicated by Laurence Olivier's letter that says that he'd 'just read your exciting and highly original play that Vivien (Leigh) and I would like to do'. They didn't, unfortunately, but so much of his work was far too good and far ahead of its time.

I was now ready for senior school. Had we stayed in the Channel Islands I might have gone to the senior part of Vauxblets, but having moved back to England, another Christian brothers' establishment was sought for me to attend. The nearest, Mayfield College, was only 20 miles away. I had got used to being a day boy for the time we were in London and couldn't bear the thought of yet another boarding school, especially of this kind. Mayfield College reminded me of Colditz, stark, red brick, in a hollow and facing wooded, undulating land which sloped away, down to the playing fields and to the permanently dirty and slime covered swimming pool. They gave it a wash and brush up once a term.

The news that I was going away again I took with a sinking heart, and I implored, cajoled and almost broke down over not being sent away again. It was no avail, to Mayfield College I went. I remember hating the place, loathing the smell of the place, its situation, the people I saw, the study, my classroom and so it was that from 1952 to 1954 I attended another establishment I vowed would get nothing from me. The more the scholastic discipline demanded of me, the more I'd make sure that my talents would not be extracted. To pay the establishment back was the only way I could in any way say, through my policy of disruption, that I hated my being sent away. Shortly after I arrived I'd heard that if you ate soap it would make you ill, which was what I wanted, as it would be time off in the sanatorium. I ate as much as I could find - a bar of Wrights coal tar soap, the school issue - and really was ill, and for two weeks I enjoyed life in the lovely clear, crisp sheets of the sanatorium, and matron's full attention, as I played the charming boy who had seen the stupidity of his ways.

War books were inescapable then. *The Colditz Story*, *The White Rabbit*, *The Dambusters* – all were very popular and I read them in the comfort of my bed. I did get better, unfortunately, and it was then back to the dormitory, the daily morning mass and evening benediction. Only occasionally was I bullied. Once I was tied hand and foot to a revolving blackboard and bombarded with chalk, dusters and missiles of all kinds for being called Sebastian, so I could suck up to the said religious master. "Repent for being called by that name," the leader of the group said. "I repent," I answered quickly. At least at that moment it was true - I really did regret it. With blood drawn from face and neck, I was undone and let loose. I was never able to organise my retribution on that boy, he seemed invulnerable and had a posse round him always. I paid the price and was left alone.

I'm far more interested in the individual and his ability to say something I want to hear or feel towards than the sweaty endeavours of lots of people all wanting the same thing. But about this time I had to join teams, for at Mayfield like everywhere else, the school had their Blue Team and their Red Team and whatever else they thought up; I had to play cricket and rugby most weeks at the appropriate times of the year for these sports and my first thought was how I could get out of these games and still be seen as honourable.

The first winter term at Mayfield I had to see the lie of the land vis-a-vis rugby and its attendant grime and at least have a bash at appearing *sportif*. I'd run madly around hoping to look willing to try to catch the ball at least, or appear to be helping my side along. After a few weeks of getting mud all over me for what seemed to me a completely dubious purpose, I worked out a knack of running like mad in the general direction of the pack towards whatever end they were heading for. By so doing, if the charge was on the wooded side of the pitch, I could disappear into the trees and not even be missed. Naturally I didn't want to be found out, that wouldn't have seemed to be playing the game, so I dropped back in again the next time they all were to be found heaving, panting and puffing away on the wooded side again a quarter of an hour later. In this way rugby days were spent running up and down looking busy on the open side for most of the time, and the rest of the match was spent watching muddy bodies getting pummelled and bashed about from the wooded side of the pitch.

In the summer term we went after school down the long sloping field towards the filthy swimming pool which, as I mentioned before was usually very dirty and badly looked after, but at the beginning of term it got pretty crowded for it was clean. We would usually not have an attendant or supervisor after school and some of the boys would have cigarettes that they would secrete in their towels that we would puff away at or taking turns when only one was available. Talk was of how to get more cigarettes, the inevitable dirty jokes, girl talk. I took it all in, but only contributed usually to subjects like how to disrupt classes by humming or tapping under desks, or with completely incapable teachers, how to ask very provocative questions deliberately to embarrass them. I seemed to have the knack of never getting caught and some of my schoolmates would ask how I did it. I did it by making noises, coughing suddenly and extremely loudly when the brother's back was turned, so he would practically jump out of his skin but could not identify a culprit. I also persuaded a whole group of the class to say in unison, from different parts of the classroom, "He did sir!", so that for a split second the master thought that someone was actually owning up or treacherously pointing the finger at the boy concerned. Another trick: on being asked a question I would put my hand up and put on an awful stutter on the first letter of the answer, then change the answer to, "Could I be excused sir?"

All this was passed on to my parents when I saw them at half term or terms' end, but I think behind the scenes I was to remain there by hook or by crook. I hadn't quite left the school for good when a notice went up, that a school in the East End of London had been asked to present a boxing tournament between their chosen fighters, and volunteers were asked for at the College. I volunteered I think, or was made to feel that I'd be good at it, so I did. Very nervous underneath about the whole thing, while feigning enthusiasm, I did some training with punch bags and some sparring partners. I suppose they thought after a few weeks that I'd be alright on the night, and as the first of the two nights over which all the matches were to be held approached, I felt quite confident about the prospect. There were to be twelve bouts on the first evening, with two bouts in each weight. I was the flyweight. My opponent, who came from Clapham, spoke with a broad nasal cockney accent. We were the first match of the evening. The winner of the first evening would fight the second six who had won the night before.

The night arrived, and as the lights went down in the hall, we climbed into the ring. The bell went for the first of three by three minute rounds. I came out fighting, and this Clapham boy Williams got a real bash on the nose fairly early on, but apart from that punch my role was one of sparring, deflecting, and a bit of holding. As our fight was the first of the evening, I knew that if I won this one I could step out and know that that was my contribution for the evening. The Londoners thought they were in a very posh place and naturally put on imitiation loud, snobby accents which didn't quite come off and used this and other jokes to try to warm up the atmosphere for the coming tournament. The second round he hit me somewhat harder but without a good aim. Then I saw an opportunity and let fly with what I had to offer against his solar plexus. This last seemed to do the trick for as the round was nearly at an end and he looked winded, the referee stopped the contest and I was declared the winner. My right hand held aloft, "The blue corner has it," he shouted to the cheering of Mayfield and the booing of London. So there it was, this mini gladiator, of getting on for six minutes' experience, lighted by the floodlights, led out to the shower, clapping my opponent on the back when we met outside, I felt my day had come. In the end it was six all the first evening, so the tie was the starting score for the second evening. My opponent in the red corner this time was an Italian called Manzini, an Eastender of unsmiling and quite unflappable disposition, or so he seemed. Again we were the first contest being the lightest, and into the ring we went. Eyeing each other across the ring, listening to the advice from our respective corners about the honour of our respective sides, gumshields in, laces checked at the gloves, sawdust for the boots, spitoon for the breaks, we attacked each other. Manzini came at me, I deflected. I'd beaten Williams, I'd do the same again: a punch to the jaw. I was still thinking of the previous night's victory, being seen as a hero, hard into the stomach came the next blow, deflection - the bell.

This was not my cup of tea; the second bell, and out came this Italian with fire, and the same thoughts in his soul as mine, with one glancing crash he broke the bridge of my nose and profuse bleeding came forth down my nose. I'd had enough, the second bell had not been rung but that would do me I thought, humiliation openly to see, and with the blood streaming down, I walked across the ring, lifted the ropes and left the hall, to the surprise of a flabbergasted Manzini, the seconds, the timekeeper and the whole school. As it happens, it didn't concern me what people thought and when I think back to this very strange occurrence and how I coped with public humiliation I feel that my justification is that it was the right thing to do at the time. Naturally one wouldn't brag about giving up in such circumstances, but it was not held against me.

Mayfield College had a separate girls' establishment in the same village and rumour had it that nightly dormitory visits were made; this information I found highly tempting, and wanted to get myself involved, but I was only twelve years old, uninitiated, green, and certainly not tall enough to scale the great outer walls, all of which militated against experimenting with a subject that was slowly but surely taking over in rank of importance. In any case, at this moment the time had come to leave not only Mayfield but also Smarden too, for the beautiful house had been unfortunately beyond the financial means of my parents to keep up, and so we went back to London for a while.

My parents still had the lease on the Manresa Road Studio at the time and my father would use the place as a very useful *pied à terre* when earlier over from Sark and later from Smarden. Right in the middle of Chelsea, the road ran due north-south from the colourful Kings Road end, with its Georgian houses, to the Kensington end and the Fulham Road. The Queen's Elm pub where many writers and painters went, was at hand, just around the corner but he didn't ever drink there – at least I never saw him do so, except a glass of cherry brandy once at Christmas.

The studio, with one enormous north light, the great 40 foot high ceiling and the smell of turps, oil paint and charcoal of the painter's refuge, this was home once again for my nomadic family. There were five of us, and my sister born on Sark and brought into the world by my grandfather like myself, was now about three years old. At this time between schools I was at home like my sister, but my brother, not old enough for changing to a senior school still attended preparatory school. So here we all lived for a while, six months or so, until the arrangements were made for selling Smarden, that wonderful house. We were sad to leave and not all that keen to move into the Surrey suburbs, which were to be our next destination.

CHAPTER 6

WALLINGTON IN THE SOUTHERN SUBURBS

*– Where someone said of one of my father's best
oil paintings: "That's funny, I dabble too"!*

The move to Wallington, Surrey, came about with dispiriting speed, and the Smarden house was, sadly, sold back to the bank from which the loan for its purchase had been taken out in the first place.

When my grandfather had retired from medical work in China, he had had built a large house in which he would have his surgery. His nurse lived in and until she died, his wife ran this Victorian Gothic house, a house into which we were now going to move. There were six bedrooms, a very large garden, a tennis court, a mosaic tiled conservatory and a half moon drive with great wide cross and bar gates at either side of the frontage. The local bus which was to take me to my next school every day stopped at the request stop just outside one of the gates, under a great oak tree, and later on my job was to weekly clear hundreds of bus tickets, sweet papers and detritus of every kind stuffed into our hedge or just thrown into our drive. Once when no one was looking my father stuck a ten shilling note to the pavement with very strong glue. We would then watch from a window that gave a view of the bus stop the wary attempts to pick it up. People would sometimes kneel down pretending to be doing up their shoe laces but really trying to prise the note from its grip. Others would openly bend down and try to get their finger nails underneath it; all manner of methods - surreptitious, furtive, open - were used, but the note held firm and a week later at a quiet time of the day, my father got a thin blade and slicing under the note from one side to the other, retrieved his money. He had several money tricks. He could flick coins up his sleeve with great dexterity and we children never could work out how the coins could so easily disappear if his shirt sleeves or jumper were not loose.   Another, more vocal, trick won my complete admiration: his ability to belch through the alphabet was a magnificent feat, one it took us ages to master, although I don't think my sister ever tried.

What a change from the urban colour, the sights and sounds of London, the very quiet rural elegance of the Georgian house in Kent, or the wild brown lanes and cliffs of Sark, was this south London commuter town.

A school had been found for me to attend, this time run by fully fledged men of the cloth, priests who had had the ability to pass the Latin exams at their places of instruction, but were nevertheless representatives of the constriction of practical education that is classrooms, rules, hierarchies, masters and power.   At least this place was a day school.   As the bus stop was just outside our gate and as the journey to school lasted only 15 minutes, this was a wonderful change from the often appallingly rough journeys on the ferry from Weymouth to St Peter Port, or by plane from Blackbush to Guernsey, or the many sad and heart-rending separations at Creux harbour.

The bus journey, on that first morning in 1953 through the leafy roads and the short walk from the main road near the school entrance to the aptly named Peeks Hill, was pleasant. My new uniform bright, crisp and the school emblem on the breast pocket of the dark blue blazer was worn with less of the dislike for which I held the Vauxblets and Mayfield uniforms.

This first day there brought, at least subconsciously, a relief from a naturally fairly destructive attitude to schools. The day school meant that I was where I really only ever wanted to be, at home, where I had my extensive collection of model cars, some pistols, knives and swords I'd been given, valuable old flint boxes - since stolen - and swashbuckling and dangerous, two killer battle swords, all these in my den. I kept my rooms always very tidily and would have displays for friends to see if they came to visit me. That day I did my best to maintain a solid and progressive feel in my inner attitude towards the classroom, masters and schoolmates.

As the days and months went by, this initial fine attitude waned, as awful marks in papers, and no sign of any apparent improvement in my progress, came forward. When I had been there six months or so, and I had been asked so often at home to try to concentrate, to try to be less interested in being disruptive, I think, in a way, I threw in the scholastic towel once and for all.

There was a French teacher who at the beginning of each new term would say that as there had been so much fooling about in the previous term (often due to me) that for this term there would be no repetition of it. "I will not repeat myself, do you hear me laddies? I will not repeat myself." This sentence, in which he never saw the humour, was repeated every term for the years I was at the school and was the sentence immediately prior to his next entreaty that, "Now for dictation laddies and I will not repeat the words." As the dictation was always the same we could prepare missiles for future classes - he was a type of teacher who was at once totally consistent in his repetition but was completely unpredictable as far as violent, physical outbursts were concerned. So although we could be getting prepared for the next poor chap's hell, with the French teacher we had to watch our step. The dictation started with the words we pretended we didn't hear and it was always 'Ve cow', 'Ve 'orse' and the side-splitting 'Ve sparkling plug'. The man, who was Polish and was a prisoner of the Germans for several years during the war, should have been treated with more respect. But if after ten years he still didn't know that it was the 'sparking' and not 'sparkling plug'; still gave the same 10 words he'd always done; said 'Ve' and not 'the' and still did not know that one said 'the horse' and not 'Ve 'orse', then maybe I shouldn't just blame myself for my less than scintillating academic progress.

This propensity towards sound as language, the apeing of sound, the mimicry of the different accents and dialects was as yet some way off and at that time, with the Polish French teacher, my horizons were pretty confined. The gift of the mispronunciation of the French teacher's English, and the vocal problems of the teacher who could not say the letter 'R' (so when a school friend called Rogers got things wrong, the teacher's anger with him, bursting out always with, "Wearly Wogers, can't you get anything wight?" was greeted by unrestrained guffawing) both prompted my involving others in my aim of disrupting the course of the period. After the third or fourth time of hearing, "Wearly Wogers", I repeated it using a technique of appearing as though I agreed that Rogers was an idiot and that I should join the teacher in his admonition. Of course for a second it appeared to the others that I really was siding with the teacher, but after turning round and making a sign that they should join in, they grasped that a great deal of fun was to be had by producing a gradually mounting chant of, "Wearly Rogers, can't you get anything wight?" This inexorably mounting chant finally causing the poor teacher to fetch the tougher Maths master who was in the next door classroom, he came in to complete silence. Remarking, "Well they had been shouting at the tops of their voices before I came for assistance", didn't put him in a very good light as far as anyone was concerned.

This Maths teacher, a nasty looking man, was very short, had rimless glasses and a crew cut and maintained total discipline by meting out strap notes, or 'chits' as they were called then, at the slightest provocation. Provocation to him could be, "Excuse me Father, could you explain that again?" This was either taken as ignorance, or as a questioning of his capacity of making himself quite clear the first time. He chose the absolute opposite approach to teach his subject from the lax or ineffectual ones. His method was the iron ...od and was as inefficient as a way of imparting knowledge ...e opposite was for others. Naturally these different approaches were not based on whims, but the only way in which their personalities were able to be projected or otherwise through teaching. In any case as I don't think I can remember a single one of them from any of the schools that gripped my attention, except Brother Charles, and he only as a man not as a master, it didn't seem to matter at the time.

What I needed, wanted and would have worked hard with was a person who straddled the subject, who radiated his belief and lured me into his grip. He would have needed the ability to root me to the spot, to fire me with his powerful personality. But it was not to be and the days passed at this school were as at any of the others, lost in idleness my mind wandering and waiting in a way for life to begin. At school all I found was the different classrooms with their individual smells, and features, were the daily drudge, the regimed and statutory years of incarceration.

I did a bit of sport; the teams were picked and I liked the idea of the fast bowler. Denis Compton and, somewhat later, Freddie Truman began to appear as heroes in my life, especially Compton, who had a physical presence I could respect, for I needed the man to appear like a larger than life character, someone in whom I could see no flaw, and if he had one, which he like anyone else would have had, it would have been so subservient to the total image of achiever and hero. In his case the flowing dark hair as he tore down the pitch with style, speed and personality, powerfully put into action his ability. For in the singular competence that places the highly talented person apart from the rest lies the lure. Sometimes I'd look for the signs of weakness in the hero, something I could dislike so as to make his achievement less of note, make him in short less distanced through his talent and so become more able to be caught up with, copied, imitatable, someone I might be able to equal – in short, to make the hero my equal.

I got involved in quite a few fights which again I would orchestrate, wanting to prove my worth at something other than fooling and disruption, at which I was second to none. Surreptitiousness was my trade, the art of innuendo, deviousness, implication, and attendant schemes to deflect from commitment or just the real hard work of it all.

Once or twice I went camping, which I loathed; all the mud, grubbiness, the 'team spirit', kettles boiling over, cold nights, hard work and camaraderie was not for me. Pitching tents in wind, finding flat ground, the apparent spirit undaunted, marching on to nowhere, with continual freezing goose pimples, all seemed to me as irrelevance. I joined the Scouts one evening; it was also to be the last evening with them. I tried the morse code explained by someone who seemed uninterested himself in the subject. I asked if I could try out 'Help me please' by making the relevant taps. By the end of the evening I still didn't get what one was supposed to do, feigned a bad stomach, went home and the Scout movement continued on its way without me.

My scouting days being over, the school Army Cadet Corps caught my eye. They met once a week in a hut. This army cadet gathering was run by a very tough corporal who used to drill us and show us weapons, touched as though they were the rarest of objects. One week there was a bren gun which was taken to bits and put back together again. Then next week we would put it together and then dismantle it again. The Corporal would arrive in all weathers half an hour before we all arrived, all seven of us that is, and put in 30 minutes taking each piece out and polishing it, then placing all the component parts along in lines ready for the evening puzzle. As each week he put everything in the same order, we fairly soon got the hang of it.

We were to have polished our boots until they shone like mirrors, the webbing and straps as new and the blancoing perfect, to complete this Army Cadet's dreary uniform. I often wondered why he would polish and expect all of us to spend ages before the evening's drill polishing, only to meet in a hut near the railway station in Purley. It's like the doctors' surgeries or solicitors' front office doors, I felt: this paying the cleaner to polish practically out of sight the brass handle on the door, but at the same time not noticing that the door was practically falling off the hinges, being so rusty. Once inside, some doctors' and solicitors' offices sport naked light bulbs, peeling outdated wallpaper, and provide the honoured clients or patients with dog-eared and scruffy old magazines. The Corporal was like that: he would polish, polish and polish again, but when out of uniform would be seen in shapeless clothes with his elbows sticking very nearly out of the worn out jumpers he wore.

The Cadet period lasted somewhat longer than the Scouts, getting on for a term, and on the day that the annual mock battle came around, held in some woods near Dorking, I was quite excited. Blanks were to be used and we really would be firing at our enemy, the Waddon cadets, from behind trees and from banks in the wood. This was to be the day the Corporal saw as the vindication of his claim that the Purley Cadets were of the competence of the S.A.S. or crack commando battalions at the very least. Poor chap. The day of the battle began with overcast skies that fell as torrential rain by the time we got in the coach taking us to the place of combat. He tore about in the mud, blasting out shots at figures seen fleetingly darting from tree to cover, and from cover to hollows. A draw was declared when we looked like the water buffalo in the Lower Ganges and no-one could tell who was on the Waddon or the Purley side. The great battle between the 8th Army and the Afrika Corps in miniature was over, and filthy, wet, dripping in the pure awfulness of it, this was my last go at soldiering, and back we went to the hut in Purley for a mug of tea.

One day my parents did receive a communication from the Home Office stating that His Majesty's forces would not be requiring my effort for National Service, as being born on the 7th January 1940 I had missed that hell by eight days. If I had had to join I would like to have become involved in some aspect of music. And it was on being asked to put some bamboo sticks in the ground to hold the french beans up straight, that I started my life long interest in drumming. On pressing the stick into the rather hard earth it broke in two and I started tapping it on any flat surface I could find. Meanwhile, the cadets, the scouts, sports, all faded out to be replaced by the slowly mounting intense interest in women and girls. Of course as any other boy, awareness of the more beautiful sex had started by one's awareness of the role of mother and the impact on seeing her as a woman for the first time.

Naturally one's parents would be seen going in and out of the bathroom, and my elegant mother, who had a very attractive shape and slim, well shaped legs, was my yardstick. Sometimes as I was walking past, or early on in the main bedroom of wherever we were living, her elegant and fine female form would be visible through the silken nightclothes she would wear. When I was still very young we had gone over for a short holiday, back to the small hotel in Burpham whilst living in Chelsea. We went out in a party with some people also staying there and their daughter of twenty or so. They took us in their car to Littlehampton beach, and there, while collecting some shells the daughter had an accident with her costume. One of her very ample breasts dropped out. It was very exciting for me, but she quickly put it in her hands and made an attempt to stuff it back into her costume. I don't know why I felt that that small act of replacement should have been handled in any other way, but the period between exposure and being secreted again I suppose was far too short. On another occasion walking up Oxford Street, my mother noticed that the woman ahead of her had her skirt tucked into her knickers. She pointed this out to the woman, who turned aggressively to her and said, "What's it got to do with you, mate?" These two incidents surely show that for some people temporary slips in their physical emplacement are not as important as to others.

It was at this time when at the age of about 13 that

I'd noticed a girl around who seemed to be often in male company, either older boys or grown-ups. I think I must have seen her on buses or walking about on Saturday mornings when the youth of the area would amble up and down the main street talking and arranging parties and things to do in the weekend evenings. She was quite tall, slim and had a good shape; she had long dark hair and was from a large detached house further up the Woodcote Road where I lived. I had found out her house by noting that she would get off the bus a hundred yards or so further up from the bus stop outside our gate and go up the drive to her door. It must have taken some time and observation to notice all this, but plucking up courage one evening when I saw her on her own, I asked if I could take a stroll with her. It wasn't possible that day, but if I would like to see her the best way would be to meet her parents formally since, as I lived in the same road, it would not look like her being just picked up.

So not wanting to, but feeling that to wait a week or so would make me seem less eager, I nodded once or twice from the other side of the road sometimes, but held my beating body in check until I felt she would maybe find me more interesting. The third week after she'd made her offering and having mouthed, "This evening?" across the road, to which she nodded, I walked up to her house. She opened the door to me and took me up to the first floor where her parents were sitting, the father was reading the paper, the mother knitting.

"This is Sebastian," Suzanne said and her father, a solicitor I think, greeted me quite amiably and the mother looked up and nodded. It was the beginning of my life as a man.

• • •

This marks, I think, the beginning of the end of my childhood. My childhood is the first part of my life, under the spell of my father; my early adulthood the second part, one in which my life, though completely different, was still ruled by being my father's son.

I was well into my late twenties when I left home literally, rather than metaphorically. Although I had spent some four years abroad after leaving school and tutors, I never felt I'd actually really left. I couldn't. The pull of the atmosphere, the lure of its smell, the essence of home was too strong to give up. Although the years abroad gave me three fluent languages, opportunities to play my drums and piano in jazz clubs all over Europe, and myriad encounters with girls and women, the call of something stronger always seemed to pull me back. All the houses, flats and cottages are now owned by others, all are changed out of all recognition, gone forever into memory. There stalks abroad in those Channel Islands, Kent and Sussex, Chelsea and Kensington houses, a uniqueness that is indestructible, the treasure of being a child of bliss in the Peake household.

On leaving home I left the oils and pencils, the pine table and the green covered Georgian chairs – their only furniture of worth – I left the smell of something dear, precious, untranslatable. A mystery, something to die for, to kill for, to protect, to cherish, to which to remain fearlessly loyal, to revere and be proud of, something which was irreplaceable. At the end of *Gormenghast*, although he is physically walking away, Titus is, I think, walking forwards and backwards at the same time. Away from his home, the castle, his mother the countess; but back to them at the same time. I think of a ship in a great storm that is further back than when the storm broke despite seeming to go forward, for the power of the elements is pulling it back. And this pull, what is it? I don't know, and sometimes I wished it would release me. Why couldn't I have fallen in love and said goodbye smiling and running expectantly into the new? What was/is the hold of that which has gone?

What is the explanation for my feeling which runs deep like the river in *Titus Alone*? A never ending flood going nowhere, coming from nowhere, destined to beat always at the heart's door of those whose insatiable need for love prevents them from seeing what is there before them. Blinded by the illusion of rejection, unjust, in its assumption that the people who produce emotional misfits like me are destined to tramp the same road in one direction as I am in another. Not meeting because a rendezvous is impossible. I do not believe I was loved, although it was patently obvious I was. Like St. Thomas I cannot believe even when I see the holes in Christ's hands. I will end my days and get in the box like everyone else with the absolute conviction that intrinsically I am unlovable. And so on leaving home I aimed like the successful salmon to leap the highest rapids but I was dragged back by the underflow and the pull of the sea, so that, like the unsuccessful salmon, I languished in the shallows.

Moments of adventure, crossing the Sahara, Lapland in summer, being shot at in Lisbon, being cheered in a Bordeaux bar playing African poly-rhythms on a table in a bar to lunchtime break grape pickers or taking my first £1,000 private sale order 20 years ago: these examples of moments of isolated thrill compete with the dream of home but never replace it.

EPILOGUE

My father had a very philosophical attitude to physical pain, and on hitting his thumb hammering, would say nothing. The puce face and the rising colour it caused would, of course, be as painful as it would be for the person who screams out, swears or reacts by throwing the hammer across the room or toolshed. He gave no indication of being in pain and took it all, whether hammer blow, glass cut or simply falling over, as though the event simply had not occurred. He would not shout obscenities, as he did not like to swear, but tried whenever possible, even during particularly trying times with wife or children, to keep his outbursts to something harmless. The most violent utterance I can ever remember was the expletive 'Jehozaphat'.

Towards the final years of his life, he could not make his speech understood. His pathetic slurrings of the voice were incomprehensible. The years of institutional care took their toll on his mind, for he could lash out, physically and verbally at the nearest thing in sudden frustration, and therefore needed constant supervision. I remember going to awful places like Banstead and Friern Barnet to see him before a more humane place could be found to look after this genius, the State institutions which were free but horrifying; the private houses (and this was the early 1960's) cost from £100 to £200 per week, which my mother could not afford. At Friern Barnet the main door to the closed section of the institution would be unlocked to admit us into the inner, darker part. The padded cells, where he was several times incarcerated 'for his own good', had a menacing, dark and frightening finality about them. When my mother visited him, alone or with my brother and I, it necessitated a trip from Central London with several changes of bus - and she visited him every day of the years he was in home, hospital, mental home or institution. Sometimes bruised or with black eyes after fights between inmates, my father just couldn't recognize any of us, would make strange sounds and, because of a multiplicity of drugs, would have saliva coming out from his mouth. He had to take drugs against depression, outbursts, frustration; different colours, types, strengths; all to no avail – he died at 57, a cadaver before his time. Dignified to the end, he would stagger up on seeing my mother. Mary Rose sat on a pin, Mary Rose: a little joke between them.

From the first medical prognosis – wrong at first, as most of them were – as to the exact nature of his pornographic and debilitating illnesses, the advice was, "Go away to be looked after by private institutions that can cope". "How can I pay?" asked my mother. "Find the money," was the answer. Help did come to her from various sources, but was intermittent and irregular, certainly not consistent enough to pay the regular fees required. At an age younger than the current writer, he was already on the slope towards senility. In a corridor at the Priory Nursing Home in Priory Lane, Roehampton, a doctor after examining him for the first time, detachedly told my mother, "Premature Senility," and walked off down the corridor. My father was in his late 40s.

Before he began the period of permanent incarceration, because of his accelerating infirmities, he had tried rest as a possible cure to his need to be very, very active in very different artistic enterprises concurrently. He wrote to my mother very often from a priory in Aylesford, one of the first places he went to. Run by nuns, this institution provided quiet and tranquillity, where a person could be alone to relax and meditate, think and rest. He wrote a postcard to me almost on arrival in January 1958 at the place and because he spoke very often about the art of perspective, did a drawing of a strange fish with lots of bubbles, diminishing in size, emanating from its mouth. The writing on the postcard above the fish reads; 'Here's some perspective for you.'

After a period at home, he went to another institution when he became, despite the constant and dedicated love of my mother's attention, too much for her to handle. He wrote to me on a scrap of paper:

Dear Sebby,

   This isn't a letter. It isn't even a note. It's a notelet.

   But it brings my love to you and wishes you all the best for the next few weeks - and after.

               Love to you
               From Daddy

I treasure these and the other few letters and cards I had from him, because I know now the mental and physical agonies he went through. At the time a teenager, and younger, I was sometimes unaware of his real illnesses and their toll on him and my mother. He was my father whom I loved so much that the very memory of him and his dignified forebearances can bring tears to me. My mother was once told by a relation that she should feel 'honoured' to be able to care for someone so special and that the hand of God was on her and him. This eyewash was, of course, at one remove from actually seeing the pencil falling from his hand on trying to draw or on hearing incomprehensible sounds through his drugged system. This 'honour' was a 24 hour hell, especially when my father could not sleep, for the clock of his physical body started to become very different from ours as soon as the drugs - he called them bombs - became the sine qua non of his existence. From the early, retreat-like weekends away to try to expunge, even temporarily, the need to work, to the middle period of constant nursing at home, to the final and deadly slope to full, unadulterated hell alive, the period of decline took some 8 years. For the month preceding the departure to a series of institutions, homes, psychiatric homes, the tension we lived under in our house in Wallington was awful. He would walk all over the house, up and down the stairs, get into bed and out again, get dressed and undressed, want a pencil to draw, paint and then not want to, call my mother the moment she had just put him to bed at 2.30 p.m. in the afternoon, asking to put back on the clothes she had just taken off and so on. When people came to see him - admirers, students, fellow writers, painters - he would be still for a while then with a movement of his eye, indicated to my mother he had had enough and leave. Always extremely polite and well mannered, he had a fairly short tolerance of other people. Simply put, the 'feel' of the other, unless it were someone who was patently dear, an old friend or family member, didn't really quite fit in. The loyal friends and family watching helplessly as the illnesses took their course towards his death in November 1968, were always profoundly and genuinely moved by the sight of his decline and many offered to help as he got worse.

When the arbitrary shouting and loud cries which would echo around the house, and the constant and debilitating demands upon my mother became no longer tenable, it was a strange sort of relief and sadness that came to settle over us all. There laid in his work room on his old mahogany table, (on which a thousand illustrations had been born, where *Titus Alone* was written, where *The Glassblowers* poems were put together for the collection, on which the great *Treasure Island, Ancient Mariner, Quest for Sita* were drawn) his attempts at drawings, some of them waiting for his vitality that was never to return. The smell of paint, charcoal, crayons, pencils, canvasses, paper, his utensils, his own world, at which he was a master, sat like Miss Haversham's wedding guests' room. The tragedy of it all, the waste of those last years, the languishing of his talent. When I visit his grave, which I do frequently, I am uplifted when reading his words: 'To live at all is miracle enough' and feel that he did live, he did have a happy marriage, he was someone who left a legacy that is for the nation to see, feel and experience. If the establishment, the museums, are so insensitive to his contribution to English Art, if they choose to wear blindfolds, and if his works do not provoke an excitement in them, moved and changed by his contribution, then they are as foolish as I hold them to be.

He died in a home in Burford near Oxford, run by a wonderfully committed uncle of mine who as a man wanted to care for the lonely and old and as a doctor to help them painlessly end their days. On days that I visited my father, towards the end, there he would be, sitting somewhere in a row of octogenarians in his fifties, looking the same age as them. In the final days I went to see him and on reaching out my hand for his, tears welled up in me, but I controlled myself and pretended to be interested in the other patients, hiding, I thought, my depth of sorrow. On regaining my composure, I looked at him and his moist eyes opened and on recognizing me, he cried and mouthed the word 'Sebby'. I never saw him alive again and I did not want to see him in death. Two days after my last visit we all went back to my uncle's home the moment we heard he'd died. Death **was** for him such sweet sorrow, for he had had enough: nearly eight years of shifting from place to place at a stage before L Dopa. He had had an operation on his skull - a practice for Parkinson's disease now abandoned, which did no good, left a dent in his forehead the size of a golfball and did not keep the intense sporadic shakings at bay, as had been promised, and which had left my mother in the deepest of dilemmas as to whether to put my father through the terrifying ordeal.

My uncle, who died recently, was the kindest and most considerate of Christians and the token £25 weekly my mother paid for the last year or so of my father's life, was a relief financially, but also in a spiritual sense, as he promoted the ideal of the Hospice, long before this idea became as well known. Assisted by his wife, Dr Gilmore gave 'The Close' an atmosphere of love and caring, free of bureaucratic pettinesses, concentrating on the things that really matter; the little appropriate joke at breakfast, the helping hand of real care. I have personally canonized him, for my Uncle James brought relief to my mother and love to my father when he really needed it.

At the funeral in Burpham in Sussex, where Dr. Peake had lived and practised, grown old and died, and where he, his wife, my father's brother and sister-in-law and now my mother and father lie together, there was a large congregation. Later, at the Memorial Service in St. James's, Piccadilly, Sir John Clements, an old friend, read some of my father's poetry from the lectern. He was buried at the age of 57 looking nearer 90, leaving behind him over 10,000 drawings, 200 oil paintings, books, poems, short stories, illustrations, plays, film scripts, stage designs, and ideas that are as radiant in concept and execution as they were from their inception. Projects now underway in film, play and written word began to a great extent in the little cluster of houses that make up Warningcamp and Burpham, nestling under the South Downs beside the Arun on the chalk soil of the hilly beauty of Sussex near the sea.

At times when I remember the man I loved that was my father, I produce from the past the naive but simple, profound but evocative, Catholic prayer that we said at Vauxblets, kneeling on the stone floors in our pyjamas with the windows of the dormitory wide open for the good of the soul. We would pray out loud in unison:

Jesus, Mary and Joseph, I give thee my heart and my soul

Jesus, Mary and Joseph, assist me in my last agony

Jesus, Mary and Joseph, may I breathe forth my soul in thy
    sweet company.

This helps sometimes, because it evokes naivete and the simplicity of childish belief, but it also lies deep in received belief that remains and keeps me cool when I want to explode with the unfairness of the story I have just told.

Boy on a donkey, 1948

Also available in Vintage

Mervyn Peake

TITUS GROAN

With an introduction by
Anthony Burgess

Stranger than fiction, larger than life – welcome to the weird world of Gormenghast

Titus Groan, heir to Lord Sepulchrave, has just been born. A Groan of the strict lineage, Titus is seventy-seventh, he will inherit the miles of rambling stone and mortar that form Gormenghast Castle, and its surrounding kingdom. His world will be predetermined by complex ritual, the origins of which are lost in time; it will be peopled by the dark characters who inhabit the half-lit corridors. Lord Sepulchrave, a figment of melancholy, and his red-haired Countess; Swelter the chef and his bony enemy Flay; Prunesquallor, castle physician, and his etiolated sister, Irma, and Steerpike, the Machiavellian youth.

Dreamlike, fantastic and macabre, Mervyn Peake's extraordinary novel – the first in the Gormenghast trilogy – is one of the most astonishing sustained flights of the imagination in modern English fiction.

'It is uniquely brilliant and we are right to call it a modern classic'
Anthony Burgess